Gender Shifts in the History of English

How and why did grammatical gender, found in Old English and in other Germanic languages, gradually disappear from English and get replaced by a system where the gender of nouns and the use of personal pronouns depend on the natural gender of the referent? How is this shift related to "irregular agreement" (such as *she* for ships) and "sexist" language use (such as generic *he*) in Modern English, and how is the language continuing to evolve in these respects? Anne Curzan's accessibly written and carefully researched study is based on extensive corpus data, and will make a major contribution by providing a historical perspective on these often controversial questions. It will be of interest to researchers and students in history of English, historical linguistics, corpus linguistics, language and gender, and medieval studies.

ANNE CURZAN is Assistant Professor of English at the University of Michigan. She has written extensively on history of English, lexicography, and pedagogy, and is co-author of *First Day to Final Grade: A Graduate Student's Guide to Teaching* (2000). Professor Curzan is also co-editor of the *Journal of English Linguistics*.

STUDIES IN ENGLISH LANGUAGE

General editor
Merja Kytö (Uppsala University)

Editorial board
Bas Aarts (University College London)
John Algeo (University of Georgia)
Susan Fitzmaurice (Northern Arizona University)
Richard Hogg (University of Manchester)
Charles F. Meyer (University of Massachusetts)

The aim of this series is to provide a framework for original work on the English language. All volumes are based securely on empirical research, and represent theoretical and descriptive contributions to our knowledge of national varieties of English, both written and spoken. The series covers a broad range of topics in English grammar, vocabulary, discourse, and pragmatics, and is aimed at an international readership.

Already published

Christian Mair
Infinitival complement clauses in English: a study of syntax in discourse

Charles F. Meyer
Apposition in contemporary English

Jan Firbas
Functional sentence perspective in written and spoken communication

Izchak M. Schlesinger
Cognitive space and linguistic case

Katie Wales
Personal pronouns in present-day English

Laura Wright
The development of standard English, 1300–1800: theories, descriptions, conflicts

Charles F. Meyer
English corpus linguistics: theory and practice

Stephen J. Nagle and Sara L. Sanders
English in the Southern United States

Kingsley Bolton
Chinese Englishes: a sociolinguistic history

Gender Shifts in the History of English

ANNE CURZAN

University of Michigan

CAMBRIDGE
UNIVERSITY PRESS

PUBLISHED BY THE PRESS SYNDICATE OF THE UNIVERSITY OF CAMBRIDGE
The Pitt Building, Trumpington Street, Cambridge, United Kingdom

CAMBRIDGE UNIVERSITY PRESS
The Edinburgh Building, Cambridge, CB2 2RU, UK
40 West 20th Street, New York, NY 10011-4211, USA
477 Williamstown Road, Port Melbourne, VIC 3207, Australia
Ruiz de Alarcón 13, 28014 Madrid, Spain
Dock House, The Waterfront, Cape Town 8001, South Africa

http://www.cambridge.org

First published 2003
Fourth printing 2004

Printed in the United Kingdom at University Press, Cambridge

Typefaces Ehrhardt 10/12 pt and Melior   *System* LaTeX 2$_\varepsilon$ [TB]

A catalogue record for this book is available from the British Library

ISBN 0 521 82007 3 hardback

For my parents,
who have always believed
their daughters could do anything

Contents

Acknowledgments

The history of this book spans two institutions, many more than two years, and even more patient friends and colleagues willing to listen to me talk about gendered words in the history of English – and reassure me that others would be interested as well. The book was made possible in part by the generous support of the Walter Chapin Simpson Center for the Humanities and the Royalty Research Fund at the University of Washington; I appreciate all the efforts by both institutes to support the research of faculty in the humanities and social sciences. I am also enormously grateful to the staff at the Humanities Text Initiative at the University of Michigan, in particular John Price-Wilkin, Christina Powell, and Nigel Kerr, who created a web-accessible version of the Helsinki Corpus and helped with the research in innumerable other ways. Special thanks also go to Judy Avery and Barbara Beaton at the University of Michigan Libraries, Kathy Welsh at the Center for Statistical Research at the University of Michigan, and Paul Schaffner at the *Middle English Dictionary*.

This book would not have been possible without the help and support of many wonderful friends and colleagues. I would like to thank in particular some of my colleagues and former mentors at the University of Michigan, who fed and informed my passion for pursuing questions about the history of English: Richard W. Bailey, Frances McSparran, Lesley Milroy, Karla Taylor, Theresa Tinkle, and Thomas Toon. I am indebted and immensely grateful to Anis Bawarshi and Mary Curzan, who have read and commented on this book chapter by chapter, with incredible care and insight, providing invaluable observations, commentary, and suggestions. I would also like to thank the anonymous reviewers for Cambridge University Press, whose feedback and questions showed me new ways to discuss some of the issues in this book. I received valuable research assistance from Elizabeth Falsberg and Andrew Hsu. I would also like to acknowledge the ways in which I continue to be inspired by the curiosity, enthusiasm, and discernment of so many of the students with whom I have had the opportunity to discuss questions about language and gender. Many thanks also to Merja Kytö, a member of the editorial team responsible for the *Studies in English Language* series, for her meticulous reading and comments on the manuscript and to Kate Brett, linguistics editor at Cambridge University Press, for her unwavering support of the project. I take full responsibility for any errors that remain.

My friends and family have given me unflagging support, counsel, and love throughout the entire process of creating this book. For all this and more, I am immeasurably grateful.

Introduction

"I think she's got it!" exclaimed a participant at the American Dialect Society's annual meeting in January 2000, after the final vote for the "Word of the Millennium." The early candidates for the honor ranged from the lofty (*truth*, *freedom*, *justice*) to the academic (*science*), from the political (*government*) to the seemingly mundane (*the*). The debate was heated, with members concerned whether the vote was based on the words themselves or on the concepts that the words represented. Rather late in the discussion, the word *she* was proffered and it quickly began to gain momentum – perhaps oddly parallel to what *she* seems to have done in medieval times when it entered the language. *She* gathered support from all sides: *she* represents a linguistic innovation of this millennium (*she* is first cited in 1154 AD); the introduction of *she* is change at the very core of the English vocabulary; the mysterious origins of *she* seem best explained as a combination of distinctive phonological processes in English and the effects of language contact, a crucial force in the history of English; *she* as a feminine linguistic marker represents a fundamental social category and its ascendance can be seen as symbolic of the gains by women at the end of the millennium; and *she* allows us to celebrate the pronoun, a type of mundane function word that tends to get taken for granted, albeit a critical linguistic building block. And *she* did get it. *She* prevailed over all rivals to be crowned Word of the Millennium.

She is just the kind of word that is the focus of this book.

The study of gendered linguistic forms

With the election of *she* as the word of the millennium, a personal pronoun gained the kind of recognition and acclaim usually reserved for open class or content words – not everyday function words like pronouns. While much of English vocabulary has been studied extensively, the first comprehensive book on Modern English personal pronouns, written by Katie Wales, was not published until 1996. As Wales's book demonstrates, personal pronouns in English are fascinating both linguistically and socially. Take, for example, the current confusion over phrases such as "between you and _ (me?/I?)": this confusion and the resulting

1

variation exemplify a change in progress throughout the pronoun system as speakers struggle to distinguish contexts for subject and object forms, as well as the stigmas that speakers are willing to attach to those who "misuse" their pronouns. In fact, the history of personal pronouns is as interesting as their current status in the language, as the mysterious appearance of *she* in 1154 AD suggests, and to understand the critical workings of the largest gender shift in the history of English, from grammatical to natural gender, we must examine the third-person singular forms.

In Modern English, the third-person singular pronouns *he, she*, and *it* are the only grammatical forms to retain or maintain the gender system. As such, they have been the focus of sexist language debates as well as definitional debates, as explained in Chapter One: does Modern English have a true linguistic gender system when it is upheld only by these pronouns and seems to correspond to biological sex? As Chapter Two demonstrates, the shift in gender systems, from grammatical to natural gender, has also been a focus in the creation and main-tenance of historical ideologies about English, from notions of progress and linguistic imperialism to counter-claims of creolization. Chapters Three and Four examine how these third-person pronouns came to carry natural gender in the history of English, unlike their Old English predecessors *he* 'he,' *heo* 'she,' and *hit* 'it,' which carried grammatical gender. In other words, these chapters address the question of when *he* and *she* became restricted to animate beings (as well as when *he* became a default pronoun) and when *it* came to refer to all inanimate things – or at least almost all things.

Pronouns should not steal all the attention away from content words in exam-ining the history of gender and gender shifts in English. The lexical items that refer to men and women, as well as girls and boys, have also been the source of much modern debate and are in need of historical contextualization. For example, generic *man* is often paired with generic *he* in discussions of the masculine as un-marked in English, and the gender binary reflected in *he/she* plays out in perhaps even more dramatic ways in the lexicon, as masculine and feminine words often follow notably different semantic paths over time.

Now that English follows a natural gender system governing personal pronoun agreement, there is only a subset of nouns that "carry gender" at all – and this is almost entirely semantic, because they refer to gendered beings. (There are also some morphologically gendered suffixes such as *-woman, -man, -ess*.) The focus of Chapter Five is a subset of these – a set of common words that have been used to refer to men and women, boys and girls since Old English, as well as some of the more contemporary synonyms (although I will argue that there is no such thing as a "true" synonym). These formally "invisibly" gendered nouns – gendered because their animate referents are gendered – provide a different perspective on how attitudes about gender can and have played out in English, not only in the construction of masculine and feminine categories but also in the positive or negative meanings that words in these categories tend to acquire.

At the heart of this book, Chapters Three, Four, and Five, are three studies that examine linguistic shifts related to gender in the history of English, all related to the overall shift of English from a grammatical to a natural gender system. The studies also focus on the linguistic histories of these three features of Modern English usage because they are often the focus of discussion and debate about how gender plays out in the language: the use of generic *he* to refer to people of unknown or unspecified gender; the use of *he* and *she* as well as *it* to refer to inanimate objects; and the semantic shifts and asymmetries in male–female word pairs (e.g., *man* and *woman*, *bachelor* and *spinster*).

This book works from the premise that we should not take the language of gender for granted. These linguistic forms have complex, interesting, and sometimes controversial histories; and as Suzanne Romaine (1999: 293) points out: "Debates about language are really about issues of race, gender, class, or culture." The history of gender in English, of the gender categories assumed and/or revealed in the language and of the words used to refer to men and women, reveals syntactic, semantic, and cultural forces at work as the language changes. The findings in the following chapters put language in the foreground, examining the linguistic forms and categories and reconsidering the role that gender plays and has played in how we categorize, name, and refer to the world and specifically to men and women. Gender proves to be a very productive focal point for what it reveals not only about grammatical mechanisms and language change but also about cultural attitudes.

The context of language and gender research

The topic of "language and gender" is becoming almost commonplace, with a proliferation of published books and college courses on the subject. The focus is more often on discourse rather than grammar; when there is a treatment of gendered or generic language, it rarely takes a historical perspective. Overall, questions such as whether or not there is such a thing as "women's language" and how gender plays out in conversational interaction and rhetorical style have attracted the most attention. As a case in point, a book published in 1998 titled *Rethinking Language and Gender Research* focuses entirely on investigations of speech communities and the ways in which researchers need to re-examine the gender dichotomies that tend to underlie the questions they pose. The goals and arguments of the articles in this book provide important insights about the development and direction of the field; and, in fact, they apply not only to discourse but also to gender categories in language itself. In this case, as in so many others, the gender of the speakers steals the limelight from gender in the language spoken.

This emphasis highlights the new, now prevalent meaning of gender as a category of animate beings related to biological sex. I was, in fact, intrigued to read Mary Talbot's introduction to her book *Language and Gender* (1998), in which she writes: "In linguistics and language learning, the label 'language and gender' sometimes causes a bit of confusion because people naturally think of gender as a grammatical category. Not in this book. Gender, in the sense I am using it here, is a social category, not a grammatical one" (Talbot 1998: 3). My experience is the opposite: what confuses people about gender in language is their assumption that gender is a human trait, not an arbitrary linguistic category. So while Talbot's book is about gender as a purely social category, this book will attempt to negotiate between the two: gender as a social construct/category and gender as a linguistic construct/category – and how and when the two should be put in dialogue.

A gap in existing scholarship

Theoretical models and insights in linguistic theory and in feminist theory all too rarely inform each other, particularly in the more traditional areas of language study such as historical linguistics. (Feminist theory has made more successful inroads in newer areas such as discourse analysis.) Yet each has much to gain from the other. As the following chapters demonstrate, understandings of gender in feminist theory can help to rethink concepts of gender in language. And an understanding of the history of gendered linguistic forms can help to reread the role and meaning of gender in the language of our cultural texts.

At the most fundamental level, *gender* itself often remains ill-defined in linguistic theory. The word *gender*, popularized by modern feminist theory as a way to distinguish socially constructed meanings of masculine and feminine from biological designations of sex, became a buzzword in late twentieth-century academia. As such, *gender* is now often used indiscriminately to replace the perceived "politically incorrect" word *sex*, thereby obscuring or obliterating the originally intended (and always politically correct) distinction between the two. The distinction is also pervasively misunderstood or dismissed. The second edition of the *Oxford English Dictionary* (*OED*), often viewed as one of our most authoritative sources on the language, itself seems to treat the distinction between sex and gender as a trivial one; the definition (3b) of *gender* reads: "In mod. (esp. feminist) use, a *euphemism* for the sex of a human being, often *intended* to emphasize the social and cultural, as opposed to the biological, distinctions between the sexes" (italics added). Gender is no euphemism, and the distinction that it creates between the biological and the social is critical, in linguistic theory as elsewhere. Sex is biological, "a matter of genes, gonads and hormones," as Mary Talbot puts it (1998: 7); gender is socially constructed, involving sets of traits that we learn and perpetuate as "masculine" and "feminine." The *OED* editors seem to prefer traditional linguistic definitions of gender as only a system for categorizing nouns (see Chapter One). And while there are important distinctions to be made between linguistic gender and other forms of gender at times, there are also important connections to be made.

Few linguists outside discourse analysis have pursued the connection between feminist descriptions of gender in other academic disciplines and traditional descriptions of gender in linguistics, but the link is obvious and crucial, especially in studies of the English language. The gender constructs in the English language reflect social constructs of gender in the world of its speakers; if gender in the language is isolated from its extralinguistic motivations, it proves impossible to explain in all its variation, both synchronic and diachronic. As the next few chapters describe, the recognition of this connection between linguistic and extralinguistic gender requires a redefinition of "natural gender," and this revised definition immediately helps to explain the exceptions in the Modern English gender system and the patterns visible in the rise of natural gender in the history of English personal pronouns.

Approach of this book

The contents of this book blend the empirical and the literary, the theoretical and the anecdotal. I find these approaches complement each other. I have drawn on different methodologies and theoretical approaches, from corpus linguistics to prototype theory, from historical syntax to sociolinguistics to feminist theory. As this book crosses traditional disciplinary boundaries, I hope it will be as informative to trained linguists and literary scholars as it is to more general readers interested both in gender and in language change.

Some feminist linguistic scholarship that addresses questions of gender in the English language has been fairly criticized for its generalizations about patriarchy and language control, for the sometimes strident tone and agenda that can seem to determine the direction of the scholarship.[1] While this book tackles some of the same controversial issues, I hope that the nature of the historical linguistic analysis presented here is not vulnerable to such a critique. The goal of historical linguistic scholarship is to unravel and seek to explain the complexity of language change. The complexity of speech communities and the nature of most language changes makes clear the difficulty and undesirability in most cases of "assigning responsibility" for particular changes to particular speakers, particularly at the conscious level. The relationship of prescription to language change otherwise occurring in the speech community is an interesting and fruitful area of inquiry within historical language study, and one that proves to be relevant to several of the linguistic changes discussed in this book.

These statements are not meant to deny that I am in some way politically invested in this work. No historian, linguistic, cultural or otherwise, is ever a

---

[1] One common target of such critiques is Dale Spender's well-known book *Man Made Language* (1985), which attempts to expose the connection between patriarchy and the language – a language that Julia Penelope has referred to as the "Patriarchal Universe of Discourse." Mary Daly's *Wickedary* (1987) works from the premise that women cannot find a place or voice in this language created and dominated by men. Many of these works are discussed in more detail throughout the book; I mention them here as evidence for how inflammatory the kind of material that appears in this book has proven to be for some scholars in the field and how tangled the relationship of language, attitudes, beliefs, and social structures can become.

completely impartial observer, and one could argue that this may not even be entirely desirable. Scholarly investment does not indicate bad scholarship; in fact, one could argue that the best scholarship requires investment on the part of the researcher. Romaine (1999: xiii) eloquently defends this scholarly stance: "I do not accept the accusation . . . that personal and political commitment to a topic means it cannot be treated as a serious academic discipline." As scholars in language and gender research, as in many other disciplines, have articulated, we must recognize that we all bring particular questions and perspectives to bear on the material we study and simultaneously strive to provide the most accurate analysis possible. In the field of historical linguistics specifically, particularly when working with a topic such as gender, it is critically important to work carefully with the language and with the relationship of language to speakers, within the linguistic frameworks established for how we believe language functions, both structurally and within speech communities.

Organization of the book

No book should or could claim to tell the entire story of gender in the history of the English language. In this book, I have chosen to focus on three developments in English that are all related to the larger shift in English from a grammatical to a natural gender system, two focused on grammar and one on lexicon:

- the development of personal pronoun reference to animate beings;
- the loss of grammatical gender and the related rise of natural gender in personal pronouns referring to inanimate objects;
- the semantic shifts in the lexical fields of words for 'man,' 'woman,' 'girl,' and 'boy' – the lexical forms that most clearly retain gender semantically in a natural gender system.

While the focus here will be on language, it quickly becomes apparent that these linguistic developments are intertwined with and reflective of cultural and social developments for English speakers. They become a site from which to view other phenomena such as some of the repercussions of heavy language contact and mixing in the history of English, sexist social structures and practices, and English speakers' attitudes toward their own language. In this way, these studies complement Dennis Baron's valuable book *Grammar and Gender* (1986), which examines how attitudes toward men and women become attitudes about language.

Chapter One lays the groundwork by exploring the thorny issue of defining gender in the first place. It begins with a general review of the scholarship on linguistic gender as well as specific theoretical models for the Modern English gender system, in order to expose the ways in which we need to rethink the definition of gender in English. It may seem odd that the apparently "simple" gender system of Modern English has been the source of such scholarly confusion and frustration; it is the exceptions to the rule – the inanimate nouns that can still be referred to with gendered pronouns – that have proven so difficult to explain. Personal pronouns now carry the weight of the history of English gender, and by examining how the "natural" gender system of these pronouns came to be, we can come to a better understanding of what the variation in the system means, both linguistically and socially.

Chapter Two begins with a critical survey of the ways in which the loss of grammatical gender and the emergence of the modern gender system have been framed in histories of English. This historiography shows the ways in which gender often blurs the lines between the linguistic and the social, and the ways in which the descriptions in these histories reveal underlying ideologies and belief systems. This survey sets the stage for a discussion of how to rethink the framework for the history of English – both ideologically and linguistically – in order to explain the gender shift and semantic changes that gendered words have undergone.

The discussion of gender then takes a more empirical turn to look specifically at the history of English personal pronouns (the only forms to retain gender agreement in Modern English) and of English gendered nouns for people (the nouns that clearly retain semantic gender in Modern English). In a broad linguistic context, Chapters Three and Four are devoted to historical syntax, specifically the transition from grammatical to "natural" gender in the history of English ("natural" being a term that will be problematized in Chapter One) and its repercussions in Modern English. The corpus-based study presented in Chapter Three historicizes the generic pronoun question by providing a broader examination of agreement patterns between pronouns and nouns referring to human beings in Old and Middle English. The chapter ends with a survey of grammatical prescription on the pronoun question to frame the debate historically and provide perspective on the ways in which attitudes about gender can play out in descriptions of gender in the language.

Chapter Four, also based on a corpus study of pronouns, offers historical linguists a new model for understanding the English gender shift from grammatical to natural gender. It focuses specifically on when and how English lost grammatical gender in the singular third-person pronouns *he, she*, and *it*, used anaphorically to refer back to gendered nouns. The gradual loss of Old English inflectional endings, all of which served to mark case, gender, and number, is clearly a major factor in the loss of the grammatical gender system: once noun phrases no longer overtly marked gender, personal pronouns were left as the only grammatical forms carrying gender, and by the end of Middle English (at the latest), they were following natural gender. The findings of this study clarify when and how the personal pronouns shifted away from grammatical gender agreement and how our understanding of "natural" gender is historically contingent. These facts about the grammatical progression of the shift in the personal pronouns also contribute important new evidence to the ongoing discussion about the influence of language contact in the dramatic changes between Old and Middle English, as well as to theoretical work in historical syntax.

Chapter Five turns from pronouns to nouns, from grammar to the lexicon, from syntax to semantics, in order to examine the history of a core set of terms used to refer to men and women, boys and girls. The study serves to historicize the debate about generic *man*, often linked to generic *he*, and about the sexism of words such as *girl* when applied to women. The premise of this chapter, like those that precede it, is that we can better understand the history of individual words within a broader context of related forms, and this chapter specifically examines the ways in which the masculine–feminine gender binary plays out in the core of the lexicon. It also pulls together a range of more technical linguistic scholarship in an attempt to create more accessible histories of semantic change with real implications for modern concerns about gender and language, both in public debates and in feminist scholarship. The chapter focuses first on words for younger gendered beings, specifically *boy* and *girl*, *child*, *knave*, *knight*, *maid*, *maiden*, and *wench*, as well as other more peripheral terms. The discussion then turns to general terms for adult gendered beings, treating in particular the words *man* and *woman*, *wife* and *husband*, *bachelor* and *spinster* and other fundamental gender pairings, as well as words such as *lord* and *lady*, *harlot*, *hussy*, *hag*, and *crone* as their histories become intertwined. Looked at in the wider context of their lexical fields, the histories of these words reveal patterns of semantic change that are simultaneously fascinating and potentially disquieting in what they reveal about our beliefs and attitudes about men, women, and children. Woven into this chapter are examinations of the treatment of these terms in a historical range of dictionaries, often compared with evidence of actual usage from both literary and more vernacular texts.

The concluding chapter addresses the ways in which these historical questions are playing out in the debates about Modern English. The chapter briefly comments on attempts to "reform" the language so that it will be less sexist as well as a commentary on these very efforts. From a historical perspective, feminist language campaigns have been surprisingly successful as political agendas and linguistic changes have fallen into line. This final chapter considers the implications of calling particular terms, from generic *he* to *history*, sexist, as well as the implications of these studies of gender in the history of English for feminist work on language. The historical framing of these issues, in the final chapter and throughout the book, aims to provide a critical perspective for speakers participating in attempts to change the language and for speakers whose language is changing, as well as the linguists who study these very speakers and their language.

A note on terminology

I have intentionally not played with the word *history* in the title. This book, as it works to describe the development of gender in the history of the language, is not designed as an attempt to set an agenda for feminist language reform. This is not to say that this material is not relevant to language reform movements or that this book is completely apolitical. The motivation behind this book is to provide the historical information that can contextualize current debates about gender, as well as sexism, in the language and debates about language reform. This book works to explain how, for example, the pronouns *his* and *her* have been used differently over time, and why "reforming" a word like *history* is an example of an ahistorical (mis)understanding of sexism in the language. (The word *history* was borrowed into English in the fourteenth century, adapted from the Latin *historia*.) I do not want to deny the potential rhetorical effects of this word, but I also do not want to ignore the fact that opponents of language reform often gather their ammunition from this kind of re-parsing of history (italicized or not).[2]

Readers will also notice that I use the term *gendered*, an adjective derived from a verb with which not all speakers – let alone lexicographers or spell checkers – feel comfortable. But *gender* as a verb effectively captures the ways in which scholars such as Judith Butler have argued that gender is a kind of performance – sets of repeated behavior through which we create gendered selves and perpetuate gender categories. In this way, the functional shift of this word in the language, from a noun to a verb, reflects new ways in which scholars have conceptualized gender in the world. The adjective *gendered* also serves as a convenient means of categorizing the set of linguistic forms that carry gender in a given language.

A note to the reader

A reader can "read" this book in a number of ways. A reader with linguistic training can read the material as presented. For readers less familiar with the history of the English language, the more general background on the history of English included in Chapter Two, although far from comprehensive, should provide a historical linguistic context for the detailed analysis of earlier stages of the language presented later in the book. In addition, Appendix 1 provides useful background on the history of English personal pronouns. A specialized reader may choose to concentrate on Chapters Three through Five, which include the empirical studies. In addition, Appendix 2 contains technical information about the Helsinki Corpus and about the methodology used for the studies in

---

[2] Deborah Cameron justifiably disagrees with me on this point, asking why feminists should not play with language for political ends. As she writes: "*Herstory* is an excellent word, pointing out with wit and elegance that history has too often been the story of men's lives . . ." (1990: 111). I do not want to discourage speakers from deliberately playing with words for political ends or deny that speakers may easily misparse this word as a sexist compound; as a historical linguist, however, I find myself reluctant to extend language reform in such a way, when most speakers will not know to distinguish this deliberate wit from more serious attempts to create a more generic or gender-equitable language.

Chapters Three and Four. While the material in Appendices 1 and 2 is situated at the end of the book so that the results of the studies themselves can be highlighted in the chapters, I encourage readers to turn to the appendices for this background information. Throughout the book, readers will find brief summaries of relevant studies and a wide range of references so that they can further pursue questions of particular interest about language as well as language and gender.

1   Defining English gender

1.1   Introduction

In the fifth century BC, according to Aristotle's account, Protagoras first created the labels *masculine, feminine*, and *neuter* for Greek nouns, and language scholars have been trying to explain the relationship of grammatical gender categories to the world around them ever since.[1] Protagoras himself, apparently anxious that the grammatical gender of nouns and the sex of their referents did not always correspond in Greek, is said to have wanted to change the gender of Greek *menis* 'anger' and *peleks* 'helmet,' both of which are feminine nouns, to masculine because he felt the masculine was more appropriate given the words' referents (Robins 1971 [1951]: 15–16). Despite Aristotle's subsequent proposal of grammatical reasons for nominal gender classes, the original labels persisted in the descriptions of gender in classical grammars – and, therefore, in all the later Western grammars modeled on them – and these labels have created the pervasive misperception that grammatical gender categories in a language reflect a connection between male and female human beings and masculine and feminine inanimate objects. The terms deceptively imply a link between the categories in the natural gender system of Modern English – in which there is a clear correlation between masculine and feminine nouns and biological traits in the referent – and the categories in the grammatical gender systems of other Indo-European languages; in fact, these two types of systems are distinct. The shift of English from a grammatical to a natural gender system is highly unusual and involves a complex set of related grammatical transformations in the language.

Despite their descriptive labels, noun classes in a grammatical gender system, unlike those in a semantic gender system, do not correspond to conceptual categories, no matter how creative the grammarian. In other words, there is no way

---

[1] For more detailed descriptions of the Greek and subsequent Latin treatments of grammatical gender, see Robins (1971 [1951]) and Vorlat (1975). Vorlat provides the most comprehensive treatment of early English grammars (1586–1737) currently available, grounding these works in the classical tradition from which they stem and identifying areas of grammatical conservatism and innovation.

(or at least no linguistically justifiable way) to explain why in French a table is feminine and a necklace masculine based on the features of the referents (e.g., the appearance of the table or the shape of the necklace). Yet in languages with two or three grammatical genders and the misleading labels *masculine, feminine*, and *neuter*, it can seem only logical to equate grammatical gender and biological sex – especially when there often is a correlation between grammatical gender and biological sex for nouns describing human beings (grammatical gender is not always arbitrary). But attempts to do so, particularly for inanimate objects, usually yield little more than nonsense.

The mysteries of how European languages such as German, French, Spanish, or Italian categorize nouns as masculine, feminine, and neuter are at best a source of amusement and more often a source of bafflement and frustration for Modern English speakers, who are often unaware that their own language used to have these same kinds of noun categories. To English speakers, having been brought up in a linguistic universe where sexless objects are almost always *it*, it can seem arbitrary and absurd to talk about such objects with language normally reserved for male and female human beings and perhaps for animals. And the idea that grammatical gender is not supposed to "make sense," that it is semantically arbitrary, often makes even less sense. Grammatical gender categories serve to divide the nouns in a language into formal classes, which serve as the basis for agreement with other elements in the sentence (e.g., adjectives, pronouns, verbs). They seem as natural and functional to native speakers of these languages as any other grammatical feature. It is the terminology that is deceiving: *gender* no longer simply means 'kind,' and *masculine, feminine*, and *neuter* cannot serve unambiguously as generic labels for word classes. In response, linguists have attempted to develop specific, less ambiguous terminology for gender systems in the world's languages, as the following section describes.

The natural gender system of Modern English – in which only nouns referring to males and females generally take gendered pronouns and inanimate objects are neuter – stands as the exception, not the rule among the world's languages. In this way, the descriptive term *natural* for Modern English implies a pervasiveness that is, in this case, inappropriate: the English gender system is unusual in the family of Indo-Germanic languages, as well as among Indo-European languages more generally. Indeed, one does not have to turn back too many pages in the history of English to find a grammatical gender system: Old English (750–1100 or 1150 AD) had grammatical gender categories very similar to those of Modern German, its "sister" language. ("Sister" is a gendered reference that may have an etymological motivation, for although Old English *spræc* 'language' is a masculine noun, the Old French word *langue*, from which *language* is derived, is a feminine noun.) Old English had three grammatical genders – masculine, feminine, and neuter – and all inanimate nouns belonged to one of the three classes, sometimes for morphological reasons but often for no obvious reason. For example, *Englaland* 'land of the Angles' is a neuter Old English noun (its root *land* is a neuter noun), but *mægð* 'tribe, race, country' is feminine, and *cynedom* 'kingdom' is masculine (the suffix -*dom* is masculine); synonyms often have different genders (*ecg* 'sword' is feminine, while *sweord* 'sword' is neuter), which underscores the fact that this gender system is not principally meaning-driven. (There also exists a subset of Old English nouns that appear with inflectional morphology associated with two or three different gender classes – e.g., the masculine-feminine noun *sæ* 'sea.') By the time of "Chaucer's English" or most dialects of Middle English, however, the "early English" with which Modern English speakers are most familiar, the English grammatical gender system is all but gone.

While recent work on gender has clarified much of the relevant terminology, the term *natural gender* has to date not been adequately explained. It is here that a historical perspective, as presented in this book, has much to offer. Examining the historical development of the English gender system provides a new understanding of the development of natural gender. This chapter, drawing on a range of earlier scholarship devoted to defining linguistic gender and the Modern English gender system specifically, frames important possible ways to redefine natural gender for English. It is only within this context that we can make sense of the gender shift in the history of English, of the variation still present in the system today, and of what it means for the masculine to be unmarked in the grammar and lexicon.

1.2 Definitions of linguistic gender

Gender in language, which can be referred to by the general term *linguistic gender*, can be defined at the most basic level as a system of noun classification reflected in the behavior of associated words (Hockett, quoted in Corbett [1991: 1]). Stated differently, the essential criterion of linguistic gender is taken to be *agreement* (also known as *concord*), or systematic and predictable covariance between a semantic or formal property of one grammatical form and a formal property of another. Gender only exists if grammatical forms with variable gender (e.g., adjectives, pronouns, numerals) regularly adopt forms to agree with grammatical forms of invariable gender, usually nouns (Fodor 1959: 2). Given this definition of linguistic gender, there is no determinable limit to the number of genders possible in language, and in the known languages studied to date, linguists have recorded gender systems ranging from two to over twenty gender classifications.[2] We see this kind of gender agreement in French in the sentence:

---

[2] Speakers of many Western languages tend to have a limited view of gender, restricting it to the familiar two- or three-gender systems of Indo-European languages. And they are often supported in this by language authorities. For example, the second edition of the *OED* privileges Indo-European gender systems in its definition of grammatical gender. The primary definition begins: "Each of the three (or in some languages two) grammatical 'kinds', corresponding more or less to distinctions of sex (and absence of sex) in the objects denoted . . ." It is important to note with respect to this first definition that, in fact, the treatment of sexless nouns – many of which are grammatically masculine or feminine – does not usually correspond to distinctions of sex in these systems. For sense (b) under this definition, the editors provide the explanation:

French: Une petite boîte est arrivée de Paris.
'A small box has come from Paris.'

Within the noun phrase, the indefinite article *une* and the adjective *petite* both appear in the feminine form to agree with the feminine noun *boîte* 'box,' and the past participle of the verb (*arrivée*) also takes the feminine *-e*.

Old English demonstrates very similar types of agreement patterns both inside and outside the noun phrase. For example, in this highly contrived Old English sentence:

Old English: Seo brade lind wæs tilu and ic hire lufode.
'That broad shield was good and I loved her' (literally: 'her loved').

The demonstrative pronoun *seo* 'the, that' and the adjectives *brade* 'broad' and *tilu* 'good' appear in their feminine form to agree with the feminine noun *lind* 'shield'; in the second clause, the shield is then referred back to with the feminine pronoun *hire* 'her' in accordance with the noun's grammatical gender. As the Modern English translation demonstrates, this kind of grammatical agreement for gender has been lost; only the personal pronouns still mark gender and it is semantically, not grammatically, based.

The role of personal pronouns in systems of linguistic gender has remained something of a question mark. Agreement in gender usually involves a noun and associated adjectives, demonstrative pronouns, definite and indefinite articles, possessives, or verbs, although it also occurs with, for example, associated adverbs and numerals. Anaphoric pronouns, referring back to noun phrases headed by gender-marked nouns (e.g., *hire* 'her' in the Old English example above), could hypothetically be argued to agree with the referent, not the preceding antecedent noun phrase, so that the covariance of the noun and personal pronoun are not grammatically linked but both dependent on the extralinguistic referent (Cornish 1986).[3] This theory, however, cannot explain anaphoric pronoun concord in most grammatical gender systems because there is no "natural" gender

By some recent philologists applied, in extended sense, to the 'kinds' into which sbs. [substantives (nouns)] are discriminated by the syntactical laws of certain languages the grammar of which takes no account of sex. Thus the North American Indian languages are said to have two 'genders', animate and inanimate. With still greater departure from the original sense, the name 'genders' has been applied to the many syntactically discriminated classes of sbs. in certain South African langs.

If one takes the "original sense" of the word back to the Latin *genus* 'race, kind,' it applies as well to the grammatical categories in North American Indian languages as it does to those in French or in English.

[3] The distinction between anaphora and deixis is fairly complex and fuzzy around the edges. There appears to be no maximum allowable distance between an antecedent and its anaphoric pronoun, and the farther the pronoun occurs from its antecedent, the harder it becomes to differentiate it from a deictic pronoun. *Anaphora* is traditionally defined in contrast to *deixis*, based on the differentiation between intralinguistic and extralinguistic reference (Huddleston [1984: 274–84] well exemplifies this traditional approach). Anaphoric pronouns are dependent on their linguistic

link between the referent and the nouns that describe it; in other words, the gender of a noun – on which the anaphoric pronoun depends for agreement – is not necessarily predictable from any features of the extralinguistic referent. Most scholars, therefore, consider the control of anaphoric pronouns by their antecedents to represent a form of grammatical agreement; it is clear that the same gender categories, be they grammatical or semantic, apply for pronominal agreement as elsewhere in the grammar, although their pattern of application may differ on the continuum of grammatical to semantic agreement.[4] (This idea is discussed in detail below in the description of Corbett's agreement hierarchy.) Given this inclusive definition of agreement, languages in which gender surfaces only in the personal pronouns (e.g., Modern English) would still be regarded as possessing a gender system; Corbett (1991: 5) labels these *pronominal gender systems* in order to emphasize their unique (and contested) status.

context for interpretation; they are anaphoric to the antecedent, and their gender, therefore, reflects the linguistic gender of the noun or noun-phrase acting as the antecedent. Deictic pronouns are situation-dependent and refer outside the linguistic context to the "real world" referent. Cornish (1986), however, argues that purely syntactic explanations of anaphora are insufficient; anaphoric agreement patterns cannot be adequately explained using only syntactic rules and constraints because anaphora is fundamentally a discourse phenomenon: not only does its domain exceed the sentence, but it carries specific discourse functions, which are as predictable as syntactic constraints and can override them. Anaphora presupposes a common pre-existing focus and it serves as a mechanism for the *maintenance* of a common object of focus within a discourse. Deixis involves the introduction of a new object of focus within the discourse, so it serves to *shift* the pre-existing focus to a new object, which will become the focus of the subsequent stretch of discourse (and hence a possible object for anaphora). These alternate definitions of anaphora and deixis do not rely exclusively on the notion of an antecedent because, as he argues, it is not a necessary or sufficient condition for anaphora:

> The discourse entity to which the anaphor refers . . . need not, however, have been explicitly introduced by linguistic means within the discourse model which each participant is constructing as the discourse progresses: it may have been derived via an inference on the basis of some such explicitly realised linguistic expression, or via the participants jointly focusing upon some perceptually available entity within the context-of-utterance, or it may already have been available through general or specific socio-cultural real-world knowledge, or simply by being an issue of continuing mutual concern to the participants involved. (Cornish 1986: 3)

According to this definition, the power of anaphoric elements to "refer back" need not be limited to the syntactic structure. The distinction between intralinguistic and extralinguistic reference remains fundamental to this definition of anaphora and deixis, but intralinguistic reference is extended to include larger elements of discourse. The studies in this book, which are entirely text-based, do not necessarily require this wider discourse-based definition of anaphora, but it does benefit from its flexibility in determining a pronoun's antecedent or basis for agreement. See Newman (1997: 63–116) for a valuable, more detailed discussion of anaphora and theoretical accounts of pronouns.

[4] An alternative framework for analyzing these patterns is the distinction between *lexical* and *referential* gender (cf. Dahl 1999: 105–106). Lexical gender can be semantically, formally, or idiosyncratically determined; referential gender is dependent on the characteristics of the referent. This distinction is perhaps particularly useful in analyzing animate nouns in a grammatical gender system, when lexical gender and referential gender may conflict.

Gender, although a common feature in languages throughout the world, is not essential to language; many languages have never had gender systems and others have lost them with no lethal repercussions. Ibrahim (1973: 26) describes gender as a secondary grammatical category (i.e., one that is not vital to the proper functioning of the language), or, less neutrally, as an "unessential category, which serves no useful purpose that cannot be served by some other means"; unlike other secondary grammatical categories such as tense and number, linguistic gender is a category with no "authentic relation" to conceptual categories. This statement demands qualification. Corbett (1991), in the most comprehensive cross-linguistic study of gender systems to date, equitably concludes that noun classification often corresponds to biological distinctions of sex, although frequently it does not. He defines two basic types of gender systems: (1) strict semantic systems (here referred to as *semantic gender*), in which the meaning of the noun determines its gender and, conversely, in which aspects of a noun's meaning can be inferred from its gender; (2) formal systems (here referred to as *grammatical gender*), in which large numbers of nouns do not follow semantic assignment rules and their assignments depend on formal criteria, either word-structure (derivation and inflection) or sound-structure. Even in formal systems, in which the bulk of gender assignments rest on morphological and phonological factors, there is a semantic core to the system; in this way, all linguistic gender systems are at some level semantic, although in only some systems is meaning sufficient for gender assignment (Corbett 1991: 8). Dahl (1999: 101) postulates as a universal property of gender systems that there is a general semantic-based principle for assigning gender to animate nouns.[5] The assertion

---

[5] The fact that all gender systems are at some level semantic has led many scholars to postulate that linguistic gender originates in conceptual categories of sex and this initial logical order was only later made chaotic by linguistic developments (e.g., sound changes, analogy). Through the early twentieth century, the most popular explanation of the origin of grammatical gender was that it represented the personification of objects by "primitive man." Ibrahim (1973: 50) decisively dismisses this romantic notion:

> [G]ender in its origin was an accident of linguistic history, and that as a grammatical category gender owes its emergence and existence to various linguistic (and no extralinguistic) forces. We have seen how phonetic changes, morphology, and syntax worked together in some languages to bring about gender. . . . [G]rammatical gender is merely a means for classifying nouns according to their suffixes without, in the beginning, any allusion to sex; the sex reference of gender was always posterior to the emergence of grammatical gender.

The question of the origin of grammatical gender is too complex a matter to be discussed in any depth here. Two of the most thorough works written on the subject are Fodor (1959) and Ibrahim (1973), both of which summarize much of the scholarship that precedes them. The juiciest bone of contention between Fodor and Ibrahim is whether the three genders of Indo-European arose simultaneously (as Ibrahim argues, based on work by Lehmann and Brugmann) or whether there was initially a separation of animate and inanimate, after which the former category further divided into masculine and feminine (first suggested by Meillet and promoted by Fodor). Weber (1999), returning to and rethinking a theory proposed by Brugmann in 1897 that the Indo-European

that grammatical gender categories have *no* authentic relation to conceptual ones may, therefore, be misleading.

Where does the term "natural gender" fall in this dichotomous classification system of formal and semantic gender? Corbett (1991: 9) defines a *natural gender system* as synonymous with a strict semantic one: "a system where given the meaning of a noun, its gender can be predicted without reference to its form." Given the very different and widespread use of this term in most gender scholarship, particularly work focused on English, it is preferable to define natural gender systems as a subset of strict semantic ones: a tri-partite gender system (masculine, feminine, neuter) in which the classification of nouns corresponds for the most part to the real-world distinctions of male animate (or male human), female animate (or female human), and inanimate (or non-human). In other words, while semantic gender systems are predictable based on features of the referent, the relevant features are not necessarily biological sex, and the categories can be much more numerous. For example, Dyirbal, a language spoken by Aboriginal Australians in North Queensland, has four genders, in which men are categorized with kangaroos, bats, the moon, etc.; women with the sun, water, fire, bandicoots, etc.; all edible fruit with the plants that bear them, wine, cake, etc.; and meat, body parts, most trees, and many other objects comprise another class (for a summary, see G. Lakoff 1987: 92–96). These are semantic classes, but not ones that native English speakers would predict. Other languages with semantic gender systems (e.g., the Bantu languages) have between ten and twenty noun categories. So the three-gender "natural" system is only one type of semantic gender system.

Given the semantic core in all gender systems, it seems logical to assume that strict semantic systems are more common – especially if one happens to be a native English speaker, for whom grammatical systems often appear absurdly arbitrary. But, in fact, semantic gender systems comprise a comparatively small percentage of the languages of the world,[6] and grammatical gender is not as arbitrary as it may first appear. Erades (1956: 9) typifies the prejudice of Modern English speakers against the unfamiliar mechanics of formal agreement when he dismisses grammatical gender as a "largely traditional, archaic, perhaps essentially primitive system of prescriptions and taboos. A part of the linguistic reality, no doubt, but a dead part, a petrification." He has, either intentionally or unintentionally, translated Meillet's description "dénuée de sens" in reference to grammatical gender (cited in Erades 1956: 9) as 'nonsensical' rather than

---

feminine originally functioned to form abstracts and collectives, argues that gender corresponds to the basic distinction [± particularized]. She explains: "[G]ender has the function of qualitatively more precisely defining a quantity. Gender offers the opportunity to refine the crude perspective of number – singular versus plural – into distributive versus collective plural. It is this aspect of quantity that links gender so closely to number" (Weber 1999: 506).

[6] Corbett (1991) notes that there are several strict semantic systems in the Dravidian family and others "scattered about" (e.g., in the Australian Aboriginal language Diyari and in the Germanic language English).

'non-semantic.' Grammatical gender is not a set of memorized prescriptions – the facts argue against it (Corbett 1991: 70–104). Native speakers make no or few mistakes with noun gender, borrowed words regularly acquire gender, and speakers can consistently assign gender to invented words (see the study of Italian gender in Ervin 1962). In the languages with grammatical gender systems studied to date, the gender of at least 85 percent of nouns is predictable by morphological or phonological information required and stored independently in the lexicon (Corbett 1991: 68).

Another fairly predictable characteristic of grammatical gender systems is that for animate nouns, when formal and semantic features – specifically biological sex – conflict, semantic gender (i.e., the gender of the referent, sometimes referred to as referential gender, as opposed to lexical gender) usually prevails, either for both attribute and pronoun agreement (e.g., Russian *djadja* 'uncle,' which is feminine in form but requires masculine agreement) or only for some select types of agreement (e.g., German *Mädchen* 'girl'). Corbett labels this latter group *hybrid nouns*, and he has done ground-breaking work on their patterns of agreement. Hybrid nouns do not follow the agreement paradigm of one gender, nor do they alternate between two or more consistent gender paradigms. Their agreement (i.e., grammatical or semantic) depends on the type of agreeing form involved (the *target*). To return to the example of German *Mädchen*, the type of agreement it elicits depends on whether the target is an attribute, in which case it follows grammatical gender and is neuter in form, or whether the target is a personal pronoun, in which case it can either follow grammatical gender (neuter *es*) or follow semantic gender (feminine *sie*). These nouns typically arise when semantic and formal assignment rules conflict, and Corbett argues that it is possible to specify or predict agreement given the target in question. He has created a model called the "Agreement Hierarchy" (shown below), in which, moving from left to right, there is a consistently increasing likelihood of semantic agreement.[7]

The Agreement Hierarchy

attributive < predicate < relative pronoun < personal pronoun

The agreement pattern of *Mädchen* perfectly exemplifies this system, as do Spanish titles for men, which require the feminine for attributes but take the masculine elsewhere (see Corbett 1991: 225–60 for more examples and explanation). Moving from left to right along the hierarchy, there is increasing flexibility in reference, so that the congruent form of personal pronouns can follow either

---

[7] Newman (1997: 92–93) provides a revised interpretation of Corbett's hierarchy within the framework of Barlow's Discourse-Linking Theory. He quotes Barlow (1992: 224) on the distinction of pronouns from other agreement targets: "Moving to the right, the more likely it is that the targets will contribute new properties; the more likely it is that the targets will be associated with multiple mappings; and the more likely it is that agreement targets will indicate salient properties of the described object."

formal or semantic rules (as with *Mädchen*). Certain nouns in Modern English demonstrate the varying levels of rigidity and flexibility in the two right-hand categories (the other two categories are not applicable to Modern English): for a word such as *ship*, the anaphoric pronoun has the potential to fluctuate between *she* and *it*, but the relative pronoun is restricted to *which* or *that*, not *who*. (The form of agreement chosen can be influenced by the spoken or written register, sociolinguistic variables, and pragmatic considerations.) The personal pronouns, situated on the far right of the hierarchy, are both the most tenacious targets, for they retain gender agreement longest when the system is being lost from a language, and the most volatile targets, for they are, as Corbett (1991: 242) phrases it, "the major initiator of changes in the balance between syntactic and semantic gender."

This description of how personal pronouns function as agreement targets perfectly captures their role in the transformation of the English gender system. As grammatical gender erodes in the noun phrase in early Middle English and remaining gendered forms in the noun phrase potentially take on new discourse functions (see Jones 1988), the personal pronouns are the only forms to retain gender, and they shift to natural gender. Pronominal gender systems, in general, tend to favor a shift to semantic assignment. The form of anaphoric pronouns can be determined either by the form of the antecedent or by the semantic features of the antecedent/referent; in a system with no attributive agreement and with the potential for nouns of different genders all denoting one referent, the pressure is on the pronouns to follow semantic assignment rules (Corbett 1991: 247). The deictic use of personal pronouns only enhances this tendency towards semantic agreement. In Modern English, the personal pronouns alone retain linguistic gender and it is clearly semantic gender agreement that they follow – but in modern scholarship on English, this seems to be where scholarly agreement on the gender system ends.

1.3   Proposed models for the Modern English gender system

The Modern English gender system is clearly based on semantic criteria, unlike its Indo-European ancestors. Many Indo-European languages other than English have witnessed a noticeable decay in the original grammatical gender system, although few are as dramatic as English (Ibrahim 1973: 84–86).[8] The triple-gender system has been maintained in, for example, German and some of the Slavic languages. It has been reduced to a two-gender system in the Romance languages, and it has disappeared in Persian. Ibrahim (1973) notes that the neuter was always only "vaguely" distinguished from the masculine; its paradigm of inflectional endings often differed in only two cases, so the merger of the two gender classes did not involve the restructuring of entire paradigms. The shift from

---

[8] While decay is the overall trend in Indo-European gender systems, there have been a few languages, notably those in the Slavonic group, which have added subgenders to the system (Corbett 1991: 2).

grammatical to natural gender renders English unusual among Indo-Germanic languages. Having lost most nominal and adnominal inflectional endings by the Middle English period, English has become a pronominal gender system, in which the personal pronouns *he/she/it* reflect a triple-gender system and the relative pronouns *who/which* distinguish only between the animate and the inanimate. While many speakers and scholars have remarked on the system's superficial simplicity, those who have tried to describe the system in detail have been struck by its complexity. As Erades (1956: 2) states, "[T]he gender of English nouns, far from being simple and clear, is complicated and obscure, and the principles underlying it are baffling and elusive, no less, and perhaps even more so, than in other languages."

Such a statement might seem absurd given that most nouns in Modern English follow the traditional semantic formulation of the system in which pronominal gender corresponds to distinctions of "real-world" biological sex. But most is not enough: the key to understanding the natural gender system in Modern English lies in the exceptions, the inanimate nouns that can take gendered pronouns and the human or other animate nouns that can take *it*. As Erades correctly notes, these exceptions do not prove the traditional rule of natural gender, but rather they prove the rule wrong (although *rule* is probably too strong a word to apply to natural gender agreement in any circumstances). The natural gender system is not a simple one-to-one correspondence between biological sex and linguistic gender with scattered exceptions. Theoretical notions of gender in other disciplines complicate the role of biological sex in the construction of gender in useful ways here; and they support the argument that, in fact, the exceptions to the system as traditionally defined form patterns that need to be addressed in any formulation of the system, because English speakers are consistently inconsistent in their choice of gendered pronouns according to strict natural gender rules (see, for example, Marcoux 1973).

The difficulty in describing the English system is two-fold. First, the traditional idea that gender is a fixed property of the word must be abandoned, along with the idea that, on a grander scale, all gender systems must operate in perfectly similar ways (Joly 1975: 238). Second, the new formulation of the gender system must be based on features that may not be immediately obvious either to speakers or linguists because there are few formal clues. Whorf (1956) draws the important distinction between overt and covert grammatical categories: an overt category is one having a formal mark that is present in every sentence containing a member of the category (e.g., English plural); a covert category includes members that are marked only in certain types of sentences. (Whorf labels the distinctive treatment required in such environments "reactance.") In English, gender is a covert category marked only by the reactance of singular third-person pronouns and the relative pronouns *who/what/which* (which indicate animacy). Despite this limited presence in the surface structure of English syntax, gender is nonetheless a grammatical category and requires a systematic analysis of the patterns of anaphoric pronoun use for clues about the structure of the categories within the system. Intuitive assumptions about the relationship between sex and gender are not sufficient, for while biological sex is a good indicator of gender class, it is not absolutely predictive.

The exceptional nouns, those that can flout the biological sex-linguistic gender correlation, have traditionally been divided into two basic types: conventionalized references and emotive (or affective) references. The conventional gender assignments of certain inanimate nouns seem to hold irrespective of the attitude of the speaker, and they are fairly consistent within speech communities (e.g., *ship* as *she*). Proper names could be included in this category, given that their genders are learned and conventional, and they apply even when the name is used for an inanimate object (Whorf 1956: 90–91). Whorf argues strongly that English gender represents a grammatical category because the distinctions it creates are not always natural, non-cultural differences, but they must instead be learned; he lists a series of exceptions, which has been heavily cited in subsequent literature on linguistic gender:

> Nor would knowledge of any 'natural' properties tell our observer that the names of biological classes themselves (e.g. animal, bird, fish, etc.) are 'it'; that smaller animals usually are 'it'; larger animals often 'he'; dogs, eagles, and turkeys usually 'he'; cats and wrens usually 'she'; body parts and the whole botanical world 'it'; countries and states as fictive persons (but not as localities) 'she'; cities, societies, and corporations as fictive persons 'it'; the human body 'it'; a ghost 'it'; nature 'she'; watercraft with sail or power and named small craft 'she'; unnamed rowboats, canoes, rafts 'it,' etc. (Whorf 1956: 90)

Whorf's attempt at gender categorization, however, potentially muddles the situation more than clarifies it. With the phrase "as fictive persons" appearing throughout the description, Whorf undermines the distinction between conventional gender, personification, and colloquial variation due to emotive gender assignments. Personification accounts for some gendered references to inanimates, particularly in literary registers of the language; here allegory and poetic diction effectively create gendered objects. And occasionally these uses pervade more colloquial registers, but the bulk of gendered inanimate references occur in everyday speech with no conscious personification. While the use of *she* for *nature* seems fairly clearly conventional, the use of *he* for dogs, to pick one example, is more problematic because the pronoun references for dogs have more potential to fluctuate from *it* to *he* and for many speakers, also to *she*, depending on the dog, the circumstance, and the speaker. The choice of pronoun depends greatly on the psychological and sociological attitude of the speaker toward the referent as well as the attributes of the referent. Much of the twentieth-century scholarship on Modern English gender recognizes the dependence of English gender on speaker attitudes (e.g., Svartengren 1927, Erades 1956, Kanekiyo 1965, Joly 1975, Vachek 1976, Morris 1993), but the research comes to dramatically different conclusions about the implications of this dependence, ranging from the assertion that English has no system of gender to the formulation of multiple formal gender classes.

Structuralist attempts to describe Modern English gender have often required the creation of new classification systems with categories based on the personal and relative pronouns that can be applied to a given noun: for example, Strang (1970: 95) proposes seven gender classes and Kanekiyo (1965) outlines twelve (e.g., *he-they-who*; *she-they-who*; *he/she-they-who*; *it-they-which*; *it/he/she-they-who/which*). Joly (1975: 234) dismisses these theories as "no more than a methodical arrangement of facts previously collected by traditional grammarians." They cannot provide a description of any larger systematic pattern; they can account for which pronouns are required by certain nouns, but they cannot account for how or why nouns have been classified in this way. As justification for his new classification system, Kanekiyo pushes the idea of gender variability to its limit and thereby destroys the possibility of effectively describing a *system*. He initially claims that there is no clear correlation of gender with sex: the choice of the pronoun depends not on characteristics of the noun or of its referent, but depends instead entirely on speaker-dependent factors, which are variable and unpredictable. Kanekiyo (1965: 235) qualifies this last assertion by stating that there exists "some element" of semantic consistency based on sex, animateness, size, shape, and speaker attitude: for example, "nouns *obviously* denoting male human beings and animals are *usually* referred to by *he*" (italics added).

Erades (1956), in the face of the same speaker-based variation in gender, concludes that, in fact, English has no gender at all, a conclusion echoed by Markus (1988: 242) and cited by Greenbaum (1996: 583). English gender cannot be a system of concord between nouns and pronouns because not only do nouns never overtly mark gender (which is not always the case since, for example, the suffix -*woman* unambiguously marks feminine nouns) but also antecedent nouns do not always grammatically appear before anaphoric pronouns (according to the strictest definition of anaphora, as discussed above). In this case, Erades explains, if gender were a system of concord, it would be between pronouns and ideas (notional gender); but clearly gender is not even inherent in ideas because it fluctuates from speaker to speaker. With such a dependence on speaker attitudes, English gender, while "alive" in the language, cannot be regarded as a system: "Can we speak of gender in a language where the same may at one moment be masculine, at another feminine of [sic] neuter, and, let us mark it well, in the language of the same speaker and sometimes in one and the same sentence?" (Erades 1956: 9). Erades concludes that English has no gender, unless the term is reinterpreted "beyond recognition"; the "system" is that pronoun reference varies with the mood, temper, frame of mind, and private circumstances of the speaker (his or her psychological attitude), which are usually neutral (hence English gender's apparent stability) but not always so: "The old schoolbook rule to the effect that a male being is a *he*, a female being a *she* and a thing an *it* only applies when the speaker is emotionally neutral to the subject referred to; as soon as his language becomes affectively coloured, a living being may become an *it*, *this* or *what* and a thing a *he* or *she*" (*ibid.*: 10).

In his comparisons of English to French and German, Erades makes no distinction between grammatical and semantic gender systems, implying that there is one grammatical gender system and those languages that do not comply have no system at all; in addition, by limiting anaphora to antecedents present in the syntax, he too quickly dismisses the possibility of English nouns carrying gender. Erades claims that gendered pronoun reference is based on "momentary and individual psychological associations" in the mind of the speaker, with no discernible patterns in individual or community usage. Erades rightly emphasizes speaker attitudes and the variability inherent in the English gender system, but he too sweepingly abandons systematicity in favor of speaker whims. Contemporary sociolinguistic research has shown that speech patterns within communities are often systematic and explicable given information about extralinguistic factors. In short, speaker-based theories are not inherently irregular.

The recognition of its variability is a crucial component to understanding Modern English gender, but it is equally important not to overemphasize unpredictability: although biological sex is not absolutely predictive, there are regular, identifiable patterns that are both semantic and sociolinguistic. English gender is not a completely "momentary," unpredictable phenomenon, a fact that Vachek nicely summarizes in his account of gender's sociolinguistic predictability: "The fact is that if all factors that co-operate in determining the pronominal reference are duly considered and if their hierarchy is carefully established, the apparent confusion becomes clarified and the knotty relations disentangled. In other words, if the situation of the speaker and his [sic] approach to the extra-lingual reality he is handling are satisfactorily stated, his pronominal reference to this reality should be perfectly predictable" (Vachek 1976: 389). There must be a system of gender, he concludes, if it can be so systematically manipulated; the gender category may not be strictly grammatical but it is lexico-stylistic (by which he seems to mean semantic and affective).

Attempts to describe the semantic and extralinguistic factors determining English pronoun reference, most of which postulate emotional involvement on the part of the speaker, have met with limited success. Svartengren, one of the earliest scholars to study Modern English gender variation in detail, examines exceptional uses of feminine pronouns in the "homely style" of speech or the "vernacular" (as opposed to literary language). Working from the premise that the use of the feminine for inanimate objects is an American phenomenon that has influenced British English, he devises three categories of objects that can take the feminine: (1) concrete things made or worked upon by man [sic], e.g., machinery, industrial plants, receptacles, motors, rooms, houses, money, roads; (2) substantive actions, abstract ideas, e.g., "whooping her up"; (3) nature and natural objects not worked upon by man. The feature that unifies the categories is that the use of *she* reflects emotional interest on the part of the speaker, a bond of living and working together: "[W]e must come to the conclusion that the emotional character is the distinguishing feature of the phenomenon. Consequently, *she* (*her*) does not so much mark the gender of a more or less fanciful personification – though there are more than traces of such a thing – as denote the object of an emotion" (Svartengren 1927: 109).[9] While Svartengren's dismissal of personification as the root of "exceptional" gender references and his conclusions about the emotional uses of gender are productive, they inappropriately limit these uses to the feminine and ignore larger patterns of gender agreement including exceptional masculine and neuter references.

Subsequent attempts to pinpoint the factors determining emotive gender references have often proposed that masculine and feminine references to inanimate objects reflect negative and positive attitudes on the part of speakers toward the referent. Vachek (1976), noting that exceptional gendered associations cluster around some typical invariants and have social values, formulates a scale with a neutral, unmarked reference between two polar extremes for positive and negative feelings toward the facts of any given reality. About these marked uses, he states:

> The reason why the feminine set was chosen to refer to the positive kind of approach (signalling the thing referred to as amiable, intimately known, delicate, etc.), while the masculine set serves to denote the opposite, negative kind of approach (signalling, in its turn, the concerned thing as huge, strong, unwieldy or generally unpleasant) is too obvious to need detailed specification – it reflects the common conception of the femine [sic] *vs.* masculine features regarded as typical of each of the two sexes. (Vachek 1976: 388)

Traugott (1972) concurs with this model of the affective gender system, also assuming the correlation between feminine and positive, masculine and negative to be transparent. The consensus is that for animate nouns, the masculine and feminine are both unmarked (and only one is possible), which means there is no polar opposition available for emotive reference. Speakers can, therefore, express

---

[9] According to late nineteenth- and early twentieth-century grammarians, there were lists of nouns (other than humans and animals) that took the feminine in the "homely style." But Svartengren claims that these lists do not match the usage patterns he has discovered; he argues this use of the feminine is a fairly modern phenomenon, possibly with "slender roots" in Elizabethan England, and he explains that the gendered usage by Milton and Dryden is personification due to literary associations (i.e., it is not colloquial) and the emotional function is only vaguely present. The line between colloquial usage and personification is difficult to draw and perhaps harder to defend, and Svartengren's assertion about the modernity of such gender usage cannot account for the long history of flexibility and fluctuation that has characterized the natural gender system throughout the history of English. Joly rejects the idea of gender fluctuation as an American development, stating, "Parallel developments point to a common origin: in other words, the tendency to use *she* (or *he*) for inanimate nouns, and conversely *it* for animates, was a possibility already included in the system of gender when the English-speaking community started breaking up in the seventeenth century" (Joly 1975: 233). The material presented in Chapter Four confirms this statement, proving that the tendency was more a reality than a possibility, long before the seventeenth century.

negative feelings toward an animate referent by downgrading him or her to *it*, and all other positive or negative feelings must be inferred from context.

The associations between feminine and positive, masculine and negative are not, however, obvious. Feminine references can reflect positive emotions toward a referent, but they also can reflect negative attitudes, about, for instance, frailty or weakness; in addition, masculine references can be positive about, for example, size and strength. The polar positive/negative distinction these scholars try to delineate is too neat, sharp, and simplistic (see Mathiot [1979] for a more detailed study of referential gender that blurs this dichotomy).

Joly (1975), combining structuralist principles and speaker involvement, downplays the role of the sex distinction in his description of the gender system.[10] According to his model, animacy and humanity are the top two parameters for determining gender, a reflection of fundamental distinctions in Indo-European, which are revealed once the language "did away with" morphological gender (Joly 1975: 248). To explain the fluctuation in the gender of discourse, Joly relies on speaker attitudes and perceptions of the referent:

> My contention here is that Modern English reproduces very consistently at least part of the Indo-European pattern of gender, viz. the basic opposition *animate-powerful* vs. *inanimate-powerless*. In English, whenever the speaker feels that an object or any inanimate notion possesses some kind of power, the neuter anaphoric pronoun it may be replaced by one of the two animate pronouns *he* or *she* pertaining to the sphere of humanity which is the proper sphere or power. (*Ibid.*: 254)

Likewise, when a human is deprived of power and/or personality, speakers use *it*. Joly distinguishes two degrees of power within the field of animation: major power (masculine) and minor power (feminine). So, he argues, the choice of a gendered pronoun for an inanimate is not based on sex distinction but power distinction, and there is the tendency to use the lower power first for an inanimate (it is closer to its original no-power status) unless compelled to do otherwise. All fluctuations in gender reflect speakers' emotional attitudes, from affection to contempt.

The theoretical weakness with this model lies, once again, in the attempt to reduce the semantic and sociolinguistic factors involved in English gender assignment to definable binaries, such as powerful–powerless. Morris (1993)

---

[10] Joly relies heavily on Gustave Guillaume's dichotomy between *tongue* and *discourse*, in which *tongue* is a closed set of conditions in a language that allows an unlimited number of consequences at the level of *discourse* – a framework that echoes Saussure's original distinction between *langue* and *parole*. His representation of gender in tongue includes the possibility for gender changes in pronoun reference which then appear in the gender of discourse. Interestingly, these fluctuations occur more often in direct speech and interlocution, showing the effect of standardization on narratives; speech exemplifies a gender of discourse which adapts to situational and extralinguistic facts. But the fluctuations are not completely free, as they are limited by the finite number of possibilities incorporated in tongue.

makes a useful move in relabeling the referent as the *denotatum*, in order to contrast it with the *designatum*, or the speaker's extralinguistic mental construal of the object. This distinction allows the useful separation of biological traits in the denotatum from individual speakers' experience or impressions of it, and it is on the latter conception that gender assignment is based. But Morris, while rightly emphasizing speaker experience in the assignment of gender, still relies on binaries in the analysis of "exceptional" gender references, in this case based on predictability or lack thereof.

It is impossible to pinpoint precise factors in gender assignment, although it is very possible to recognize patterns. As importantly, there is no reason to postulate a dichotomy between natural (unmarked) gender and affective gender in English (cf. Baron 1971, Traugott 1972). To do so is to treat the fluctuations in gender as exceptional, as excluded from the base or unmarked system. Instead, the formulation should involve only one system, which incorporates "unmarked" and "marked," "neutral" and "emotive," "natural" and "unnatural" gender references. This one system for English gender can be described as semantic, with the understanding that not all of semantics can be broken down into componential binaries. In a well-pointed reminder, Corbett (1991: 32) remarks that in all semantic systems, "it is important to bear in mind that the world view of speakers determines the categories involved, and that the criteria may not be immediately obvious to an outside observer." And they may be even less obvious to insiders trying to describe their own language.

1.4   A re-understanding of Modern English gender

Beyond all the specific features that scholars have tried to isolate over the years to explain variation in Modern English gender references lies the broader concept that gender in the language reflects the social constructions of gender learned, maintained, and perpetuated by speakers. This description of linguistic gender clarifies the correlation between gender as defined in other academic disciplines and gender as it should be defined in the grammar of Modern English. It redefines the terms by which gender in Modern English is a semantic category. In feminist theory, it is a given that social constructions of gender represent combinations of features inherent in "reality" and of society's attitudes toward those features. Members of a given culture or society create the categories of masculine and feminine and determine what those ideas represent. They are not fixed categories – they fluctuate through time, by context, and by speaker. There is, however, consistency in the core features generally attributed to these categories (e.g., biological sex) and in the shared beliefs and attitudes about them within a culture. This description of the semantic categories in a natural gender system corresponds to the formulation of semantic prototype theory described by George Lakoff (1987), drawing heavily on work by Eleanor Rosch. In this model, categorization is a matter of both human experience and imagination: "of perception, motor activity, and culture on the one hand, and of metaphor, metonymy, and mental imagery on the other" (G. Lakoff 1987: 8). Both fuzzy and radial categories, as defined by Lakoff, have central members and fuzzy boundaries, which allow for partial membership and variability, just as we find in Modern English gender categories.

Four decades ago, Ervin (1962) recognized this correlation between gender in the language (semantic gender) and gender in the culture.

> Taking gender as an example, there is an anatomical distinction, but we assign sex by these ultimate criteria only at birth or with animals. Most of the time we judge human sex on the basis of secondary, imperfectly corre-lated contrasts such as size, type of clothing, hair style, and voice. Finally, cultural experience and verbal practice differentiate the sexes and the mas-culine or feminine nouns which refer to them. We may therefore expect to find three different bases for meanings which might be generalized: (a) sexual symbolism associated with anatomical differences or sexual rela-tions; (b) physical properties varying in their correlation with sex, such as size; (c) cultural associations such as contrasts in beauty, slowness, laziness, and stability. Within a given culture, we can predict systematic contrasts in meaning between masculine and feminine words with no animate referent. (Ervin 1962: 253)

The three different bases of gender assignment Ervin lists are fundamental to cultural constructions of gender, and it is not surprising, therefore, to find them reflected in linguistic distinctions of gender. While they closely correlate to sex, they are not wholly dependent on it, and they carry the potential for synchronic and diachronic variation. Suzanne Romaine (1999: 73–82) also creates a series of connections between notions of femininity and the feminine gendering of inanimate objects (e.g., cities, like women, being in need of conquest). Neither, however, pushes as hard as is possible on the obvious connection to theoretical social constructions of gender – an overarching concept beyond lists of features and examples – nor does either take a historical perspective on the question, which in fact helps to reveal this theoretical connection for the modern system.

"Animacy" tends to be assumed as a given entity in distinguishing genders – if not cross-culturally, at least inter-culturally – but it is not nearly so stable a con-cept. For example, the Ojibwa gender system relies on animacy, but their notions of animacy are not the same as ours (e.g., snow, snowshoes, and cooking pots are animate), which clearly reflects a different culture and world view (Romaine 1999: 69–70).[11] Nevalainen and Raumolin-Brunberg (1994: 182–84) note that animacy distinctions in the early Modern English period were different from those today, as higher animals as well as trees, water, and various human body parts were often seen as animate, which allowed for more frequent gendered reference to

---

[11] Dahl (1999: 101) describes the hypothesized "animacy hierarchy" HUMAN > ANIMAL > INANI-MATE and postulates that "animacy" with respect to gender assignment may be defined differently, cutting off at different points in the animacy hierarchy.

these non-human antecedents. If, as Nevalainen and Raumolin-Brunberg argue, the choice between personal and non-personal gender is determined by whether a being is felt to possess characteristics associated with a member of the human race, then the choice between genders should be similarly determined; the assignment of gender will, therefore, correspond to some degree to contemporaneous constructions of gender in the culture, which may not be immediately obvious to speakers or to historical linguists.

Laqueur (1990: 134–42), in his history of the body and gender, points out that sex as defined in early modern England shows greater similarities to what today would be called gender, because biological, anatomical differences between men and women were inextricably intertwined with gendered characteristics. One of the two was not necessarily seen as more fundamental or "biological" than the other. This lack of a distinction between essential gendered traits and biology may provide one explanation for how certain inanimate nouns were classified as masculine or feminine in Early Modern English and earlier, after the semantic gender system had taken hold. Although these inanimate objects did not have any biological sex, they could exhibit a sufficient number of characteristics associated with one sex to be "naturally" classified under that gender.

Ben Jonson provides an extended list of gendered inanimate nouns in his description of early Modern English gender in the *English Grammar* (1640):

> Of the *Genders* there are sixe. *First*, the *Masculine*, which comprehendeth all *Males*, or what is understood under a *Masculine species*: as *Angels*, *Men*, *Starres*: and (by *Prosopopoeia*) the Moneth's, Winds, almost all the *Planets*. Second, the *Feminine*, which compriseth Women and *femal species*: I'*lands*, *Countries*, *Cities*, and some *Rivers* with us: as *Severne*, *Avon*. &c. Third, the *Neuter*, or *feined Gender*: whose notion conceives neither *Sexe*; under which are compriz'd all *inanimate* things; a *ship* excepted: of whom we say, *shee sayles well*, though the name be *Hercules*, or *Henry*, (or) the *Prince* . . . Fourth, the *Promiscuous*, or *Epicene*, which understands both kinds: especially when we cannot make the difference; as, when we call them *Horses*, and *Dogges*, in the Masculine, though there be *Bitches*, and *Mares* amongst them. So to *Fowles* for the most part, we use the Feminine; as of *Eagles*, *Hawkes*, we say, *shee flies well* . . . Fift, the *Common*, or rather *Doubtful gender*, wee use often, and with elegance: as in *Cosin*, *Gossip*, *Friend*, *Neighbor*, *Enemie*, *Servant*, *Theefe*, &c. when they may be of either Sexe. Sixt, is the *Common of three* Genders: by which a *Noune* is divided into *Substantive* and *Adjective*. For a *Substantive* is a *Noune of* one only gender, or (at the most) of two. And an *Adjective* is a *Noune* of three Genders, being always in the infinite. (Jonson 1972 [1640]: 57)

Jonson's assertion that English has six gender categories may seem absurd enough to dismiss the entire description, but it must be contextualized: the early English grammarians, such as Jonson, were working within the fairly constrictive classical grammar tradition, which compelled them to copy or mold Latin grammatical categories to fit English usage. In constructing the masculine as representing the "male sex and that of the male kind" and the feminine as the "female sex and that of the female kind," Jonson and other grammarians seem to assume various inanimate nouns fall into these gendered "kinds" (Curzan 1999). Personification, residual confusion, and classical allegory are not sufficient explanations, as many scholars now recognize in discussions of similar fluctuation in the Modern English gender system. An alternative explanation is that what the early grammarians label "kind" is synonymous with what today is labeled "gender"; in other words, "kind" refers to the socially constructed attributes assigned to a given sex.

What is also striking about Jonson's description is the correlation of his list of exceptional nouns with similar lists of exceptional nouns in Modern English. As Chapter Four describes in more detail, Jonson's list includes many nouns that also prove to be exceptions in the diffusion of natural gender through the lexicon in early Middle English. In sum, there appears to be a lexical subset of nouns, which will be referred to as *resilient nouns*, that retain gendered references with greater tenacity than other nouns throughout the history of English. It is a semantic category, and it is difficult to define with exactitude: it is comprised of nouns such as *sun, moon, earth, city, month*, and *church*, which continue to take masculine and feminine pronouns through Middle English and even into Early Modern English. The consistency of these exceptions goes beyond *prosopopeia* 'personification,' to use Jonson's terminology; clearly a level of systematicity underpins these fluctuations in gender, and it is linked to contemporaneous social constructions of animacy and gender in the English-speaking community. In any description of Early Modern English and Modern English, it is more productive to consider these nouns as *part of*, rather than as *exceptions to*, the English gender system.

1.5   Conclusion

Much of the current work on Modern English gender maintains that pronoun selection depends on speaker attitudes and involvement as well as cultural prototypes; the facts presented here suggest that all of these factors in turn rest on the same foundation: the concepts of sex and gender held by language users and the society in which they express themselves. The way in which English language users make distinctions between male and female and between masculine and feminine in their culture will be reflected in the distinctions they make between masculine and feminine in their language, as long as the gender system is a semantic one. Like gender in society, gender in the English language represents a set of constructed categories, categories whose boundaries will change over time, reflecting the evolution of ideas about sex and gender. The criterion of animacy is now more heavily weighted so that gendered characteristics are often subsumed under non-personal reference, but they still surface in the well-documented gendered references to inanimate nouns throughout the spoken language and occasionally in the written language as well. These gendered references depend on the context and register of discourse as well as the attitudes of speakers, all of which are affected and in many ways determined by social concepts of sex and gender.

Nevalainen and Raumolin-Brunberg (1994) refer to the English gender system as *notional gender* in an attempt to move away from the misconceptions bound up with the description *natural gender*, and this new terminology may better capture the psychological and social aspects of gender assignment in the language.[12] It is possible, however, and I think pragmatically preferable to retain the description *natural gender* with the understanding that its definition rests not purely on biological sex but instead on social concepts of sex and gender, and the flexibility in reference that this system allows speakers is natural and highly patterned. The argument that changing erroneous or offensive terminology relating to an issue is a necessary component to changing conceptions about the issue itself is certainly a valid one. Changing accepted forms of language is a way to shape how speakers linguistically formulate or articulate their ideas, even if it does not immediately alter the ideas themselves. Conscious language change is not always successful, particularly if it is not supported by a strong political or social movement. As a result, employing specific new terminology to suit one particular agenda can obscure the more important points motivating the shift in terminology. In this case, given the clear correlation between linguistic and social gender, and the growing understanding of what the latter involves, the description *natural gender* for the English language could naturally come to encompass and appropriately refer to both biological sex and the social constructions engendered by it.

Corbett (1991: 32), as quoted above, notes that semantic gender categories reflect the world view of speakers, and while these categories in Modern English cannot be broken down into binary features for analysis, it is possible to predict variation to some extent given knowledge of extralinguistic factors. Instances of gendered anaphoric pronouns that cross biological lines are not exceptions to an underlying "real" or "unmarked" system of natural gender; they are part of a natural gender system which is natural *because* it corresponds to speakers' ideas about and constructions of gender in the world about which they speak.

---

[12] Jespersen (1924: 55, 230) introduces the term *notional categories* as opposed to syntactic ones in his description of English gender, but it quickly becomes apparent that he is making no distinction between notional and natural gender for English: "I am chiefly concerned with the relation between notional (that is, in this case, natural) and grammatical categories, and shall try to show how here and there languages have in course of time developed other and more rational groupings than the old traditional ones" (Jespersen 1924: 230).

2 The gender shift in histories of English

2.1 Introduction

In 1936, A. C. Ross succinctly stated, "The loss of grammatical gender in later English is one of the most difficult problems of English philology" (Ross 1936: 321). There is no doubt about the endpoint: in the past millennium, English has shifted from a morphological gender assignment system to a semantic one, so that when Modern English speakers think of "gender" in their language, they think of the pronouns and nouns that refer to gendered entities. But the exact nature of the shift – of what stages it involves – is complex and has never been described or understood in full detail. The next two chapters provide technical details to begin to fill some of the gaps in knowledge of the historical shift from grammatical to natural gender in English, sometimes referred to as "the gender shift" in the history of English. This chapter focuses on the ways in which the gender shift has been framed before – a historiography of histories of English focused on their telling of the story of the gender shift – and what this can tell us about attitudes toward language and gender, as well as language change more generally.

In the history of the English language, the shift from Old English to Middle English is often cited as one of the most important defining periods in the evolution of the modern language. It is also one of the most difficult to study. The apparently sweeping nature of the linguistic changes between Old and Middle English, as typically described, results in large part from two important factors: the discontinuity of the written record, which telescopes a series of changes undoubtedly occurring over several centuries into about a 200-year period; and the shift from a fairly consistent and fairly conservative literary version of the surviving West Saxon dialect in Old English to a wider variety of recorded Middle English dialects. The linguistic transition from Old to Middle English, which appears to occur relatively abruptly during the first two centuries of Norman rule, is often categorized into three major developments (although there are many other, less conspicuous morphological and syntactic changes, as well as significant phonological changes). The first major linguistic change is the extreme simplification of inflectional endings through all word class paradigms in English, to the point of morphological loss and increased reliance on fixed word order. Noun endings were reduced to the extent that they came to distinguish only the plural and the genitive, eventually both with a final -*s* (all other oblique cases became indistinct); adjectives and demonstrative pronouns lost all distinctive endings; and personal pronouns lost the distinction between the accusative and dative forms (i.e., between direct and indirect objects). Second, and apparently simultaneous to the demise of inflections, the language lost grammatical gender and adopted, in its place, the modern natural gender system. And third, the language witnessed an enormous influx of borrowed words and word-forms from Scandinavian, French, and Latin. These developments for ever changed the face and nature of the language, and they determine some fundamental ways in which English differs from its Germanic cognates. In the academy, over the past two centuries, these distinctive features of English's development have also often been touted as praiseworthy elements of the language's lineage.

Now at the beginning of the new millennium, it is revealing and instructive to write a history of histories of English: to review ways in which both trained grammarians and untrained language observers over the past few centuries have described the "evolution of English," specifically with respect to grammatical gender, and to review the ways in which these descriptions of the language's early history reflect cultural assumptions and biases in our more recent history. Grammars have at times taken pains to explain grammatical gender, and histories of English have tended to stigmatize grammatical gender as they have framed its loss – and the language's gain. In turn, more radical creole theories, often motivated by a desire – or perceived need – to overturn conventional wisdom, have contributed important ideological considerations to the ways in which we frame the history of English.

2.2   Pre-scientific attempts to explain grammatical gender

The understanding that grammatical gender categories in language have no real-world analogues has become a fundamental premise in linguistic theory (see Chapter One). But over the centuries, given the deceptive terminology for categories in grammatical gender systems, many Western grammarians have struggled to find semantic reasons why in various Indo-European languages, certain nouns are masculine while others are feminine. Perhaps the most popular and enduring semantic explanation of grammatical gender describes it as a set of distinctions based on the active and passive quality of things.[1] As Thomas of Erfurt writes in his Latin grammar *Grammatica Speculativa*, composed between 1300 and 1310:

---

[1] For an extended, engaging, and well-informed discussion of the grammars mentioned in this section as well as other early treatments of gender, see Baron (1986: 93–105).

We shall now discuss gender. First it must be noted that two general properties are found in things, *ie* [sic] the property of acting and the property of being acted upon which, although they are found in all things made up of matter and form, are yet seen to be contained more readily and distinctly in separate things . . . Masculine gender is the mode of signifying the thing by means of the property of acting . . . Feminine gender is the mode of signifying the thing by means of the property of being acted upon. (Thomas of Erfurt 1972: 179)

Within this general framework, grammarians have often attempted to find specific reasons for the gender of individual nouns. James Harris, in his universal grammar *Hermes*, takes pains to make sense of the gender of ships and of the ocean in English.

Among *artificial* Substances the SHIP . . . is *feminine*, as being so eminently a *Receiver* and *Container* of various thing, of Men, Arms, Provisions, Goods, &c. . . . As to the OCEAN, tho' from its being the *Receiver* of all Rivers, as well as the *Container* and *Productress* of so many Vegetables and Animals, it might justly have been made (like the Earth) *Feminine*; yet its *deep Voice* and *boisterous Nature* have, in spite of these reason, prevailed to make it *Male*. (Harris 1765 [1751]: 48–50)

Harris describes masculine nouns along the same lines as Thomas of Erfurt: "conspicuous for the Attributes of imparting or communicating; or which were by nature active, strong, and efficacious, and that indiscriminately whether to good or to ill; or which had claim to Eminence, either laudable or otherwise." Feminine nouns are then contrasted with the masculine: "such as were conspicuous for the Attributes either of receiving, or of containing, or of producing the bringing forth; or which had more of the passive in their nature, than of the active; or which were peculiarly beautiful and amiable; or which had respect to such excesses, as were rather Feminine, than Masculine" (*ibid.*: 44–45). The interchangeability of *masculine* and *male* in Harris's explanation of the gender of the ocean underscores his merger of formal categories of gender in the language and biological categories of sex in the world.

Thirty-seven years after *Hermes* was first published, James Beattie, in his *Theory of Language*, refutes Harris's claim that speaking of death as feminine would be absurd (it is, after all, feminine in Latin, French, Italian, and Spanish) and points out the weaknesses in Harris's explanation for the gender of the ocean.

If it is merely because the *earth* is the common mother of all terrestrial productions, that her name is feminine, it will be difficult to assign a sufficient reason, why the *sea* should not also be feminine; since it is probable, that as many animals and vegetables may be produced in the sea, as on the land. Its deep voice and boisterous nature entitle it (according to Mr. Harris) to a masculine name: but in Virgil, the fury Alecto, who was a female, and sufficiently turbulent, utters a more terrifick yell than ever proceeded from the most tempestuous ocean . . . And the common people of Scotland, when expressing the sea by a pronoun, often call it *She*, but I think never *He*. (Beattie 1968 [1788]: 139)

Beattie concludes (one senses with frustration): "It were vain to attempt to reduce these peculiarities to general principles . . . [A]llegories are fantastick things; and genders, that have no better foundation, cannot be expected to be uniform in different countries" (*ibid*.: 140).

In his introduction to noun gender in English, Beattie is equally pragmatic about what gender categories are necessary and desirable:

Another thing essential to nouns is gender. For language would be very imperfect, if it had no expression for the sex of animals. Now all things whatever are Male, or Female, or Both, or Neither. The existence of hermaphrodites being uncommon, and even doubtful, and language being framed to answer the ordinary occasions of life, no provision is made, in any of the tongues we are acquainted with, for expressing, otherwise than by a name made on purpose, or by a periphrasis, Duplicity of sex. The genders therefore are only two, the masculine and the feminine: for what we call the neuter gender implies properly the negation of sex . . . (*Ibid*.: 134)

Modern debates over politically correct language often focus on the need for a singular generic pronoun in English, and only recently have they returned to the language's lack of a duplicitous singular pronoun!

Perhaps due to these peculiarities and the overall elusiveness of grammatical gender in the face of grammarians' attempts to explain it, the loss of grammatical gender in English has been the source of little mourning. In fact, it has proven fodder for praising English and often deriding other languages. Mark Twain speaks for many of his fellow English speakers when, in a longer critique of the German language entitled "The Awful German Language," he allows himself an extended diatribe on what he considers to be the absurdities of German grammatical gender:

Every noun has a gender, and there is no sense or system in the distribution; so the gender of each must be learned separately and by heart. There is no other way. To do this one has to have a memory like a memorandum-book. In German, a young lady has no sex, while a turnip has. Think what overwrought reverence that shows for the turnip, and what callous disrespect for the girl . . .
"*Gretchen*. – Wilhelm, where is the turnip?
"*Wilhelm*. – She is gone to the kitchen.
"*Gretchen*. – Where is the accomplished and beautiful English maiden?
"*Wilhelm*. – It has gone to the opera."

To continue with the German genders...a person's mouth, neck, bosom, elbows, fingers, nails, feet, and body are of the male sex, and his head is male or neuter according to the word selected to signify it, and *not* according to the sex of the individual who wears it – for in Germany all the women wear either male heads or sexless ones; a person's nose, lips, shoulder, breast, hands, and toes are of the female sex; and his hair, ears, eyes, chin, legs, knees, heart, and conscience haven't any sex at all. The inventor of the language probably got what he knew about a conscience from hearsay.

Now, by the above dissection, the reader will see that in Germany a man may *think* he is a man, but when he comes to look into the matter closely, he is bound to have his doubts; he finds that in sober truth he is a most ridiculous mixture; and if he ends by trying to comfort himself with the thought that he can at least depend on a third of this mess as being manly and masculine, the humiliating second thought will quickly remind him that in this respect he is no better off than any woman or cow in the land. (Twain 1921: 272–73)

While recognized as a wonderful humorist, Twain made no claims to being a linguist, and he freely interchanges biological sex and grammatical gender in this passage to emphasize – if not create – the absurdity he describes. The fact that turnips are feminine nouns in German does not imply any equation of turnips with females in size, shape, color, taste, nature, or anything else, either in the world or necessarily in the minds of German speakers. Shoulders, noses, toes, and other body parts are, of course, of no particular sex – despite their various grammatical genders – and their grammatical status has never been known to cause more personal identity crises in German men (or women) than in English-speaking ones. Grammatical gender, a syntactic means of categorizing nouns for the agreement of adjectives, determiners, complements, and pronouns, seems as natural to native speakers of such languages as natural gender does to English speakers. The beauty or beastliness of grammatical gender is all in the eye of the beholder (or the ear of the behearer, as the case may be). And the way English speakers choose to describe grammatical gender in other languages, or in the history of their own language, can be deeply revealing of their linguistic biases, if not their underlying attitudes toward both English and non-English speakers.

2.3   Framing of the gender shift in standard histories of English

A review of published histories of English reveals a wide and culturally revealing range of descriptions and explanations of the history of gender in English. Recent sociolinguistic work has emphasized that the ways in which speakers talk about and evaluate language are as critical a part of language use and language study as the linguistic signs and sounds speakers use to make these commentaries. When we as speakers talk about language, we are often talking about much more – and this is as true for published works on language and its history as it is for more casual comments about the language use around us.

In the past few decades, histories of English such as those written by Georges Bourcier (1981), Roger Lass (1987), C. M. Millward (1996), and Barbara Fennell (2001), just to name a few, take a more empirical, descriptive stance to current knowledge about the loss of grammatical gender. (There are older examples as well, such as Emerson's *History of the English Language*, written in 1895.) But in many standard histories of the English language, sometimes less technically or scientifically oriented but some more linguistically descriptive ones as well, from the eighteenth century to the present, grammatical gender both in Old English and in other languages with similar systems has been described with a broad array of derogatory adjectives (boldface added).

> In the older form of the language we cannot by any means conclude that males will be masculine, females feminine, and things without life neuter. There an ox was masculine, but a sheep neuter; one word for a woman, *wif*, was neuter; while other, *ides*, as well as *fæmne* (borrowed from Latin *femina*), are feminine. *Child* (*cild*), *maiden* (*mæden*), are neuter. Old age (*ildu* or *eldu*, Modern English *eld*) and a street are feminine, a brook masculine, though a burn is feminine. The genders seem as **unreasonable** as those in Latin, Greek, French, and German. (Champneys 1893: 103)

> [Alfred's English] had the same **irrational** system of genders: *hand* was feminine, *fot* (foot) was masculine, while *mægden* (maiden) and *wif* (wife, woman) were neuter. (Bradley 1924 [1904]: 9)

> One of the consequences of the decay of inflections described above was the elimination of that **troublesome** feature of language, grammatical gender. (Baugh and Cable 1978: 166)

The descriptive terms *unreasonable* and *irrational*, while arguably neutral terms used to refer to the arbitrariness of Old English grammatical gender, are, in fact, highly evaluative; and the word *troublesome* allows no neutral interpretive spin, capturing the negative connotations implicit in the other two adjectives. The authors of these histories carefully distinguish between biological sex and grammatical gender, implying, if not directly stating, the undesirability or absurdity of having the two not correspond as they do in Modern English. The descriptions fairly consistently begin with the most striking examples in Old English of the lack of concord between grammatical and natural gender – usually the masculine and neuter words for women – and then often provide a few examples of masculine and feminine inanimate objects. Champneys (1893: 237–38) tries to reassure his readers that this disjunction between biology and grammar does not have extralinguistic implications: "We have seen that in English before the Norman Conquest certain words for woman and child were neuter. But our ancestors did not think any less of them on that account; this gender was a matter of grammar only, of terminations in the substantive and its adjective, and, with the loss of special inflexions to mark it, it passed away as a matter of course." In a footnote, however, Champneys hedges his bet and adds, "Though the gender may have originated in some such feeling. But we cannot enter sufficiently into the feelings of our very remote savage ancestors to explain the genders which are attached to words in Old English." With one sentence, the distinction between the linguistic and the extralinguistic with regard to gender has been obliterated – not to mention the civility of our ancestors.

These generally unflattering portraits of grammatical gender in Old English and in other languages provide the backdrop and justification for singing the praises of Modern English. Prior to the "modern" period, the English language benefited from a fairly dramatic reversal in attitudes toward the language itself. In the late sixteenth century, the rhetoric describing English shifted from deriding the language as "rude" and "barbaric" to lauding its eloquence (for more details, see R. F. Jones 1956: 168 ff.). It was only after English was recognized as an eloquent tongue with its own literary tradition that the first rhetorics, dictionaries, spelling books, and grammars were written in an effort to enhance, regulate, and standardize the language (for more details, see Green 1996, Vorlat 1975). By the nineteenth century, histories of English could laud English as indubitably a superior tongue, rather than lament its imminent or already ongoing decay (see Bailey 1996). Since the nineteenth century, narrative histories of English have often framed the language's abandonment of grammatical gender in its "primitive" past as an important step in the language's evolution toward an ever-more ideal state, outstripping its Indo-European relatives in a steady progress towards rationality. For examples:

> In Old English, as in all the old cognate languages, each substantive, no matter whether it referred to animate beings or things or abstract notions, belonged to one or other of the three gender-classes . . . Anyone acquainted with the intricacies of the same system (or want of system) in German will feel how much English has gained in clearness and simplicity by giving up these distinctions and applying *he* only to male, and *she* only to female, living beings. (Jespersen 1912: 203)

> We now come to what is the most remarkable, and one of the most beneficial, of all the changes which the English language has undergone – the substitution of 'natural' for 'grammatical' gender. It is not easy for us English people to understand what a wonderful change this really was. We are apt to look on it as the most natural thing in the world that 'gender' should correspond to sex: that masculine and feminine nouns should be those denoting males and females respectively, and that neuter nouns should be those which denote objects which are not regarded as possessing sex. (Bradley 1924 [1904]: 47)

> English enjoys an exceptional advantage over all other major European languages in having adopted natural in place of grammatical gender. In studying other European languages the student labors under the heavy burden of memorizing, along with the meaning of every noun, its gender. (Baugh and Cable 1978: 10)

> Above all, English is mercifully free of gender. Anyone who spent much of his or her adolescence miserably trying to remember whether it is "la plume" or "le plume" will appreciate just what a pointless burden masculine and feminine nouns are to any language. In this regard English is a godsend to students everywhere. Not only have we discarded problems of gender with definite and indefinite articles, we have often discarded the articles themselves. (Bryson 1990: 18)

These stories of English gender are written both by trained linguists (e.g., Jespersen, Baugh and Cable) and self-certified language observers writing as much for the entertainment as the education of their audience (e.g., Bryson). And while the authors' purposes may differ, the underlying language ideology and assumption of English's obvious advantages or superiority are similar.

Jespersen posits this kind of "progress" as the growing masculinity of English. This makes him almost too easy a target for exposing the ways in which the framing of gender in histories of English reveals as much about social attitudes as linguistic beliefs. Jespersen (1912) writes:

> If briefness, conciseness and terseness are characteristic of the style of men, while women as a rule are not such economizers of speech, English is more masculine than most languages. We see this in a great many ways. In grammar it has got rid of a great many superfluities found in earlier English as well as in most cognate languages, reducing endings, etc., to the shortest forms possible and often doing away with endings altogether. (Jespersen 1912: 4–5)

> Now, it seems to be characteristic of the two sexes in their relation to language that women move in narrower circles of the vocabulary, in which they attain to perfect mastery so that the flow of words is always natural and, above all, never needs to stop, while men know more words and always want to be more precise in choosing the exact word with which to render their idea, the consequence being often less fluency and more hesitation. It has been statistically shown that a comparatively greater number of stammerers and stutterers are found among men (boys) than among women (girls). Teachers of foreign languages have many occasions to admire the ease with which female students express themselves in another language after so short a time of study that most men would be able to say only few words hesitatingly and falteringly, but if they are put to the test of translating a difficult piece either from or into the foreign language, the men will generally prove superior to the women. With regard to their native

language the same difference is found, though it is perhaps not so easy to observe. At any rate our assertion is corroborated by the fact observed by every student of languages that novels written by ladies are much easier to read and contain much fewer difficult words than those written by men. All this seems to justify us in setting down the enormous richness of the English vocabulary to the same masculinity of the English nation which we have now encountered in so many fields. (*Ibid.*: 15–16)

From this perspective, the loss of grammatical gender ironically aids in the process of gendering the language as masculine.

Peyton, in his late eighteenth-century history of the language, similarly bestows gendered characteristics upon language and, in the process, glorifies English compared to its European neighbors. And while his language technically divorces these languages from their speakers, the descriptions belie cultural and ethnic stereotypes, disembodied and disguised as linguistic judgments:

> I come now to the last point, viz. the sweetness of our tongue, which will be the more conspicuous if we compare it with our neighbours.
>
> The Italian is pleasant, but without sinews, like a still fleeting water: the French delicate, but even nice as a woman, scarce daring to open her lips for fear of spoiling her countenance: the Spanish is majestical, but runs too much on the o, and therefore is very guttural, and not very pleasant: the Dutch manlike, but withal very harsh, as one ready at every word to pick a quarrel.
>
> Now we, in borrowing from them, give the strength of consonants to the Italian, the full sound of words to the French, the variety of terminations to the Spanish, and the mollifying of more vowels to the Dutch: and so, like bees, we gather the honey of their good properties, and leave the dregs to themselves.
>
> Thus when substantialness combineth with delightfulness, fulness with fineness, seemliness with portliness, and currentness with staidness, how can the language that consists of all these be found otherwise than most full of sweetness?
>
> Again, the long words which we borrow, being intermixed with the short of our own store, compose a perfect harmony, when care is taken to chuse judiciously such as are proper to frame the speech by, according to the matter to be worked upon, majestical, pleasant, or manly, more or less, in whatever sort you please. Add to this, that whatsoever grace any other language carries with it in verse or prose, in tropes or metaphors, in echoes and agnominations, they may all be lively and exactly represented in ours. (Peyton 1771: 28–30)

Here the copiousness of the English vocabulary complements the efficiency of its grammar, all to make it a more praiseworthy tongue. Appropriation here is synonymous with improvement.

It is the rare language observer who can comment on language change, particularly in his or her own native language, in a neutral, non-directional way. Evolutionary models of language change have been employed since the nineteenth century. And while many of the biological analogies have been abandoned in the latter half of the twentieth century, others remain (e.g., language death) and the idea that language change is directional often resurfaces. The language is either in a deplorable state of decay, losing crucial grammatical, lexical, and phonological features that ensured its previous eloquence and grandeur. Or the language is constantly improving – a view of language development (perhaps best exemplified by Jespersen) in which *evolution* is synonymous with *progress*, and *modern* means 'better.' The fact is, however, that older generations of speakers rarely view the linguistic innovations of their children or of any "non-traditional" language-speaking group as improvements on their own language use. New usages are, instead, seen as another example of the laziness, depravity, or general lack of respect for tradition manifested by younger generations and non-standard language speakers. Even in models of language progress, the language is still often held to be at its evolutionary pinnacle at the moment of description because it is invariably being corrupted by the younger generations of speakers (for a more detailed discussion of attitudes towards English throughout its history, see Bailey 1991).

McMahon (1994: 323), in her insightful critique of evolutionary theories of language development, dismisses the Jespersen school of thought about language progress as outdated, no longer accepted in linguistic theory, and focuses instead on the dangerous implications of Schleicher's depiction of language decay. The latter school is a disturbingly popular view of language change (Grossman [1997] and Simon [1980] provide just two characteristic examples), but the former also retains a following and surfaces fairly often in more traditional histories of English. Linguistic theory may have dismissed progress as a model for language change and, as noted earlier, there certainly are modern history of English texts that do not employ teleological models; but not all histories of English, particularly less technical ones, have abandoned this model. In 1990, Bryson describes English as "a godsend" to the world, a language previous scholars have attributed with "an exceptional advantage over all other major European languages" (Baugh and Cable 1978: 10) because it has "gained in clearness and simplicity" (Jespersen 1912: 203). Hence, English can be framed as the world's most popular second language because it is somehow better (more expressive, lexically richer, more logical, etc.), not because it is spoken in some of this century's largest, richest, and most powerful countries. It is Darwin's "survival of the fittest" theory misapplied and misinterpreted. And the loss of grammatical gender is often singled out specifically as one of the more momentous evolutionary gains by English, even if not all of the other changes in English structure over the centuries are framed as progress.

The first three of the four eulogies of the English natural gender system quoted above from written histories of the language include no consciously acting agents in the "progress" of English; in the fourth, however, Bryson describes English as "discarding" linguistic features, almost as if this were a conscious choice either by speakers or somehow by the language itself. Occasionally, historians of English are even more explicit in describing the loss of grammatical gender as a conscious effort by brave, innovative, forward-thinking English speakers. For example, Trench writes in the nineteenth century:

> It was the boldest step in the way of simplification which the language has at any time taken... We did not inherit this simplicity from others, but, like the Danes, in so far as they have done the like, have made it for ourselves... The practical businesslike character of the English mind asserted itself in the rejection of a distinction, which in a vast proportion of words, that is, in all which are the signs of inanimate objects, and as such incapable of sex, rested upon a fiction, and had no ground in the real nature of things. It is only by an act and effort of the imagination that sex, and thus gender, can be attributed to a table, a ship, or a tree; and there are aspects, this being one, in which the English is among the least imaginative of all languages, even while it has been employed in some of the mightiest works of imagination which the world has ever seen.
>
> What, it may be asked, is the meaning and explanation of all this? It is that at certain earlier periods of a nation's life its genius is synthetic, and at later becomes analytic. At earlier periods the imagination is more than the understanding; men love to contemplate the thing and the mode of the thing together, as a single idea, bound up in one. But a time arrives when the intellectual obtains the upper hand of the imaginative, when the inclination of those that speak a language is to analyse, to distinguish between these two, and not only to distinguish, but to divide, to have one word for the thing itself, and another for the quality or manner of the thing; and this, as it would appear, is true not of some languages only, but of all. (Trench 1855: 239–42)

The nationalistic – or perhaps imperialistic – notes ringing through this description are unmistakable. Language histories, much like dictionaries, are ways to legitimize, if not glorify, a language. And the loss of grammatical gender is often presented as a tribute to the English language and to the English mind believed to have molded it. The equation of a language with a nation is made explicit by Jespersen:

> To sum up: The English language is a methodical, energetic, business-like and sober language, that does not care much for finery and elegance, but does care for logical consistency and is opposed to any attempt to narrow-in life by police regulations and strict rules either of grammar or of lexicon. As the language is, so also is the nation... (Jespersen 1912: 15–16)

Trench's effusion highlights how beliefs about language, be they fact or fiction, often serve as the basis for myths about the superiority of one language and the inferiority of others. The loss of grammatical gender in the history of English was not a conscious "rejection" by English speakers, whose minds are not and never have been more practical or businesslike than those of the speakers of other languages. (One only has to look at the English spelling system for confirmation of this fact!) This linguistic development in no way symbolizes the triumph of the intellect over the imagination. Trench has merged sex and gender in this description (much as Twain did in his) so that grammatical gender necessarily carries extralinguistic implications for inanimate objects: the grammatical categorization of nouns as masculine or feminine implies a connection of these objects to biological sex when, actually, it functions as a system of noun classification. Grammatical gender systems, common in languages throughout the world, require no more imagination and no less intellect than any other grammatical feature. And English speakers were certainly not on the cutting edge of linguistic progress in "making natural gender for themselves" either in a quest for simplicity or as an intellectual exercise. As importantly, the generations of English speakers whose language underwent this gradual transition between gender systems were undoubtedly unaware of the long-term implications of the gender variation sprinkled throughout their speech, as is explained in the discussion of sociolinguistic research below.

In sum, it is clear that in discussions of English and other languages, misunderstandings of gender run wide and deep. Under the guise of "only" talking about language, speakers will say things about other speakers that they may recognize are not founded or appropriate in other contexts (for an extended discussion of the modern implications of this phenomenon, see Lippi-Green 1997). In rethinking natural gender and its history in English, language should not be divorced from social constructions and attitudes, from identity, or from the realities of language variation within speech communities.

2.4   Morphological explanations for the loss of grammatical gender in English

In traditional, more technical histories of the language, as discussed above, the shift from grammatical to natural gender is explained as the direct result of the decay of noun and modifier inflectional endings in the late Old English and early Middle English periods. And while the loss of inflectional distinctions is unquestionably a critical component of the loss of grammatical gender, it alone is not sufficient cause to explain the progression of the shift between gender systems. There appear to be other internal factors involved, in addition to the external ones described later in this chapter. Research over the past few decades has answered many questions, while posing new ones.

In Old English, gender was determined more by the form of the attributes and pronouns than by the form of the noun. There are a few significant noun-endings in the nominative singular which indicate gender (e.g., weak masculine -*a* or strong feminine -*nes(s)*; see Mitchell 1986: §61), but the gender of most nouns is not predictable from their morphology (e.g., a strong noun-ending with a consonant in the nominative singular could belong to any of the three genders). In addition, many of the inflectional endings of different genders and cases overlap. There also exists a set of nouns in Old English that can be declined like nouns of two or even three genders (*multiple-gender nouns*). Mitchell (1986: §62–65) provides at least three explanations for these mixtures of forms: errors from ignorance of a "dying system"; analogical confusion confined to a particular context; variation (or confusion) of gender and class in Germanic or in Old English. All three possibilities raise intriguing questions, particularly as to why these nouns show variation from grammatical gender agreement earlier than others. Kitson (1990) also proposes that gender in early English was a dialectal variable; using evidence from topographic vocabulary in charter boundaries, Kitson creates convincing dialect maps for the distribution of different gender agreement patterns for various multiple-gender nouns referring to topographical features. At minimum, this may all be framed as evidence for some weakness in the system as early as Old English.

One important causal factor in the inflectional endings becoming indistinct is the "Germanic stress rule," or the movement of stress toward the word-initial syllable. This fixing of primary stress early in the pre-history of English – the placement of stress was variable in Indo-European – resulted in the reduction of final vowels to /ə/ and in the loss of many final inflectional consonants (particularly final -*n* and -*m*).[2] Even after most of the inflectional distinctions for nouns had disappeared, however, the grammatical gender system remained at least partially intact in early Middle English because of continuing gender agreement in the attributes (C. Jones 1967a: 99, 107). Exceptions in attribute agreement have been explained by Ross (1936) as neutralization (the use of neuter forms with masculine or feminine inanimate nouns), by Clark (1957) as masculinization, and by numerous other scholars as gender change or confusion (*Genuswechsel*). Charles Jones (1967a, 1967b, 1988) convincingly refutes all these theories, arguing that there is rarely any complete change in a noun's gender from Old English; instead certain inflectional endings take on new, unhistorical expressive functions in late Old English and they come to indicate case irrespective of gender or they take on identifiable discourse functions. In other words, gendered inflectional endings and gendered forms of demonstrative pronouns serve to signal relationships between elements in a sentence or larger unit of discourse. Specifically, Jones notes that barred þ ("thorn," an early English orthographic form used to represent "th") and its variants *þæt* and *þet*, the Old

---

[2] Kastovsky (1999) frames these phonological and inflectional losses as impairing an already "precarious" interrelationship of gender and class distinctions, which led to the system's collapse, allowing number to become dominant and case recessive, as well as moving the language toward word-based morphology. He concludes: "The dissolution of the OE gender system thus has its first and foremost root in the disintegration of the class-based inflectional system involving paradigm profiles and the establishment of a default system based on the realisation of the category 'plural', which was independent of the categories of case and gender" (Kastovsky 1999: 721–22).

English neuter forms, are used with masculine and feminine nouns as discourse markers or "trackers" to refer to nouns previously introduced in the discourse ("shared information") and to refer to nouns of specific lexical subsets (e.g., geographic localities, parts of the body, etc.). Jones also claims that these forms serve to introduce new material into the discourse in the *Lindisfarne Gospels*, which could seem to broaden their discourse functions in potentially problematic ways, but it seems likely that these forms did come to cross gender lines in order to carry relevant discourse information. In addition, the phonetically distinctive endings -*ne*, -*(e)s*, and -*um* come to indicate accusative, genitive, and dative respectively, irrespective of the gender of the noun. Roberts (1970), who examines adnominal inflectional endings in Felix's *Vita Sancti Guthlaci*, confirms Jones's hypothesis about unhistorical gender agreement between attributes and nouns: she finds feminine -*re* serving as a dative marker before both masculine and feminine nouns.

With the leveling of distinctions in the inflectional endings of nouns and the loss of morphologically distinct noun classes in late Old English and early Middle English, adjectives and other attributive forms could no longer sufficiently support the formal agreement system. Their inflectional endings also weakened and were leveled, and their gender-marking functions, Jones argues, came to be subordinated to their case-marking ones. Thus, "the idea of sex," in the traditional view, was the determining factor for any gender agreement that remained; in other words, sex triumphed over gender. The critical implicit assumption here is that linguistic gender assignment based on sex (natural gender) is the unmarked gender system, historically present in the language even if not manifested – a system which underlies the morphological assignment system (at least in English, but the assumption may apply to other languages as well). Natural gender is, therefore, available to triumph should morphologically determined gender break down. Given the fact that many of the world's languages exist without linguistic gender, however, there is no justification for assuming *natural gender* to be inherent in language. It is true that all formal gender systems are to some extent semantic, and studies have shown associations between grammatical gender and connotations based on attitudes toward "real world" gender (for a summary, see Romaine 1999: 81–83). And it seems to be true that in these semantic elements lie the roots of English natural gender.

Classen (1919) was one of the first scholars to challenge the traditional idea that once speakers could no longer distinguish gender by grammatical form, they had to or would naturally substitute a system based on sex. Would not the anaphoric pronouns, he asks, have been sufficient for retaining grammatical gender? In fact, the answer to Classen's question would seem to be no. The research on linguistic gender in general by Corbett (1991) and on Germanic personal pronouns specifically by Howe (1996) strongly suggests that if a grammatical category such as grammatical gender is lost in the noun phrase, it is also eventually lost in the personal pronouns: "personal pronouns cannot indefinitely uphold a grammatical category/property-based distinction alone" (Howe 1996: 63). This assertion does not provide, however, the motivation for the personal pronouns adopting *natural* gender.

The question Classen does not ask is why the pronouns did not lose all gender distinctions in parallel with, or subsequent to, the loss of these distinctions in the elements of the noun phrase. The loss of such distinctions in the third-person singular pronouns was more than a theoretical possibility in the late Old English period when masculine *he* and feminine *heo* seem to have been phonetically merging in several dialects (cf. McIntosh *et al.* 1987). Yet with the introduction of the new pronoun *she*, gender distinctions in the personal pronouns were if anything strengthened. (See Appendix 1 for a brief history of the personal pronouns in English.) The question then returns to why the personal pronouns shifted to natural gender.

Studies of gender in Old English, as in almost all languages with bi- or tri-partite grammatical gender systems, have confirmed that there existed a partial correspondence between linguistic gender and natural sex alongside gender de-termined by formal properties; in other words, nominal gender class assignments had both a syntactic and a semantic basis. Most words denoting men were gram-matically masculine (e.g., *man, secg* 'man,' *wer* 'man,' *fæder* 'father,' *cniht* 'boy, young man') and most denoting women were grammatically feminine (e.g., *mægð* 'maiden,' *cwen* 'queen,' *moðer* 'mother'), with the few notable exceptions men-tioned in most histories of English: the masuline noun *wifmann* 'woman' and the neuter nouns *wif* 'woman,' *mægden* 'maiden,' *bearn* 'child,' and *cild* 'child.' In addition, Corbett's agreement hierarchy manifests itself in Old English gram-mar, where there exist two systems of agreement, similar to many languages with grammatical gender: noun-phrase internal and noun-phrase external. Within the noun phrase, grammatical gender agreement in the inflectional endings of the noun and its modifiers is obligatory (with occasional exceptions for unnaturally gendered animate nouns such as masculine *wifmann* 'woman'). Outside the noun phrase, however, grammatical gender agreement between anaphoric pronouns and their antecedents is often variable. In the few cases in Old English where the grammatical gender of a noun referring to a human being conflicts with its gender (e.g., *wif* 'woman'), the anaphoric pronoun almost always agrees with the referent's sex. In other words, nouns such as *wif* and *wifmann* are referred back to with forms of *she*.

A more controversial question has remained about how prevalent natural gen-der agreement is between grammatically gendered inanimate nouns and their anaphoric pronouns in Old English and early Middle English. In other words, how early did inanimate objects come to be referred to with 'it' rather than with 'he' or 'she'? Chapters Three and Four examine this question in detail, tracking the story of gender variation in the personal pronouns back through the centuries. And variation is a key term here as it points to a more sociolinguistic perspective on this grammatical change. One of the other intriguing questions about the gender shift is why it happened in English and not in many other Germanic languages, and here again sociolinguistic information is helpful, specifically the role of language contact in the history of English.

2.5   Sociolinguistic factors relevant to the history of gender in English

Histories of English often work from the premise that there exists one systematic and continuous history of English, from Old to Modern, and they flourish at least in part because they bestow on the language a definable lineage and, in turn, historical legitimacy (see Milroy 1992, 2000 for an excellent discussion of these issues). The underlying assumption is that beneath all the "superficial" changes English has undergone, it has remained, at a most fundamental level, the same language throughout the past 1,500 years; all the changes can, therefore, be fit into a coherent progression of the language toward Modern English. This systematic progression of the language, whether described as improvement or more neutrally as change, is consistently toward the standard form of English which emerged in the early modern and modern period.

The history of English, however, is not nearly so coherent. To provide realistic descriptions and explanations of the linguistic developments involved, a written history of English, like that of any other language, must incorporate the potential for dialect interference and foreign interference, as well as natural drift (cf. Thomason and Kaufman 1988: 9). The story of any language is the story of evolutionary change (*evolution* in the sense of gradual development). One of the signs of change in progress with respect to any particular feature of language is variation. Speakers within one community or across different speech communities use different variants – some older and some innovative – all of which are available in their personal or in the community's collective linguistic repertoire. Eventually, some variants are favored over others, sometimes for functional reasons (e.g., maintenance of distinctions) and sometimes for social reason (e.g., prestige forms).[3]

Diachronic change can and should always be examined as a process of selection by speakers of one of several coexisting variants within the speech community – a selection dependent on grammatical factors, context, and social situation, and usually below the level of consciousness. Admittedly, recreating patterns in these selections in earlier stages of English is a difficult if not impossible task. The

---

[3] April McMahon (1994: 334–40), pursuing ideas proposed by Robert Stevick (1963), employs biological evolutionary models to help explain the apparent paradox that variation arises randomly and yet change is generally regular: "This axiom [Chance in combination with selection produces order] would help us solve our problem of perceived directionality, for which teleological explanations have previously been proposed. Perceived directionality is accepted in current evolutionary theory as resulting from random variation and natural selection, which combine to produce order with no necessary external direction: an accumulation of historical accidents may still look like a conspiracy" (McMahon 1994: 337).

limited written record of Old English demonstrates very little dialectal variation: the written texts up to 1050 AD are predominantly in West Saxon due to the political dominance of Wessex beginning in the late ninth century and the subsequent adoption, under the guiding hand of King Alfred, of the West Saxon dialect as the literary norm. Surviving Middle English texts show a significantly wider range of dialects (cf. McIntosh *et al.* 1987), but it is still difficult to determine the relationship between the written and spoken language of a particular area. The written language is probably more archaic or conservative than the spoken must have been, and the consistency of some scribes' features undoubtedly masks variation in the spoken language. Middle English manuscripts do, however, exhibit variation that is critical to understanding the progression of linguistic changes during the period.

The story of English, inherently complex in the details of dialects even at its early stages (cf. Toon 1985, McIntosh *et al.* 1987), is also not the story of one language. The first thousand years of the tale of English in the British Isles is in some ways as much about language contact as language continuity. Descriptions of linguistic change, both in English and in other languages, often emphasize language-internal (or system-based) explanations over language-external (or speaker-based) ones. The former describe most shifts – phonological, morphological, or syntactic – as phonologically determined or as inherent to the structure of the language; the latter open the possibility of cultural and social forces affecting language change, some of which may not be "native" to the language or its land. The foregrounding of the speaker's role and external causal factors in such sociolinguistic approaches does not preclude language-internal factors in an analysis of linguistic change; rather, it adds to structural theories a new dimension for explaining how linguistic change begins and spreads. Not that this problem is solved. Explaining the actuation and implementation of language change remains one of the most challenging aspects of historical sociolinguistics and sociolinguistics more generally. Current work in sociolinguistics, particularly social network theory (see L. Milroy 1980; Labov 2001: 325–65), has provided one useful framework in which to describe the maintenance of linguistic norms and the introduction of linguistic innovations – that may be either externally or internally motivated – based on the density and multiplicity of network ties within a speech community. The model of multiple causation proposed by Thomason and Kaufman (1988), incorporating the possibility of both external and internal causes in the description of linguistic change and not requiring clear boundary lines between them, allows the type of unified explanations towards which linguistic theory ideally aims. With regard to English in particular, it is impossible to understand many of the transformations the language has undergone in the past millennium – in this case, specifically the loss of grammatical gender – without considering external causes in combination with internal ones.

While there are clearly internal reasons that help explain why English lost grammatical gender, the fact that English is unusual among Germanic languages in having undergone this loss suggests the presence of contributing if not causal factors in the external history of the language. The turbulent history of the English language, during which the British Isles were attacked, settled, and ruled first by Danes and then by Normans, only strengthens the case for external causes involved in early linguistic developments. The burning of monasteries, books, and documents by the Danes in their raids on the north and east midland areas of England and the subsequent rule of England by French-speaking nobility, based in London but controlling the entire country, create a sharp discontinuity in available records of the language between the stages of the language tradition-ally labeled Old and Middle English. The fairly dramatic differences between "*Beowulf* English" before the break in records and "Chaucer's English" after it have led to speculation in modern scholarship about whether the language itself underwent a parallel "break" in its history, caused by intensive language contact. The specifics of these proposals, are often grouped summarily under the title "the Middle English creole question."

2.6   The gender shift and the Middle English creole question

The same syntactic event in English – the loss of grammatical gender – that has been used to laud English as a noble tongue with a proud lineage and history of progress has more recently been employed as possible evidence for toppling this linear construction, for disrupting more traditional notions of lineage by emphasizing the presence of other languages and heavy language contact. The Middle English creole question is perhaps most interesting for what is at stake in posing it. Middle English creole theories venture to suggest linguistic changes so dramatic that they jeopardize the very label *English* for the language that surfaces in the twelfth and thirteenth centuries in written documents. They suggest that the changes in this time period are not just superficial, but rather that they fundamentally alter the nature of the language. The literature on the Middle English creole question ranges from technical linguistic scholarship to more theoretical attempts designed to disrupt traditional assumptions about the history of English. And employing the term *creole* to describe English is an effective method of provocation because *creole* is often a stigmatized term, connoting for many "not full language" status. To suggest that English, with its prestigious position in the modern world, could be historically considered a creole brings some people up short, and sometimes sets them up in arms.

The facts of the gender shift in English potentially argue for at least some external causes. The stress rule alone cannot account for why English lost its complex inflectional system and grammatical gender system because, while other Germanic languages underwent the same stress rule and some similar phonological changes, they did not witness this particular syntactic develop-ment. Language-internal explanations do not appear to be sufficient. It is also undeniably striking that the three major changes in the English language between Old and Middle English – the loss of inflectional endings, the loss of grammati-cal gender, and the significant influx of borrowed words – are also characteristic features of modern creole languages.

Creole theories are, however, mostly speculation: no Middle English creole theory can stand up to the linguistic evidence.[4] To begin with, none of the Middle English creole theories adheres to traditional definitions of *creole*. A creole is typically described as an elaborated pidgin, formed when a pidgin is adopted as the first language of a community – in other words, when it is acquired as a first language by the children of the community – and it must fulfill all the communication needs of its speakers. No theory has seriously proposed that Middle English has its roots in a pidgin. The distinction between a creole and a mixed language, however, has become fuzzy as alternate definitions of *creole* have been applied in various theoretical models. If a creole can be alternatively described by its function, its history, or its formal characteristics (Romaine 1988), the standard distinction between pidginization and creolization is potentially destroyed because creolization can become a type of simplification. One of the broader, more inclusive descriptions of a creole is "an extreme mixture of the systems (phonology, syntax, and lexis) of two or more languages" (Görlach 1986: 333), a definition similar to that of Bailey and Maroldt (1977: 21), who describe creolization as a "gradient mixture of two or more languages; in a narrow sense, a *creole* is the result of mixing which is substantial enough to result in a new system, a system that is separate from its antecedent parent systems." So here, *creolization* refers not only to the process of building on a pidgin, but also to language contact that disrupts the continuity of a language, turning it into a "creole-like" variety – in other words, it undergoes dramatic simplification to look like a creole.

These terminological exercises – the broadening of the definition of *creole* and *creolization*, the application of new terms such as *creoloid* or *creolitic features* (Danchev 1997: 81–82), and the attempts to nuance mixed-language definitions to fit the facts of Middle English – suggest, at a more fundamental level, that the larger question about the status of Middle English is also being refined: the issue is no longer whether Middle English represents a "pure" creole or mixed language, but rather how fundamentally language contact influenced the development of English. How "extreme" was the mixture and how "new" was the resulting language system?[5]

---

[4] As Fennell (2001: 126) summarizes the scholarly discussion of the Middle English creole question: "It is something of a cautionary tale, since it shows that it is dangerous to take over an argument, however appealing it might be, without careful consideration of the factual evidence at hand."

[5] Theories based on the premise that Middle English "looks like" a creole are not convincing. To begin with, exactly what a creole "looks like" is not a settled issue. Studies of hypothesized creoles such as Afrikaans describe lists of creole features, none of which are absolutely determinative of creoleness, but a certain combination of which can justify the creole label (see Markey 1982). This approach can prove to be circular – creole features are drawn from languages thought to be creoles and then used to establish the creoleness of other languages – but the lists of features serve as useful guidelines for comparing possible creole languages. The major creole features demonstrated by Middle English include simplified segmental phonology, the disappearance of grammatical gender, the growing dominance of subject-verb-object word order, and the lack of singular nominal case inflection. Most of these features represent types of "syntactic simplification," related to the loss of nominal and adnominal inflectional endings. (The relationship of morphological simplification and the rise of

As contradictory and surprising as it may seem, Middle English creole theories have advanced both French and Old Norse as possible source languages. Bailey and Maroldt (1977: 38) push the concept of French influence to its limits by proposing that Middle English represents an Anglo-Norman-based creole. Sociological evidence argues against any creole theory involving Anglo-Norman: the language contact situation between the Normans and the Anglo-Saxons was not typical of creolization.[6] Inflectional mergers and confusion are already apparent in late Old English; and as Chapter Four describes, natural gender was already incipient in the anaphoric pronouns. The influence of French certainly may have accelerated some of these fundamental linguistic transformations already occurring in English, but it did not instigate them. Interestingly, while this creole theory is in some ways a radical one in its assertions, one could argue that it nonetheless makes a relatively conventional move in privileging French influence in syntactic changes in English over the more likely, but less prestigious language, Old Norse.

To explain the loss of grammatical gender specifically, Bailey and Maroldt (1977: 45) describe a situation of gender confusion resulting from French influence: "When these [unstable Anglo-Saxon gender distinctions] came in contact with French, with its usually or often different gender assignments, further confusion must have arisen; gender was consequently rendered so utterly complex and overmarked that it had to be given up." This obviously oversimplified explanation is echoed in less radical proposals about the impact of language contact with French and in standard histories of the language. In scholarly articles, Domingue (1977: 72) and Danchev (1997: 90) also cite French as a probable cause in the demise of grammatical gender categories, even as Domingue strongly advocates the idea that contact with Old Norse precipitated or perhaps even caused the

---

subject-verb-object word order is a classic chicken-and-egg question. Traugott [1972] suggests that increasingly fixed word order and inflectional simplification are symbiotic processes.) But Middle English fails to demonstrate some of the other phonological, morphological, and syntactic features typical of creole languages: it retains closed syllable structure, inflectional endings for the plural and genitive, and comparative adjectives formed with -er and -est; the singular personal pronouns continue to mark case and gender; the number of prepositions increases rather than decreases; and verbs continue to mark tense, aspect, and non-finite forms (see Markey 1982, Görlach 1986, Danchev 1997). Danchev (1997: 86–100) provides the most comprehensive comparison of Middle English to typical creole attributes, and he concludes that while Middle English features coincide with creole features in over 50 percent of the items included on his list, Middle English diverges with respect to some very typical creole characteristics. In addition, many of the major "creole" features of Middle English are also typical of learner inter-languages – more or less developed approximations of an identifiable target language.

[6] There were few French monolinguals and they were socially stratified in the aristocracy. Most French speakers were bilingual and after 1204, when King John lost Normandy to the French, most of the Norman aristocracy still living in England adopted English as their primary or only language, if they had not done so already (Smith 1992: 50–52). In addition, the French-influenced changes (including new English grammatical constructions, such as composite prepositions, e.g., *outside of*), generally spread out from the capital, whereas the three "creole-like" features of Middle English moved from the north and the central and east Midlands towards the South.

reduction of inflectional endings. In histories of English, the nod to the power of French contact is often subtle: the loss of grammatical gender "was the result of processes that had been steadily at work since the Norman conquest" (Lounsbury 1891: 123). On the other hand, Claiborne, in his history of English, provides an extreme example of the depiction of French influence on the English gender system:

> A no less important result of French influence, though indirect, was the loss of grammatical gender. Old French had retained the Latin masculine and feminine genders (the neuter had vanished), while Old English had all three. Confusion grew out of the fact that too often corresponding words in the two languages had different genders . . . Even worse confusion arose from the fact that both French and English adjectives were inflected for gender – and with quite different inflectional endings. Imagine, then, the problem of mentally replacing an English noun with a French one (as people must often have done) and then adding an adjective, which was supposed to agree with the noun in gender. Did that mean the gender of the English noun, or of its French replacement – assuming anyone remembered by this time? And having decided this, how was the adjective to be inflected – in the English or the French fashion . . . How much the abandonment of grammatical gender in English was due to conscious efforts to resolve this confusion and how much to the general loss of inflectional endings (which by itself would have abolished gender distinctions for most adjectives) we do not know. But certainly by the fourteenth century English had done away with these artificial distinctions entirely, and has been all the better for it ever since. (Claiborne 1983: 114–15)

Given the relatively glib tone of this explanation and the unrealistic suggestion that English speakers might have consciously abandoned grammatical gender, Claiborne may have been aiming for humor, although the book is published as a factual account of the history of English.

As Chapter Four explains, however, the rise of natural gender in English anaphoric pronouns did not emerge from helter-skelter confusion over grammatical gender categories, whether due to language contact or not. Natural gender references gradually made inroads into anaphoric reference, beginning in Old English. The often contradictory gender classifications in French and early English play a role in the rise of the Modern English gender system, but it may actually occur in later Middle English, after the major diffusion of the shift, and often alters patterns of variation stimulated by internal and other external factors. If another language were involved in the loss of inflectional endings and grammatical gender – and dialect and sociolinguistic evidence suggests this is likely – the best candidate is Old Norse.

Several scholars have advanced proposals involving Old Norse (cf. especially Domingue 1977, Poussa 1982). The close contact between the Anglo-Saxon and Viking farming and merchant communities would have facilitated language intermixing; furthermore, as Poussa describes, both Norse and the northern English dialects existed as primarily spoken languages and may have been of comparable prestige, so the communities could have used both languages in attempts to communicate through a lingua franca. There is no decisive evidence about the extent to which Old English and Old Norse were mutually intelligible during this period. There is a general consensus that the two languages were similar enough (cognate lexicons with different inflectional systems) to be at least partially comprehensible and poetic evidence would support this theory.[7] Poussa (1982: 72) draws the comparison to modern Scandinavian dialects, and while Old English and Old Norse may not have diverged that far in the centuries separating the invasions of England, it seems probable that the Danelaw areas were characterized by bilingualism, especially given the limited literary and educational tradition in either country that could have served to slow down language change. This kind of social and linguistic contact opens the possibility of both heavy borrowing and substratum interference, the two mechanisms of contact-induced change proposed by Thomason and Kaufman (1988). The fact that lexical borrowing from Old Norse was not particularly heavy in all dialects of English (although it was significant in some northern varieties) does not preclude the possibility of structural interference caused by that language. In fact, contact with Old Norse is a very likely external factor involved in the leveling of Old English inflectional endings in the northern dialects – a spoken language phenomenon, appropriate given the nature of language contact in this situation – and the related loss of grammatical gender distinctions. To explain the loss of inflections in English, Domingue cites speaker confusion in the face of two different sets of inflectional endings (often on very similar, cognate words), which led to reliance on other means to express grammatical function and the decline in inflectional ending articulation or use.[8]

---

[7] In the *Battle of Maldon*, a Viking messenger stands on the bank and yells to Byrhtnoth and his Anglo-Saxon army, demanding tribute in return for peace; Byrhtnoth responds that they will give only spears as tribute: they will valiantly defend their nation against the raiders rather than submit to them. Obviously, poetic accounts of historical events should not be viewed as factual records, but it is interesting to note that the poem assumes mutual intelligibility and mentions no "foreign tongue" for these foreign attackers.

[8] Poussa (1982) additionally attempts to provide a sociolinguistic explanation for the rise of this Scandinavian-influenced form of English from a local midland dialect to a pervasive language force throughout the country. If the creole-speaking population were as large as Scandinavian place-names might indicate, the creole could have survived the deconstruction of the Danelaw due to its "high local prestige" and its functionality in its geopolitical position between York and London, whose respective dialects may have diverged dramatically. Poussa must then rely on the influence of the second Danish "intervention" (Swein's invasion in 1013) and Knut's reign from 1017 to 1035 to explain the elevation of the midland creole from a prestigious local dialect to one source of London Standard English. Poussa's theory likely exaggerates the influence of Norse-speaking populations up to 1066 and does not incorporate the subsequent rule of the French and their language in London, but her suggestion of high local prestige for these midland dialects remains a valid possibility, and the emphasis on the presence and influence of Old Norse in the history of English is critical.

The potential validity of some details in these proposals is undermined by the overarching creole argument. Proposals for significant Old Norse influence on English syntax do not require the positing of a creole; in fact, they only suffer from the attempt to defend this radical, and it seems inapplicable, idea. Perhaps the most important argument against Middle English creole theories is that there is no evidence for any discontinuity in the transmission of the language. Linguistic change in late Old English and early Middle English may have been rapid and dramatic in nature and in scope, but it does not appear to have been disruptive. Speakers at the time were most likely unaware of the far-reaching implications of the inflectional and gender variation in their language. On the other hand, it seems that only external explanations involving language contact can account for the rapidity and the timing of the linguistic changes in late Old English and early Middle English.

In the case of Middle English, the "creole-like" features of inflectional reduction and loss of grammatical gender seem to have been incipient in the language and accelerated by language contact. The case study of the gender shift in the personal pronouns effectively exemplifies the ways in which the rapid development of a linguistic change appears to have been driven both by external factors and internal ones. Given widespread proof that language contact often promotes greater and faster change in linguistic systems (McMahon 1994: 266; Harris and Campbell 1995: 51) and dialectal evidence, it seems logical to conclude that contact with Old Norse sped and amplified this syntactic change occurring early in the midland and northern dialects.

In comparing the implications of these creole theories with more traditional historical approaches, what is particularly interesting is the selective treatment histories give these various forms of foreign influence, emphasizing lexical borrowing from prestigious languages and de-emphasizing grammatical changes influenced not only by French but also by Old Norse. Borrowings can easily be framed as enhancing the language. And while many grammarians have praised the simplification of English when it lost inflections and grammatical gender as progress, it seems somehow more praiseworthy if English simplified on its own, rather than through mixing with foreign tongues. This kind of mixing with other languages that results in simplification is often pejoratively referred to as bastardization (unfortunately a familiar term to those working on creole languages). It is no accident that if a language is cited as possibly influencing the loss of grammatical gender in English, it is typically French and it is framed as a sign of literate bilingualism.

Anti-creole evidence for Middle English does not, therefore, invalidate the importance of the question. Raising the creole question forces historians of English to reconceptualize the way we frame the early history of English as well as what we mean by "English." The significance of the question is the emphasis it is willing to give to the influence of other languages on the development of English as well as the necessity it creates to consider dialectal variation. Change happened at different rates and at different times in various dialects of English, due sometimes to different patterns of language contact. This recognition of dialectal variation immediately disrupts any linear conception of English as it affirms that "English" is, in fact, a conglomeration of related dialects, not one standard language with subsidiary dialects; the history of English is the history of its dialects.

2.7   A note on working with early English texts and new corpora

The challenges of studying linguistic change in early stages of the English language, a language so far removed from the Modern English we employ to write about it, often overwhelm the advantages. Late twentieth-century sociolinguists have informants and tape recorders to capture and preserve the details of the language in ways never before possible. And new electronic databases of written and spoken English capture the nuances of language change in invaluable ways. These records of spoken English are particularly important, both for present and future scholarship, because almost all written records of Modern English are comparatively unrevealing about the details of the spoken language: written Standard English, with its fossilized spelling system (whose relationship to pronunciation is sometimes baffling) and its conventions for syntactic expression, cannot effectively record phonological or syntactic variation, the manifestation of language change in progress. On the other hand, early written records of English, particularly before the use of the printing press, have the power to tell a different story. Without a widely institutionalized standard form of the language to follow, many Old and Middle English scribes wrote the language in ways that reveal their particular dialectal features.[9] Spelling variation, forms of inflectional endings, and signs of hypercorrection, among other evidence, can all potentially illuminate dialectal differences in grammar and pronunciation, as well as language change in progress.

The evidence presented in the following three chapters comes almost entirely from written texts, and it is critical to remember that the changes discussed undoubtedly occurred first in the spoken language. Modern knowledge about spoken varieties of early English must rest on an assumption of a correlation between the written and spoken language (McIntosh 1956). There are notable limitations to such a correlation: written forms do not offer precise pronunciation;

---

[9] The majority of Old English texts that have survived are West Saxon, written in a language probably closely linked to an early form of spoken West Saxon, but possibly significantly predating the surviving manuscripts, as this written dialect may have contained a significant number of fossilized conventions by the tenth century. The Middle English period witnesses the flourishing of written dialects – dialects that undoubtedly existed unrecorded in Old English (cf. Toon 1985) – which allows the mapping of early linguistic features (exemplified by McIntosh et al. 1987) as well as some types of linguistic change. At various early stages of English, there were fairly powerful written standards, with strong local or more widespread influence – the West Saxon manuscript tradition being one of the more powerful early standards and the most influential on the written record of Old English available to language historians today.

the written language can create distinctions the spoken language does not, and it can mask other, perhaps subtle distinctions maintained in the spoken language; the written language may also be more conservative in spelling, morphology, syntax, and lexicon than the spoken language. But written forms can be assumed to represent existing variants (at that time or earlier) in the spoken language, and changes in the written language can be assumed often to parallel developments in the spoken language, although the written record may lag fairly significantly behind the spoken.

As is the case with many of the fundamental changes in the grammatical and lexical structure of early English, the nature of the gender shift and the early history of words for men and women are obscured – or at least modern knowledge of it is hindered – by the dearth of English texts in the two centuries after the Norman Conquest, the textual "black hole" in the history of the language. Research based on the early written record of English is also hampered by its limited textual size and range. Medieval scribal production was often concentrated in monastic centers, and as a result, many of the surviving manuscripts are religious texts and many are translated from Latin. The entire Old English corpus is only approximately 3 million words, perhaps none of which could be called truly vernacular or colloquial. So, for example, we may have little or no record of colloquial or slang terms for men and women in the medieval period. And there are almost no written English records in the eleventh and twelfth centuries.

In addition, in studying the gender shift, given the limited written records available for Old English and their concentration in one dialect, the variation no doubt occurring in the spoken language across class, age, and gender of speakers as well as across dialects cannot be recovered. By Middle English, differences in patterns of gender variation across the textual evidence are more abundant and may result from the chronological progression of texts or from their dialectal provenance – or from both. For example, natural gender agreement – like the loss of inflectional endings – seems to diffuse dialectally from the north and east midland areas towards the south of England, with Kent remaining the most grammatically conservative dialect through the fourteenth century. The linguistic evidence from early Middle English, therefore, represents the gender shift at many different stages: almost complete in northern dialects as early as the end of the twelfth century, and near its very beginnings in the southern dialects. Therefore, while it is still possible to identify patterns of natural gender use as well as factors involved in the diffusion of the gender shift during this period, the details importantly get "messier" than the relatively stable development of gender agreement described for Old English – and yet not nearly "messy" enough. The descriptions of all the gender shifts in the next three chapters would be even more complex, less coherent, and more "real" if we were to have access to more records of the language change in progress, if we had access to spoken and colloquial language rather than only selected, usually more formal written texts, if we were able to dive into the complexity of explaining language change sociolinguistically. Instead, in historical sociolinguistics we must often hypothesize, assuming Labov's uniformitarian principle that processes of language change observable today can be assumed to be applicable to earlier stages of language. And we must take the limited data available and come to the best conclusions possible; as Labov (1994: 11) puts it: "historical linguistics can . . . be thought of as the art of making the best use of bad data."

There is an almost irresistible tendency in historical linguistics to slip into discussing the language as if it were changing on its own, as if it had an existence apart from speakers. In fact, a pronoun does not "shift to avoid ambiguity" but rather a speaker uses a different pronoun in order to avoid ambiguity;[10] a word does not "become more pejorative" until speakers start using it in more negative contexts. Throughout this book, I attempt to involve speakers in the workings of change as much as possible; however, there may be times that the language itself becomes so focal that speakers move to the background in the framing of the description. It is also important to foreground the caveat that forthcoming chapters will inevitably draw too neat a picture, in retrospect, of the direction of syntactic and semantic change in English, a point that is reiterated in discussions of specific corpus and text studies.

To tell a more complete story of the English gender shift than has been previously attempted and to explore in a manageable way the history of words for men and women, these studies work from the Helsinki Corpus.[11] The diachronic part of the Helsinki Corpus, finished in 1991, is the largest diachronic English text database yet compiled, comprising over 1.5 million words and spanning the Old English through early Modern English periods (for more details, see Kytö 1991). The Corpus provides as balanced and "random" a sampling as may be possible for linguistic studies of early English; while periodization was a guiding parameter, the compilers also considered geographical dialect, type and register of writing, and sociolinguistic variation as factors in terms of the coverage of the Corpus. Shorter texts are presented in full and the length of extracts from other texts varies from 2,000 to 10,000 words. The Old English part of the Corpus contains 413,250 words and is broken into four chronological blocks: pre-850 (OE I), 850–950 (OE II), 950–1050 (OE III), and 1050–1150 (OE IV). The Middle English part of the Corpus, which totals 608,570 words, is also broken into four 100-year sections from 1150 to 1500, only the first of which (ME I,

---

[10] I would like to thank James Milroy for both the wording of this example and for his emphasis on this point throughout our discussions of the history of English.

[11] Every text is tagged using twenty-four reference codes to define the textual parameters such as author, date, text type, etc. (Kytö 1991: 40–56). All foreign languages, runes, italics, editors' comments or emendations, etc., are marked. There is no grammatical tagging. The Corpus is available in several versions, one of which is WordCruncher files for MS-DOS machines. At the University of Michigan, these WordCruncher files have been retagged using SGML and made locally available on the world-wide web; it is the latter version of the Corpus that serves as the basis of the studies in this book. Some of the formatting has been changed in the process: the medieval characters for ash, thorn, eth, and yogh have been substituted for coding characters (e.g., "+t" for thorn); manuscript line breaks have not been reproduced here and the symbol for "line continues" (#) has been omitted.

1150–1250) proves particularly revealing for the study in Chapter Four. The early Modern English part of the Corpus, which totals 551,000 words, covers texts from 1500 to 1710. (See Appendix 2 for a list of the specific texts included in this study.)

The studies of the English gender shift in the next two chapters contribute a description of the variation involved in the implementation of the natural gender concord system for all English nouns, as well as insight into the internal and external factors involved in this change. The results indicate that the rise of natural gender in English perfectly exemplifies established theoretical models of syntactic change such as grammatical analogy, reanalysis, and lexical diffusion, and suggest ways in which foreign influence may have accelerated, and in some cases interrupted, this process. It argues against creole theories and simultaneously calls for a revision in the presentation of grammatical gender, natural gender, and the transition between the two in histories of English. While the loss of grammatical gender is, as Ross stated, an extremely difficult problem in the history of English, modern historians of English are aided by the insights of historical sociolinguistics, by a recognition of the important ways in which philology and historical linguistics intersect with theoretical work in other fields, and by new electronic resources for English historical semantic and syntactic studies.

3　A history of gender, people, and pronouns: the story of generic *he*

3.1　Introduction

Contemporary question

The sexist nature of generic *he* has been established in linguistic scholarship for at least two decades. (Martyna 1978, 1980a, 1980b are perhaps the most cited studies; see Newman 1997: 9–61 for a good summary.) As the brief survey of selected grammar books at the end of this chapter shows, modern grammarians and style guide writers have reached a consensus: generic *he* is sexist and should be avoided. There are, however, still grammatical pundits who hold fast to generic *he* as stylistically preferred; and findings about the sexist nature of generic *he* have certainly been contested even within linguistic circles. The Harvard "incident" in 1971 is one of the more famous instances; the head of the Linguistics department described the generic masculine as simply a feature of grammar (and a "natural" one at that) and dismissed protesting female students as having "pronoun envy" (as cited in Romaine 1999: 105–106).

Modern debate on this question has been framed as though it were a grammatical question (e.g., number agreement), and feminists have fought hard to move the debate from the rhetoric of "objective" grammar rules to a discussion of the semantic and social implications of those rules. In a natural gender system, the pronoun *he* can no longer be a purely grammatical form with no meaningful content about the gender of the referent. This debate has been informed by important and interesting studies of the grammatical, social, and psychological implications of the generic masculine, and occasionally scholars gesture back in time to early grammar books like Lindley Murray's *English Grammar* (1981 [1824]) or to examples of authors such as Jane Austen who employ generic *they*. To date, these debates have not been informed by a more rigorous historical linguistic examination of the relationship between personal pronouns and nouns referring to humans in the history of English, such as the study presented here, to determine how these historical details might inform our understanding of the modern debate and what is at stake.

Historical context

Concerted prescriptive energies were first applied to the generic pronoun problem in Lindley Murray's extremely popular *English Grammar*, first published in 1794. Murray noted the violation of number agreement in sentences where *they* is used to refer to an indefinite singular noun; he labeled the use of *they* in such a situation an error and corrected it with *he*, without providing any further explanation. A little more than fifty years later, the "correctness" of generic *he* went from being a theory to being a law: in 1850, an Act of Parliament legally replaced *he or she* with *he* to "shorten the language used in Acts of Parliament" (cited in Bodine 1975: 174).

With the loss of grammatical gender concord in English by Middle English, the generic pronoun question becomes more clearly a question of semantics as well as syntax.[1] The history of generic pronoun usage is less clearly established. Newman (1997), in his valuable corpus-based book-length study of generic pronoun use, provides a useful summary of previous scholarship on current usage of singular generic pronoun constructions as well as a survey of scholarship that examines – or at least mentions – historical usage in such constructions. As Newman describes, there has been debate about how early generic *he* appears in the history of English as well as how early and often forms of *they* appear in reference to singular gender-neutral antecedents. In his analysis of this work, Newman correctly points out that evidence for epicene *he* predates prescriptivism, so prescription of generic *he* should be seen more as a suppression of variation than as an invention of the eighteenth century (1997: 21). He dates the use of generic *he* as early as Chaucer. In fact, as discussed in this chapter, generic *he* can be found much earlier than Chaucer: it can be dated back at least to the era of *Beowulf*, another literary landmark.

Is there anything in the history of the English language that can help explain how the masculine form of the personal pronoun became the generic form? To what extent is generic masculine in English the result of prescription (see, for example, Mühlhäusler and Harré 1990) or does it have a more "natural origin," as Newman (1997: 22) describes it? And what would "natural" mean in this context – inherent to syntax or inherent to the social structure of speakers? Newman notes that the generic masculine in English is not surprising given that in many Indo-European languages "the unmarked function of the masculine gender is an integral part of syntax" (*ibid.*: 22). Many modern Indo-European languages, for example, demonstrate the general use of the masculine third-person plural pronoun to refer to a mixed-sex group. It is not a universal feature of language, however, that the masculine forms also serve as the unmarked or neutral forms:

---

[1] Languages with grammatical gender systems are not immune from debates about sexist language, including concern about the assumption of masculine as the unmarked and conflicts between grammatical and semantic gender. See Pauwels (1998) for an excellent discussion of sexist language reform efforts in many European countries and languages; see Livia (2001) for a study of literary manifestations of concern about gender and pronouns in French as well as in English.

the Iroquoian languages, for example, use feminine nouns as the unmarked terms (Frank and Anshen 1983: 70). (It is also clear that feminine-unmarked languages do not necessarily imply nonsexist language communities.) Newman goes on to complicate the relationship of syntax and culture with regard to the development of epicene pronouns: "This process [modern changes in epicene pronouns] could come about in the same way that, presumably, an androcentric world view was grammaticalized by the prehistoric peoples into the unmarked masculines that mark so many of the world's languages" (Newman 1997: 227). And he calls for more diachronic work on English generic pronouns, to complement his synchronic corpus study.

Focus of this historical linguistic study

The study described in this chapter is broader than the generic pronoun question alone. It begins a response to Newman's call by providing a historical framework of the changes in the English gender system in which to view the evolution of generic reference and by locating early generic uses within this context. The empirical study of early English usage is based on the Helsinki Corpus. (See Appendix 2 for a list of the specific texts used in the Old and early Middle English sections of the Corpus as well as an explanation of the study's methodology.)

This chapter examines specifically the nature of gender agreement in early stages of English between nouns referring to people and anaphoric personal pronouns to uncover the patterns and problems that both shed light on, and complicate the history of, the generic pronoun question. The patterns provide critical context for understanding the gender shift described in more detail in Chapter Four; and the problems are enlightening in historicizing current concerns about sexism in the language. How early does generic *he* appear? How new is generic *they*? And to what extent have prescriptive energies affected agreement patterns with nouns of unknown gender? Once English shifts to a natural gender system, personal pronouns clearly carry semantic information about the gender of referents. The converse of this statement for Old English, however, does not hold: that with a grammatical gender system, English personal pronouns did not carry semantic information about the gender of referents. This chapter examines the interplay of grammatical and natural gender agreement in personal pronouns referring to gendered nouns for human beings in early English in order to understand the context and early roots of the Modern English "generic pronoun problem."

3.2 Early agreement patterns and implications for the gender shift

The early history of agreement patterns between nouns referring to human beings and personal pronouns used anaphorically provides insights about the workings of generic references in English and about the nature of the shift from grammatical to natural gender more generally: for while the pivotal class of nouns

Table 3.1: *Frequency of different types of antecedent nouns in the Helsinki Corpus Study*

Noun type	OE II (850–950 AD)	OE III (950–1050 AD)	OE IV (1050–1150 AD)	ME I (1150–1250 AD)
Proper names	1750 (46.6%)	2495 (46.2%)	1324 (50.4%)	2557 (41.7%)
Human(-like) beings)	1359 (36.2%)	2046 (37.9%)	1051 (40.0%)	2637 (43.0%)
Animals	42 (1.1%)	96 (1.8%)	21 (0.8%)	67 (1.1%)
Inanimate objects	528 (14.0%)	754 (14.0%)	233 (8.9%)	765 (12.5%)
Personified nouns	80 (2.1%)	4 (0.1%)	—	103 (1.7%)
Total nouns	3759	5395	2629	6129

in charting the progression of the gender shift in pronouns is the inanimate nouns, it is enlightening to view the grammatical behavior of these nouns in the larger context of the gender concord system for all nouns. As this section demonstrates, the patterns of gender agreement for nouns and pronouns referring to people are much more stable historically than those referring to inanimate objects, and they provide the context for understanding the mechanics of the gender shift. They also provide the context for understanding some of the lingering questions of sexist usage in Modern English.

The agreement patterns between nouns referring to people and personal pronouns should be viewed as an important context for understanding the gender shift due to the sheer numbers: nouns describing people dominate the subjects referred back to by pronouns in the Helsinki Corpus texts included in this study. Across the Old and Middle English texts in this study, the overwhelming percentage of anaphoric pronoun references (over 80 percent) involve nouns for people, both proper names and more general terms for human(-like) beings such as *mann* 'man, person,' *wif* 'woman,' *bisceop* 'bishop,' *deofol* 'devil' (see Table 3.1). These numbers reflect the thematic concerns of most of these early English texts: historical events, religious figures and stories, and religious instructional material. Inanimate objects are mentioned but often as background, with human figures the focus of the written discourse and, therefore, referred back to more frequently.[2]

One significant implication of these lopsided numbers for the gender shift lies in the fact that for all personal names and for almost all general terms for human beings in Old English, the grammatical gender of the noun and the "natural gender" (or socially constructed gender) of the referent correspond.

[2] The exceptions are medical texts, recipe books, and scientific treatises, which often focus on inanimate objects such as the sun, moon, stars, herbs, and medicines. As discussed in Chapter Four, the material in these texts is not always revealing about the larger gender concord system because it often focuses heavily on particular nouns, some of which prove to be "resilient nouns." OE I is not included in the results presented here as the evidence collected from this small number of texts is too limited to be significant; see note 8 in Chapter Four for more details.

Table 3.2: *Agreement patterns in Old English for animate nouns with conflicting grammatical and semantic gender*

Antecedent noun	Pronoun summary
wifmann 'woman' (masculine)	16 feminine 2 masculine
mægden 'young woman, maiden' (neuter)	25 feminine
wif 'woman' (neuter)	116 feminine 1 masculine-neuter 1 neuter
bearn 'child' (neuter)	1 neuter 2 masculine 5 masculine-neuter
cild 'child' (neuter)	10 neuter 6 masculine 8 masculine-neuter

In other words, grammatical gender and natural gender are indistinguishable. Most nouns referring to males are masculine (e.g., *wer* 'man,' *bisceop* 'bishop,' *munuc* 'monk') and to females feminine (e.g., *fæmne* 'woman,' *wuduwe* 'widow'). Anaphoric gender concord for these nouns, therefore, consistently follows both grammatical and natural gender simultaneously. Some of these masculine nouns theoretically could apply to both sexes (e.g., *lareow* 'teacher,' *witega* 'prophet') but in these Anglo-Saxon texts, they invariably have male referents and it is not illogical, therefore, to claim that natural and grammatical gender coincide in these cases also. It reveals the gender hierarchy in that historical period and in these historical texts – but not in this particular study – to classify these references as "natural." And it is undoubtedly explanatory in how the masculine continues on as the "generic" pronoun in reference to such nouns after grammatical gender becomes obsolete.

For the set of well-known exceptions to this rule of gender correspondence – nouns such as the masculine noun *wifmann* 'woman,' and the neuter nouns *wif* 'woman,' *mægden* 'young woman, maiden,' *bearn* 'child,' and *cild* 'child,' for which biological sex and grammatical gender do not correspond – natural gender almost always prevails in the anaphoric pronouns. Scholars have long held that with the few animate nouns in Old English for which natural and grammatical gender conflict, the anaphoric pronouns almost always follow natural gender; the results of this corpus study confirm this hypothesis (see Table 3.2). For the masculine and neuter nouns referring to females (i.e., *wifmann, wif*, and *mægden*), there are almost no conflicts with natural gender in the anaphoric pronouns: all 25 pronoun references to *mægden* are feminine; 116 out of the 118 pronouns referring to *wif* and 16 out of the 18 pronouns referring to *wifmann* are feminine. The presence of masculine or neuter modifiers in the antecedent noun phrase seems to be irrelevant for agreement in the pronouns. For example, all 25 anaphoric references to the neuter noun *mægden* are feminine, despite the fact that nine of the antecedent noun phrases include distinctively non-feminine inflectional forms (e.g., neuter demonstrative pronouns or adjectives).

The Old English words *cild* 'child' and *bearn* 'child,' both neuter nouns, are noteworthy in their fluctuation between neuter and masculine anaphoric pronouns. The word *child* (as well as *baby*, *infant*, etc.) can still take a neuter anaphoric pronoun in Modern English (e.g., "What an adorable child! It looks just like Tweety Bird."), as Newman's study (1997: 156–57) confirms; and it has been hypothesized that the neuter reference reflects the lack of gendered characteristics in the child. In Old English, children can similarly take neuter anaphoric pronouns (in agreement with their grammatical gender) or gendered anaphoric pronouns (in agreement with the biological sex or socially constructed gender of the referent). A passage from *Alfred's Boethius* captures this idea about children and the consequent fluctuation between pronominal genders in a particularly anecdotal way:[3]

(1) þæt dysig is anlicost þe sum **cild** sie full hal & ful æltæwe geboren, & swa fullice ðionde on eallum cystum & cræftum þa hwile þe **hit** on cnihthade bið. & swa forð eallne giogoðhad, oð **he** wyrð ælces cræftes medeme, & ðonne lytle ær **his** midferhðe weorðe bæm eagum blind, & eac þæs modes eagan weorðan swa ablende þæt **he** nanwuht ne gemune þæs ðe **he** æfre ær geseah oððe geherde, & wene þeah ðæt **he** sie ælces þinges swa medeme swa **he** æfre medomest wære, & wend þæt ælcum men sie swa swa **him** si, & ælcum men ðince swa swa **him** þincð. (*Alfred's Boethius* 122)

'That foolishness is most like, that a **child** be born full healthy and full sound, and so perfectly flourishing in all virtues and skills, while **it** is in boyhood, and so forth all of adolescence, until **he** becomes capable in every art; and then a little before **his** middle-age, [**he**] should become blind in both eyes, and also the eyes of the mind should become so blinded, that **he** remembers nothing of that which **he** ever before saw or heard: and [**he**] should believe, however, that **he** be as capable of every thing as **he** ever was [when] most capable: and believes that it is for every man/person as it is for **him**; and that it seems) to every man as it seems to **him**.'

---

[3] In all exemplary passages, the Old or Middle English antecedent noun phrase and the anaphoric pronouns of interest are in boldface. A non-colloquial, fairly literal translation is provided below each passage; the vocabulary and syntax of the Modern English follow the Old English fairly closely in order to facilitate comparison with the Old English syntax. Parenthetical references correspond to the text titles and page numbers in the Helsinki Corpus excerpts (with the exception of the Old English text *Beowulf*, for which line numbers are provided). For the systematic study of gender agreement in Old English and early Middle English (OE II–ME I), all the Corpus texts included in the study appear in Appendix 2. For a full list of texts in the Corpus, see Kytö 1991.

The pronominal transition of particular interest in this passage occurs in the second and third lines: *swa fullice ðionde on eallum cystum & cræftum þa hwile þe hit on cnihthade bið. & swa forð eallne giogoðhad, oð he wyrð ælces cræftes medeme*, or '[A child shall be] so perfectly flourishing in all virtues and skills, while it is in boyhood, and so forth all of adolescence, until he becomes capable in every art.' Through *cnihthad* 'boyhood,' the child is a *hit*, but upon hitting *giogoðhad* 'youth, adolescence,' it becomes *he* and continues to be *he* until he hits old age, blindness, and the other rewards of the gendered adult world.

In another striking passage, this one from the *Passion of St. Margaret*, the gender of the child transforms with age:

(2)   And se godes þeowe Theothimus gefand þæt **cild** and he **hit** up anam and **hit** wel befæste to fedenne. And þa **hit** andgeat hæfde, he **him** nama gesette, and þæt wæs **Margareta**, and **hi** syððan to lare befæste, and **hi** þæron wel geþeah. (*Passion of St. Margaret* 14)

'And God's servant Theotimus found the **child** and he took **it** up and entrusted **it** to be well fed. And when **it** had acquired understanding, he gave **it** a name, and that was **Margaret**, and [he] afterwards set **her** to learning and **she** fully excelled thereon (at it).'

The child is neuter until it is named Margaret, at which point it becomes a *she* (the antecedent here may shift to *Margaret* as well) and remains a *she* throughout the rest of the text. This passage also includes an early use of *þæron* 'thereon' to refer to the feminine noun *lar* 'learning' – a trend that is discussed in more detail in the next chapter.

The word *mann*, unsurprisingly, appears with great frequency. It is very difficult to make a consistent distinction between the antecedent noun *mann* 'person (male or female), man, mankind, hero' and the indefinite pronoun *man* 'one, people' – the two words are, in fact, cross-referenced in the standard Old English dictionary by Clark Hall (1960). Mitchell (1986: §§363–77) summarizes five possible senses of indefinite *man* – several of which draw a fine line between the indefinite and definite individual. In the singular, all anaphoric references to *man* and *mann* (spelling variation often makes it impossible to distinguish between the two) are masculine, the non-distinctive forms *his* or *him*, or plural. Examples occur in almost every text, so the selection of one is fairly arbitrary:

(3)   Forðam for ðære orsorgnesse **monn** oft aðint on ofermettum, & ða earfeðu ðurh sorge **hiene** geclænsiað & geeaðmedað. (*Alfred's Cura Pastoralis* 35)

'Because through (that) luxury **man** is often swelled with pride, and (the) hardships caused by sorrow purify and humble **him**.'

Whether or not this use of *mann* is generic is debatable and, ultimately, unresolvable. In his *EETS* edition of *Cura Pastoralis*, Sweet (1871: 34) translates the passage with the plural forms *men* and *them*, but the Old English clearly employs the singular and masculine.

Occasionally medieval texts explicitly include both men and women under the term *mann* and the following masculine pronoun references, as in example (4), confirming that the term did still carry a generic meaning:

(4)   nu **anra manna gehwylcne** ic myngie & lære, **ge weras ge wif**, ge geonge ge ealde, ge snottre ge unwise, ge þa welegan ge þa þearfan, þæt **anra gehwylc hine** sylfne sceawige & ongyte, & swa hwæt swa **he** on mycclum gyltum oþþe on medmycclum gefremede, þæt **he** þonne hrædlice gecyrre to þam selran & to þon soþan læcedome. (*Alfred's Boethius* 107)

'I now remind and advise **every man, both men and women**, both young and old, both wise and unwise, both the rich and the poor, that **everyone** examine and consider **himself** and, whatsoever **he** has committed in great sins or in smallness of mind, that **he** then immediately turn to the better and to the true medicine.'

The singular form *mann* – as well as subsequent masculine anaphoric pronouns – can also be used to refer specifically to women in Old English, providing further evidence that the word preserves the generic meaning 'person' at least into Old English, if not later. The question of when *mann* lost its generic meaning in English and came to refer exclusively to male human beings remains unsettled and is addressed in more detail in Chapter Five. In Modern English, the use of *man* to refer exclusively to women seems awkward, if not illogical – the textbook example being "Man breastfeeds his young."

Generic terms such as *hwa, sum, hwilc*, and *oðer* (see Mitchell 1986: §378 for a more complete list) also take masculine anaphoric pronouns, even when both sexes are clearly specified. The *Cura Pastoralis* provides the following advice to both spouses for maintaining proper marital "sexual distance":

(5)   Ne fornime incer **noðer oðer** ofer will butan geðafunge, ðæm timum ðe **he hine** wille gebiddan, ac geæmtigeað ince to gebedum. (*Alfred's Cura Pastoralis* 399)

'Do not, **neither** of you, deprive the other against [their (his?)] will without consent, at the times when **he** wants to pray, but have time to yourselves for prayers.'

In many Old English texts, the audience is often understood to be male, in which case the potential generic status of *he* is in many ways irrelevant. But in instances such as example (5), which explicitly comprehend the male and female into the audience, the masculine seems able to include both genders, even if only by convention. (Sweet [1871: 398] translates the passage with an even-handedness that requires some pronominal shifts in the Modern English: "Let neither of you deprive the other against his or her will without consent, when either of you wish to pray, but keep yourselves free for prayers.")

The critical implication of these details on gender agreement for animate nouns in Old English for the gender shift more generally is that for the largest

Table 3.3: *Frequency of antecedent noun gender categories in the Helsinki Corpus Study*

Noun gender	OE II	OE III	OE IV	ME I
m	3020 (80.3%)	4322 (80.1%)	2207 (83.9%)	4234 (69.0%)
f	219 (5.8%)	563 (10.4%)	230 (8.7%)	914 (14.9%)
n	231 (6.1%)	274 (5.1%)	125 (4.8%)	614 (10.0%)
multiple gender, foreign, plural, unknown, generic	289 (7.7%)	236 (4.1%)	67 (2.5%)	367 (5.9%)

subset of antecedent nouns in this study, either: (1) the grammatical gender of the noun corresponds to the natural gender of the noun; or, (2) natural gender prevails over grammatical gender in the agreement of the anaphoric pronouns. The more arbitrary grammatical gender system of inanimate nouns exists as one part of a larger system of anaphoric reference in which for animate nouns, gender agreement in the language either already corresponds grammatically to social distinctions of gender or is no longer grammatical, but rather notional, in order to correspond to these social distinctions of gender (e.g., words for women are referred to with feminine pronouns no matter what their grammatical gender). Of course, this is true to varying degrees of other languages that have retained grammatical gender, so it is certainly not explanatory in and of itself, but it may well be a factor contributing to the gradual process of the extension of the semantic gender system, described in more detail in the next chapter.

The results of this study also suggest that the gender agreement system for inanimate nouns exists in a masculine-dominated anaphoric gender system. The masculine gender monopolizes over 80 percent of the antecedent nouns in the Old English part of this study and almost 70 percent in the early Middle English part (see Table 3.3); the overall frequency of masculine anaphoric pronouns is correspondingly high. The reasons for this gender distribution are fairly obvious. Given that the majority of antecedent nouns in these texts refer to humans and that the majority of the humans they refer to are male – mostly because of the nature of the subject matter, as the events and stories in medieval historical and religious texts generally revolve around men – it is only logical that most of the antecedent nouns are masculine (given that grammatical and natural gender coincide for these nouns). Interestingly, these results correspond to more recent findings by Romaine (1999: 108–109) about reference to men and women in Modern English; she argues that men are referred to more often in both spoken and written English (although the gap may be closing). Newman (1997: 153) confirms this conclusion in his study of twenty-four episodes of television interview programs: individual males are the prime topic of discourse.

Natural gender concord between nouns referring to human(-like) beings and their anaphoric pronouns becomes almost exceptionless in early Middle English (and animate nouns continue to dominate as the most frequent antecedents, at nearly 85 percent). The neuter nouns *bearn* 'child' and *cild* 'child' continue to be referred to with both neuter and masculine pronouns, much as Modern English *child* still does with masculine, feminine, and neuter pronouns.[4] The "unnaturally" gendered masculine noun *wifmann* 'woman' and neuter nouns *wif* 'woman, wife' and *mægden* 'maiden' consistently occur with feminine anaphoric pronouns in early Middle English; and occasionally ungrammatical gender appears in the noun phrase itself, causing these nouns to appear with feminine demonstrative pronouns, as illustrated with the noun *wifmann* in a passage from Layamon's *Brut*:

(6)   Hercne nu muchel swikedom; of þere **wimmon**. hu **heo** gon swikien þer þene king Uortimer. (*Layamon's Brut* I, 388)

       'Listen now to the great treachery by that **woman**, how **she** proceeded to deceive there the king Vortimer.'

As discussed earlier, Jones (1988) provides an interesting discussion of possible discursive (as opposed to grammatical) interpretations of gendered demonstrative pronouns during the transition period, such as *þere* 'that' in this sentence.

The "generic person," whether referred to with *mann, hwa*, or another indefinite pronoun, or whether it is an understood reference, still generally appears with masculine anaphoric pronouns in the early Middle English part of the study, although there are exceptions depending on the text and the intended audience. In the *Ancrene Wisse*, an instructional text for anchorites, the word *hwa* appears with both masculine and feminine pronouns. If the audience is specifically the sisters, the reference is often assumed to be feminine, even when the antecedent is the grammatically masculine *hwa se* 'whoever':

(7)   iheren ich segge. for **hwa se** spekeð ham; nis **ha** nawt ancre. (*Ancrene Wisse* 44)

       'I say "heard," for **whoever** speaks them, **she** is not an anchoress.'

But even when directly addressing the anchoresses, as in the following warning about their susceptibility in the face of temptation, the writer sometimes employs highly masculine language, both in the choice of metaphor and in the choice of generic pronoun:

(8)   **Hwa se** is siker of sucurs þt **him** schal cume sone. & ȝet tah up **his** castel to **his** wiðeriwines; swiðe **he** is to edwiten. (*Ancrene Wisse* 120)

       '**Whoever** is certain of help that will come to **him** soon, and yet brought up **his** castle to **his** enemies, much is **he** to be reproached.'

---

[4] In order to maintain consistency with the Old English part of the study and to facilitate comparison, the Old English dictionary headword spellings (based on Clark Hall 1960) are used for Middle English words of native origin.

Another passage from the *Ancrene Wisse* contains a use of both masculine and feminine pronouns to refer to a generic person – a construction that may look strikingly familiar to modern readers – as opposed to using only *he* for the generic. In a discussion of the numerous sins associated with backbiting, the narrator quotes one prototypical type of backbiter:

(9)   weila he seið wa is me þt **he** oðer **heo** habbeð swuch word icaht . . . þt is muchel sorhe. for i feole oðer þing **he** oðer **heo** is swiðe to herien . . . (*Ancrene Wisse* 47)

 ' "Oh dear," he [the backbiter] says, "Woe is to the one that **he or she** has caught such talk . . . that is a great sorrow, for in many other ways **he or she** is greatly to be praised" '

The backbiter (*bacbitere*, a masculine noun) in example (9) consistently takes a masculine pronoun – despite the narrator's pointed message to the anchoresses that they could easily slip into this sin – but the victim of the back-biting is explicitly either male or female, demonstrated grammatically by the juxtaposition of the masculine and feminine pronouns. Such an example suggests that the masculine pronouns were not necessarily generic during this period: authors sometimes seem to find themselves going to more awkward lengths to indicate clearly a reference to a person of either sex. There are still examples, however, where authors (here, once again the author of the *Ancrene Wisse*) comfortably use *he* as a generic pronoun, explicitly encompassing both men and women (and here *mon* is clearly functioning as a gender-specific term):

(10)   **Euch** efter þt **he** is segge hit totagges. **Mon** as limpeið to **him**; **wummon** þt **hire** rineið. (*Ancrene Wisse* 164)

 'Let **each** according to who **he** is say the circumstances, a **man** as it happens to **him**, a **woman** as it touches **her**.'

Michael Newman (1997: 94), drawing on work by Corbett (1986), argues that anaphoric pronouns in Modern English carry discourse meaning and affect how the referent is to be viewed. Interestingly, the same argument could potentially be made for some examples of anaphoric pronouns from this earlier period of English. For example, the term *unwiht* 'evil creature, demon,' whose root *wiht* is historically neuter but fluctuates between the feminine and neuter in Old English, most often appears with masculine anaphoric pronouns in these early Middle English texts, and it generally refers to the devil who comes to test saints and layfolk. The word does occasionally appear with the neuter, and these instances usually seem to carry discourse implications. For example, in *Margarete*, the *unwiht* who visits her regularly to taunt and tempt her is depicted in the narrative as masculine, but when Margaret herself is disparaging him/it in direct speech, she uses a neuter pronoun:

(11)   aʒein þis eisfule **whit** þt **hit** ne eili me nawt help me mi la-lauerd.
(*Margarete* 69)

'Against this awful **creature**, that **it** not cause trouble for me, help me, my
Lord.'

For animate antecedent nouns, neuter anaphoric references can function as
marked discourse forms, usually in a pejorative way.

Slightly different discourse factors seem to influence the anaphoric pronoun
choices for the "semi-animate" neuter noun *bodig* 'body' in a passage from *Juliane*.
The body in question is that of Juliana, a saint who is referred to with the neuter
noun *mægden* and feminine anaphoric pronouns throughout the text. After her
death, Eleusius is concerned about the status and whereabouts of the dead body:

(12)   þer lette sophie from þe sea a mile. setten a chirche & duden hire **bodi** þrin
in a stanene þruh hehliche as hit deh halhe to donne. þe reue sone se he
wiste. þt **ha** wes awei ilead. leup for hihðe wið lut men into a bat & bigon
to rowen swiftliche efter. forte reauin **hit** ham. (*Juliane* 126)

'There Sophia had a church established a mile from the sea, and [they] put
her **body** therein in a stone [coffin] as highly as it avails to do with a saint.
The reeve as soon as he knew that **she** had been taken away, leapt with
haste with a few men into a boat and began to row swiftly after [them] for
to steal **it** home.'

The first anaphoric reference to the saint's body, with the feminine nominative
form *ha* 'she,' acts as the grammatical and rhetorical subject (albeit of a passive
construction) in a more animate role; although the body is no longer living, it
is grammatically active, which is reflected in the pronoun carrying the gender
of the maiden herself. The second reference, with the neuter accusative form
hit, refers to the same antecedent body, but in this case, it is the object being
retrieved. These discourse considerations of prominence, perceived animacy,
and grammatical function resurface in the patterns of use for different anaphoric
pronouns with inanimate objects, described in the next chapter.

These findings and observations provide important context for understanding
the overall shift of English to a natural gender system. Clearly, Old English
itself does not represent a "pure" or entirely consistent grammatical gender
system (if "pure" is appropriate for any such concord system given the semantic
core of all gender systems). Nouns referring to people show a strong tendency
toward natural gender agreement in anaphoric pronouns, and nouns such as
body, arguably inanimate nouns that refer to people, demonstrate the interaction
between the two gender systems as realized in discourse. Importantly, these
results mean that there was another gender system in place and available in Old
English, which could serve as the basis for reanalysis of grammatical gender in
reference to inanimate nouns (see Chapter Four). It also means that early pronoun
reference to nouns with referents of unknown or unspecified gender existed in

a variable system, in which both grammatical and natural gender could apply in reference to nouns for human beings, where both grammatical and semantic features could come into play.

3.3   Early history of generic pronoun use

As several of the examples in the previous section make clear, generic *he* occurs as early as Old English and seems to appear consistently and continuously through later stages in the history of English. Example (10) from Middle English seems to demonstrate the writer's comfort with the masculine serving as the generic, encompassing both genders. Yet in the same text, as shown in example (9), the writer occasionally opts explicitly to include both genders in the reference with the conjoined *he or she*. In other words, the generic status of the masculine is not always clear, particularly given that the nouns *mann*, *hwa se* 'whoever,' and other generic terms are masculine nouns in Old English, and in these early texts, these nouns also often have male referents. The context makes it clear that religious instructions or laws or historical observations often refer to a male audience and/or male participants in events, and this potentially has explanatory power. McConnell-Ginet (1988) theorizes "prototypicality" as an explanation for the generic masculine: a prototypical or "best example" member of the larger class comes to represent the class generically. And this prototypical embodiment will reflect cultural practices and beliefs about the nature of this class. Moulton (1977) makes a similar case in theorizing "parasitic reference" as an explanation of the generic masculine:

> Tissues are Kleenex; petroleum jelly, Vaseline; bleach, Clorox, etc. to the economic benefit of the specific brands referred to and to the economic detriment of those brands that are ignored by this terminology. The alleged gender-neutral uses of 'he,' 'man,' etc. are just further examples of this common phenomenon. A gender-specific term, one that refers to a high-status subset of the whole class, is used in place of a neutral generic term. (quoted in Newman 1997: 30)

Clearly both these arguments undermine notions of "grammatical neutrality" for the generic masculine, as they link speakers' and society's values with grammatical constructs. It is important to note here that these usage patterns of generic *he* in earlier forms of English are from written texts; the extent to which generic *he* was used and in what contexts in the spoken language is unknown.

Generic *they* occurs as early as Old English in written texts as well, as can be witnessed in the following example from *Alfred's Introduction to Laws* – its antecedent a disjunctive noun phrase and, as is often the case in Modern English, perhaps "semantically plural."

(13)   Gif oxa ofhnite **wer** oððe **wif**, þæt **hie** dead sien, sie he mid stanum ofworpod . . . (*Alfred's Introduction to Laws* 32)

'If an ox gores a man or a woman, so that they be dead, may he [the ox] be killed with stones'

As example (5) above demonstrates, a singular reference in such circumstances seems idiomatically possible, even with this explicit reference to a subject of either gender; but, as in Modern English, the pronoun *they* can also be used and interpreted as either plural (assuming a plural understanding of 'a man or a woman') or as singular and generic in this context (assuming the grammatical disjunction with "or" holds to require a singular generic pronoun). In fact, this kind of disjunctive construction seems particularly conducive to early uses of *they* to refer to a grammatically singular antecedent and it is the subject of discussion in nineteenth- and early twentieth-century grammars, as will be discussed later in this chapter. In any case, *they* is being used in at least quasi-singular generic constructions in Old English, and the evidence becomes more prominent in Middle English, although it is certainly not the only possibility for generic constructions in the period.

In Middle English, the history of use of generic *he* continues. In the two examples below, generic *he* refers to a generic person in the first example and explicitly to both genders in the second.

(14)   Swyche a persone ys ful slogh, Be he hygh, or be he logh . . . (Mannyng, *Robert of Brunne's "Handlyng Synne"* 161)

'Such a person is very lazy, be he high or be he low'

(15)   Therfor, euery lettered man and woman rede iche day these orisones of my bytter Passion for his owen medecyne . . . (Reynes, *The Commonplace Book* 266)

'Therefore, every lettered (literate) man and woman (should) read each day the orisons of my bitter Passion for his own medicine.'

And Middle English also witnesses ongoing use of generic *they*. Newman (1997: 21) provides a very interesting example of a passage from Chaucer in which different manuscripts employ forms of generic *he* or generic *they*. The Helsinki Corpus provides the following example, once again with a disjunctive noun phrase:

(16)   yff man or woman take sekenes that day, thei schuld sone recouer . . . (Metham, *Physiognomy* 149)

'If a man or woman takes sickness that day, they should soon recover . . .'

Paul Schaffner, in a more extensive survey of quotations in the *Middle English Dictionary*, has collected numerous examples of generic *they* in reference to indefinite pronouns equivalent to modern *whoso, any*, etc.; for example, there is the following instance in the *Towneley Plays* 316/326: "Whoso will of synnes seasse . . . I grauntt theym here a measse In brede, myn awne body" (unpublished paper). Another example from the Middle English part of the Helsinki Corpus proves fascinating in its recording of the kind of pronominal inconsistency so familiar to Modern English speakers (and teachers), in which strict grammatical concord with the singular gives way to semantic concord (assuming one believes *they* is always plural):

(17)   ffor whate **mann or womann** that hath **hys** mende on oure Lordis passhyon, I have no power ouer **theym** at no tyme. . . . (*The Life of St. Edmund* 168)

'For whatever **man or woman** who has **his** help in our Lord's passion, I have no power over **them** at no time'

Generic *they* continues alongside generic *he* into early Modern English, not yet condemned by prescriptive grammarians, as the next example demonstrates:

(18)   It would helpe some poore **man or woman**, who knew not how to live otherwise, and who might doe that well, if **they** were rightly directed . . . (Brinsley, *Ludus Literarius or The Grammar Schoole* 13)

Example (19), also from early Modern English, seems genuinely surprising in its strikingly modern manipulation of pronouns to create a generic reference; and the multiplication of pronouns in the odd (and awkward) construction of generic reference in example (20) may remind Modern English teachers of their students' conscientious efforts to obey politically correct guidelines.

(19)   or whose **Husband or Wife** shall absent **hym or her selfe** the one from the other by the space of seaven yeares together . . . (*The Statutes of the Realm* IV, 1028)

(20)   or take up any **dead man woman or child** out of **his her or theire** grave, or any other place where the dead bodie resteth . . . (*The Statutes of the Realm* IV, 1028)

The careful wording of early legal documents such as these, taking into account all gender and logical possibilities, foreshadow some of the careful wording encouraged by modern language reformers and were the target of language reform in the 1850 Act of Parliament.

One of the most important implications of these examples from earlier periods of English is that some form of generic *they* has been in use in the written language since Old English, as a natural solution to the generic pronoun problem. It also clearly has not been the only option and given some of the extended grammatical solutions in some of the examples above, it would seem that writers have been struggling with this construction for centuries. Generic *he* happens early, for both linguistic reasons (e.g., *mann* 'person' was a masculine noun in Old English)[5]

---

[5] Corbett (1991), as mentioned in Chapter One, argues that all gender systems are at least partially semantic. Romaine (1999: 65–90), like Corbett, notes the leakage between grammatical and natural

and social reasons (e.g., men were often the audience and referent of indefinite pronouns); and coordinate constructions such as *he or she* have a longer history than most modern grammarians mention, if they are indeed aware of it. Within this context, the history of prescription on the generic pronoun question is revealing of the ways in which grammatical rules can at times reflect cultural belief systems.

3.4 Modern prescriptive efforts on the generic pronoun question

It is only in the past couple of centuries that grammarians have attempted to intervene on the generic pronoun grammar question, to institutionalize practices of handling this construction in the written language. As mentioned above, the first known appearance of this construction as a "correctable error" of agreement in an English grammar book is in Lindley Murray's *English Grammar*. (Bodine [1975: 172–74] cites two earlier instances of "explicit advocacy" of generic masculine.) Murray actually does not explicitly state an agreement rule; he rather presents an example of incorrect usage and then simply presents generic *he* as the solution (as well as modeling generic *he* in his own prose):

> Pronouns must always agree with their antecedents, and the nouns for which they stand, in gender and number . . . Of this rule there are many violations to be met with; a few of which may be sufficient to put the learner on his guard. "*Each* of the sexes should keep within *its* particular bounds, and content *themselves* with the advantages of *their* particular districts:" better thus: "The sexes should keep within *their* particular bounds," &c. "Can any one, on their entrance into the world, be fully secure that they shall not be deceived?" "on *his* entrance," and "that *he* shall." (Murray 1981 [1824]: 135)

Subsequent grammarians in the nineteenth century, for the most part, follow suit – some explicitly stating the rule and others quietly amending sentences showing agreement with *they* to *he* (e.g., Devis 1801, Bullions 1983 [1846]). Dennis Baron (1986: 191–97) provides a very useful and interesting overview of many prescriptive efforts focused on generic *they*, and the following brief survey supplements and updates his work. Goold Brown, in his 1828 book *The Institutes of English Grammar*, which became popular enough by the mid-nineteenth century to rival Murray's grammar, categorizes generic *they* under "false syntax," with an example sentence and an explanation:

gender systems and argues that grammatical gender is, therefore, a feminist issue. She recognizes arbitrariness in grammatical gender systems; she also asserts that these categories acquired some semantic motivation. While this argument creates potentially problematic assertions about the gender assignment of, for example, 'language' and 'grammar' in many Romance languages, the recognition that not all gender assignment in grammatical gender systems is arbitrary and that there may be reflections of cultural belief systems and practices even in such grammatical (and more arbitrary) systems is an important one.

No person should be censured for being careful of their reputation.

[Not proper, because the pronoun *their* is of the plural number, and does not correctly represent its antecedent noun *person*, which is of the third person, *singular*, masculine. But according to Rule 5th, "A pronoun must agree with its antecedent, or the noun or pronoun which it represents, in person, number, and gender." Therefore, *their* should be *his*; thus, No person should be censured for being careful of *his* reputation.] (Brown 1982 [1828]: 142)

In a subsequent note, Brown relies on the traditional gender hierarchy, recorded in classical grammars and the early seventeenth-century grammars of English, in explaining the choice of the masculine: "The *gender* of pronouns, except in the third person singular, is distinguished only by their antecedents. In expressing that of a pronoun which has antecedents of *different genders*, the masculine should be preferred to the feminine, and the feminine to the neuter" (*ibid.*: 146). He goes on to assert that the masculine can include the feminine, providing what today seems an awkward example: "Or, if the gender [of conjoined antecedents] only be different, the masculine may involve the feminine by implication; as, 'If a man smite the eye of his *servant* or the eye of his *maid* that it perish, he shall let *him* go free for *his* eye's sake.' – *Exodus*, xxi. 26" (*ibid.*: 147). In these terminological shifts, Brown substitutes the term "preferred" for the word "worthier" from the classical gender hierarchy in reference to the masculine, and the notion that the masculine "involves" the feminine may simply be a restatement of the hierarchy in less transparent terms. Bodine (1975: 172) notes that the substitution of the "comprehensive" masculine for the "worthy" masculine can be found as early as Kirby's grammar of 1746.

During the nineteenth century, several published grammarians create a distinction between solutions for two different generic constructions. For generic singular nouns (be they nouns such as *pupil* or indefinite pronouns such as *someone*), generic *he* is the most appropriate (if not the only correct) choice. With conjoined antecedents (e.g., *the boy or girl*), the situation is more complex and there are more possible solutions. As Thomas Harvey explains in two passages from his popular 1878 grammar, *A Practical Grammar of the English Language*:

> There being no pronoun of the third person singular used in common for either sex, the masculine forms, *he, his, him,* are used in its place. Do not say, "Each pupil should learn *his* or *her* lesson:" use *his* alone. Say, "Should any one desire to consult me, let *him* call at my office," even though the invitation be intended for both sexes. (Harvey 1987 [1878]: 202)

When the two antecedents are of different genders [and connected by "or" or "nor"], the use of a singular masculine pronoun to represent them is improper. In such cases:

1. Use a plural pronoun that may represent both genders; as, "Not on outward charms could *he* or *she* build *their* pretensions to please."

2. Use different pronouns; as, "No boy or girl should whisper to *his* or *her* neighbor."
3. Substitute a general term, including both, for the two antecedents, and represent this general term by a singular masculine pronoun; as "No pupil (boy or girl) should whisper to *his* neighbor." (*Ibid.*: 205)

This final solution may strike the modern reader as odd: that while it is improper to refer to "boy or girl" with generic *he*, it is perfectly proper to refer to "pupil (boy or girl)" with generic *he* – but it is often just these kinds of subtle distinctions that characterize many grammar books and often separate written conventions from the spoken language. At the same time, Harvey's proposed solutions probably also sound familiar, foreshadowing some of the solutions proposed in late twentieth-century grammar handbooks for handling the "generic pronoun question": change the sentence to the plural; use *he or she*; or substitute a different term/rewrite the sentence.

In treating this same kind of conjoined construction, Samuel Greene, in his 1874 grammar *An Analysis of the English Language*, explicitly dismisses the relevance of the classical gender hierarchy in this situation although he does not actually dismiss the hierarchy:

> To use *his* alone, or *her* alone, would reveal the ownership, which is supposed to be unknown. Hence it does not avail to say that the *masculine* is preferred to the *feminine*, and the *feminine* to the *neuter*; for any pronoun would become explicit. To avoid this difficulty, it is best to recast the sentence, or so construct it as to escape such a dilemma. Yet, contrary to the general rule, frequent instances occur in which the pronoun, in such cases, is put in the *plural*, and thus the gender is concealed; as, "Then shalt thou bring forth that man or that woman unto thy gates, and shalt stone *them* with stones till *they* shall die." (Greene 1983 [1874]: 121)

Greene proves more conservative than Harvey in mentioning without endorsing the use of generic *they*, but at the same time he does not present generic *he* as acceptable written usage. Not all grammarians agree on this construction, however. Samuel Kirkham, in his *English Grammar in Familiar Lectures* (1833), specifically prescribes singular pronoun agreement with noun phrases composed of multiple disjoined nouns; he skirts the gender question by providing the example: "Neither John *nor* James *has* learned *his* lesson" (Kirkham 1833: 180).

There was room for disagreement with the prescription of generic *he* even in the nineteenth century. Baron (1986: 193) cites Alexander Bain as one of the earlier advocates of singular generic *they* with a defense of the construction in 1879 that is echoed more than a century later by modern feminists: "When both Genders are implied, it is allowable to use the plural . . . Grammarians frequently call this construction an error: not reflecting that it is equally an error to apply 'his' to feminine subjects." Bain provides examples of generic *they* from various famous authors, notes the "cumbrous" nature of *he or she* constructions, and concludes: "No doubt there are more instances of the employment of 'his', but it must by no means be maintained that this form is exclusively right" (Bain 1879: 310). However, Bain contradicts this observation earlier in the grammar, in a much less cited discussion of correct pronoun usage: "The concord of the common gender is arranged thus. For the more distinguished beings, we may use the masculine, in its representative sense; as in speaking of a member of the human family, we may say 'he', although women are also included" (*ibid*.: 122). Here Bain does not seem to see the use of the masculine to include the feminine as an "error." It is hard to know what to make of Bain's contradictory messages in the grammar except to note that the appearance of the gender hierarchy in his grammar, juxtaposed with recognition of generic *they* and the problems with generic *he*, demonstrates the pervasiveness of hierarchical ideologies in reference to gender.

Later grammarians such as Henry Sweet (1931 [1891]) and George Curme (1931) recognize the use of generic *they* as Bain did, and they relegate it to the spoken or "colloquial" (also cited in D. Baron 1986: 193). Jespersen (1933: 137–38) describes the "frequent usage" of *they* in reference to indefinite pronouns or other generic nouns and explains that "the substitution of the pl for the sg is not wholly illogical"; he goes on to note, however, that "the phenomenon is extended to cases where this explanation will not hold good" – a hint at prescription in a descriptive treatment.

In a 1938 study of current English usage, Albert H. Marckwardt and Fred Walcott detail highly mixed opinions about the use of singular *they* in reference to *everyone*. The majority of the judges recognized the sentence "Everyone was here, but they all went home early" as colloquial usage and established. However, with the sentence "Everybody bought their own ticket," the authors note: "Although a significantly large number of judges approved the expression, there is sufficient majority against it to indicate that it is not yet in good standing" (Marckwardt and Walcott 1938: 74–75). One linguist called objections to it "largely theoretical" but another explained, "But *his* doesn't sound pedantic to me, and I think I say *his* myself." The use of *his or her*, while "established" was described by two linguists as "correct but not commendable" and "a matter of pleasing the women" (*ibid*.: 73); in a footnote, the authors themselves label the usage of *his or her* as a *hyper-urbanism*: "artificial, trite, pedantic, or stilted attempts at correctness" (*ibid*.: 98). The fact that this solution to the generic pronoun question can be found as early as Middle English – that it is not simply or only a product of urbanism and feminism – would potentially complicate this description.

The most popular grammar of the early twentieth century, H. W. Fowler's *Dictionary of Modern English Usage* (1926), legislates generic *he* (and this is left in the revised version of the late twentieth century) and obliterates the distinction between singular indefinite antecedents and conjoined antecedents that was pre- served in many nineteenth-century treatments of the question. With his typical insightful and sometimes quirky commentary on the workings of the language, Fowler does recognize the variation but dismisses its validity in good prose:

they, them, their... I. *One* &c. followed by *their* &c. *The grammar of the recently issued appeal to the Unionists of Ireland, signed by Sir Edward Carson, the Duke of Abercorn, Lord Londonderry, and others, is as shaky as its arguments. The concluding sentence runs: 'And we trust that everybody interested will send a contribution, however small, to this object, thereby demonstrating their (sic) personal interest in the anti-Home Rule campaign'. Archbishop Whately used to say that women were more liable than men to fall into this error, as they objected to identifying 'everybody' with 'him'. But no such excuse is available in this case. Their* should be *his*; & the origin of the mistake is clearly reluctance to recognize that the right shortening of the cumbersome *he or she, his or her*, &c, is *he* or *him* or *his* though the reference may be to both sexes. Whether that reluctance is less felt by the male is doubtful; at any rate the OED quotes examples from Fielding (*Everyone in the house were in their beds*), Goldsmith, Sydney Smith, Thackeray (*A person can't help their birth*), Bagehot (*Nobody in their senses*), & Bernard Shaw. It also says nothing more severe of the use than that it is 'Not favoured by grammarians'; that the grammarians are likely, nevertheless, to have their way on the point is suggested by the old-fashioned sound of the Fielding & Thackeray sentences quoted; few good modern writers would flout the grammarians so conspicuously... it is needless to remark that *each, one, person*, &c., may be answered by *her* instead of *him* and *his* when the reference, though formally to both sexes, is especially, as here, to the female. (Fowler 1926: 648)

In his entry on "Number," Fowler notes that in a perfect language, there would be a singular pronoun of "doubtful" gender (thereby dismissing the possibility that *they* can function as a singular), and he tackles several of the current proposed solutions to the "generic pronoun problem." He dismisses the use of *he or she* as "clumsy" and "ridiculous," if not downright laughable ("it usually sounds like a bit of pedantic humour"), and he describes the use of generic *they* as a construction that puts a "literary man's teeth on edge."[6] The result is Fowler's explicit prescription:

he [the literary man] exerts himself to give the same meaning in some entirely different way if he is not prepared, as he usually is, to risk C [use of generic *he*]; ... C is here recommended. It involves the convention that where the matter of sex is not conspicuous or important *he* & *his* shall be allowed to represent a person instead of a man, or say a man (homo) instead of a man (vir). Whether that [convention], ... is an arrogant demand on the part of male England, everyone must decide for himself (or for himself or herself, or for themselves). Have the patrons of B [generic *they*] made up their minds yet between *Everyone was blowing their noses* and *Everyone were blowing their noses*? (*Ibid*.: 392)

---

[6] In Fowler's categorization of gender as only a grammatical term, he similarly describes misuse: "To talk of *persons* or *creatures of the masculine* or *feminine g.*, meaning *of the male* or *female sex*, is either a jocularity (permissible or not according to context) or a blunder" (Fowler 1926: 221).

The sarcasm directed at advocates of generic *they* is little softened by the rhetorical questioning of possible sexism: in this description, while speakers may be free to decide for themselves, the decision is not a neutral one, as one becomes "clumsy" and "disfavored" with the wrong decision.

Fowler proves more conservative than some of his predecessors as he rejects generic *they* for disjunctive noun phrases as well, opting for rewriting the sentence instead. In *The King's English* (1906), co-authored with his brother Francis George Fowler, they write: "Our view, though we admit it to be disputable, is clear – that *they*, *their*, &c., should never be resorted to, as in the examples presently to be given they are . . . Sentences may however easily be constructed (Neither John nor Mary knew *his* own mind) in which *his* is undeniably awkward. The solution is then what we so often recommend, to do a little exercise in paraphrase (*John and Mary were alike irresolute*, for instance)" (Fowler and Fowler 1906: 67).

Without as much rhetorical flourish as Fowler, George Kittredge and Frank Farley, in *An Advanced English Grammar* (1913), correct sentences such as the following: "Everybody has *his* [NOT *their*] faults" (Kittredge and Farley 1913: 65). In the 1956 *Modern American Grammar and Usage*, J. N. Hooks and E. G. Mathews provide a similar correct example ("*Everyone* spoke for the tactics that *he* favored") and then an explanation of the difficulty and solution in this case:

> Writers have little trouble in deciding between the singular and plural of personal pronouns except when the antecedents are indefinite pronouns. The singular indefinites . . . normally serve as antecedents of singular personal pronouns or singular possessive adjectives. Thus *each . . . he, everyone . . . he, everybody . . . his*, etc., are the usual constructions.
>
> Sometimes this valid argument is raised: "A word like *everybody*, although singular in form, actually designates a plural. Thus in 'Everybody reached for his hat,' the effect is downright misleading, because it sounds as if many persons were reaching for one hat. Besides, some of the members of the group may be feminine, and the women are left out unless we say 'his or her hat' or 'their hats.' Therefore let's say 'Everybody reached for their hats.'"
>
> In colloquial English, "Everybody reached for their hats," *a person . . . they, everyone . . . they*, etc., represent the norm rather than the exception. But in approximately two thirds of a million words of modern American nonfiction, only once did such a construction occur: "Everyone gets less and less sleep; when they do sleep, they simply drop on one of the 30 bunks" (59, 47). To be in accord with present formal written usage, then, one must use a singular personal pronoun or singular possessive adjective with a singular indefinite antecedent, as in "the existing inequalities place everybody where he biologically belongs." (Hooks and Mathews 1956: 185–86)

While they recognize the generic construction with *they* is commonly used in the spoken language, the legislation of generic *he* in the written language is unwavering. In this case, the reasoning behind the prescription is adherence with already established conventions, which skirts the question of the rationale of the conventions. In this light, it is difficult not to read the last quoted example in the excerpt about existing inequalities as at least hinting at a possible historical hierarchical justification.

As these examples indicate, the language surrounding the generic pronoun problem has changed up through the mid-twentieth century, from Brown's more explicit restatement of the classical gender hierarchy to Kittredge and Farley's rephrasing of the question as one of "accordance with present formal written usage" and what is "normally" used in these situations; the same can be seen in the shift from the "worthy" to the "comprehensive" masculine. As Elizabeth Sklar (1983: 348–58) argues, while the rhetoric of more modern grammars may be less naive and significantly less transparent, the ideas behind the rhetoric of, for example, generic masculine may be no less sexist in their implications. This survey of grammars also makes clear that the use of generic *they* has long been recognized, be it as an "error" to be corrected, as a "colloquial" feature relegated to the spoken language, or as a potential generic pronoun option in the written language.

3.5   Contemporary usage guidelines

At the turn of the millennium, the rhetoric in many grammar books on this question looks significantly different. Most current handbooks now recognize that generic *he* is sexist, advise avoiding it (often in no uncertain terms), and typically present three options for revising the construction: employ forms of *he or she*; make the sentence plural; or revise the entire construction to eliminate the need for a pronoun. Many grammars also note that using the construction *he or she* can get awkward if used too often.

Lunsford and Connors (1997) provide a fairly typical explanation of the shift away from the generic masculine: "Indefinite pronouns often refer to antecedents that may be either male or female. Writers used to use a masculine pronoun, known as the generic *he*, to refer to such indefinite pronouns. In recent decades, however, many people have pointed out that such working ignores or even excludes female – and thus should not be used" (Lunsford and Connors 1997: 141).[7] The phrase "used to use" sidesteps the role of previous prescription in

---

[7] Kolln, in the widely used *Rhetorical Grammar* (1999), is particularly descriptive of the situation with third-person pronouns in English:

> This set of personal pronouns may look complete – and, unfortunately, it does include all we have. But, in fact, it has a gap, one that is responsible for a great deal of the sexism in our language. The gap occurs in the third-person singular slot, the slot that already includes three pronouns representing masculine (*he*), feminine (*she*), and neuter (*it*). You'd think that

this usage; the authors do, however, include a discussion of the sexist assumptions that can play out in language.

Some recent style guides confront the politics of such usage questions directly. For example, Neil Daniel, in *A Guide to Style and Mechanics* (1992), devotes an entire chapter to avoiding sexist language. He begins the chapter with this strong statement:

> [N]o writer can ignore the sexist bias inherent in our language. None of us is responsible for the conventions that have dominated our language for centuries. But we are accountable for how we use the language today. Writers at all levels and in any business or social context must confront the need to include all their readers in everything they write. (Daniel 1992: 123)

He does not frame this simply as a question of prescribed or acceptable usage but explicitly recognizes the political and social implications of both the construction and the revision. At the same time, he is careful to separate accountability for English speakers' use of language from responsibility for the history of the construction.

Singular generic *they*, one option for including all one's readers in what one writes, typically remains relegated to the spoken, often not condemned as a grammatical construction but also not recognized as yet legitimate enough for formal writing. Martha Kolln, in *Rhetorical Grammar* (1999: 231), provides a relatively progressive example of such a description: "In speech we commonly use *they* for both singular and plural . . . Eventually, perhaps, the plural pronoun will take over for the singular; in the second person (*you/your/you*), we make no distinction between singular and plural, so it's not unreasonable to do the same in the third person. But such changes come slowly." This description itself reveals one reason why such a change may come slowly, as the task of legitimizing this form in the written language is left to other language authorities.

The shifts in the rhetoric of grammar books suggest that it is probably only a question of time before the written language will "catch up" with the spoken language, and *they* will be recognized as a legitimate singular generic pronoun in written prose. But it may take considerable time. The power of the tradition and the prescription of generic *he* (and *man*) has been pervasive and powerful, and in genres such as academic prose, "proper" usage can still reflect more

---

those three would be up to the task of covering all the contingencies, but they're not. For third-person singular we have no choice that is sex-neutral. When we need a pronoun to refer to an unidentified person, such as "the writer" or "a student" or just "someone," our long-standing tradition has been to use the masculine . . . But that usage is no longer automatically accepted. Times and attitudes change, and we have come to recognize the power of language in shaping those attitudes. So an important step in reshaping society's view of women has been to eliminate the automatic use of *he* and *his* and *him* when the gender of someone referred to could just as easily be female. (Kolln 1999: 230)

conservative, prescribed forms.[8] In addition (and undoubtedly not unrelated), some central style guides can be relatively conservative in their prescriptions for written prose. A striking case in point is *The Associated Press Stylebook and Libel Manual*, revised and updated in 1998. The entry under "his, her" reads: "Do not presume maleness in constructing a sentence, but use the pronoun *his* when an indefinite antecedent may be male or female: *A reporter attempts to protect his sources.* (Not *his or her* sources, but note the use of the word *reporter* rather than *newsman.*) Frequently, however, the best choice is a light revision of the sentence: *Reporters attempt to protect their sources*" (Goldstein 1998: 97). At perhaps the other end of the spectrum are linguists arguing for the inevitability and acceptability of singular generic *they* in both the spoken and written language (see McWhorter 1998: 117–24 for an adamant and accessible example). With these competing prescriptions of what should be seen as acceptable solutions to the generic pronoun problem, the one that adheres to current spoken usage – and in this case also has a long history of usage – will probably eventually prevail.

3.6   Conclusion

The still prevalent rejection of singular generic *they* in the written language raises interesting questions about the continued separation of the spoken and written language in this prescription, about attitudes that these two should not agree. Michael Newman (1997), in one of the most comprehensive studies of generic usage in the spoken language to date, concludes that *they* is the most common generic pronoun in the spoken language, although generic *he* and other alternatives do appear; gender stereotyping still occurs (e.g., *doctor* as masculine and *nurse* as feminine); and singular pronouns do not occur once in his study with notionally plural but formally singular antecedents (e.g., *everyone*).[9]

---

[8] These conservative notions of "proper" usage extend even to prose about the semantic changes involved. In a striking example, the first sentence of Mats Rydén's introductory article to the book *Male and Female Terms in English* (Rydén 1996: 1) reads: "The study of language is the study of man, of his infinite linguistic resources and of his exploitation of these resources."

[9] Newman's treatment (1997) of the generic pronoun question in Modern English is a valuable contribution to the scholarship: both the data and the analysis expand our understanding of generic usage in important ways. I must, however, disagree with one of Newman's conclusions: that singular generic *they* is not available for highly individuated definite referents (i.e., when the identity and individuality of a referent is important, as opposed to the relevance of the referent being that it is the member of a class). To support this argument, he classifies the following example as impossible: "– I'm visiting **my cousin in Connecticut.** – Where do **they**/does **he**/does **she** live?" (Newman 1997: 172). I would argue that *they* is far from impossible in this sentence, and in an informal survey, most speakers either answered that *they* sounded perfectly natural or they focused on the logical problem with asking where the cousin lives when Connecticut has already been mentioned – not even noticing the pronoun usage. In fact, Modern English speakers use generic *they* with individuated definite referents on a regular basis (e.g., "I was talking to a friend of mine yesterday and they said that the movie was terrible."), when the gender of the person

As this chapter has made clear, both generic *he* and generic *they* have a long history in the language, both written and spoken. As many linguists have noted, there is grammatical precedence for a plural pronoun to take on a singular function while retaining its plural function (i.e., the use of *you* instead of *thou*). This historical information about anaphoric pronoun references to human antecedents provides the context in which to consider the development of the many singular generic options in the language and to rethink the notion of the singular construction with *he* or even with *he or she* as somehow "better" or "more formal" – or even "older." We are, thereby, in a stronger position to consider the judgments of specific grammarians, whose predilections often become grammatical law, for social and political reasons.

in question is unknown, irrelevant, or not meant to be disclosed. Of course, when the gender of the antecedent's referent is clear from the noun itself (e.g., "Alice" or "my brother"), a generic pronoun will sound ungrammatical. It potentially overemphasizes the importance of gender as a human feature to claim that if we are referring to a specific individual whose identity is known to the speaker but not explicit in the antecedent noun itself, we must identify their gender in the pronoun – that this is always important and/or relevant to discourse.

4   Third-person pronouns in the gender shift: why is that ship a *she*?

4.1   Introduction

Contemporary question

The most cited gendered reference to an inanimate object today may be the use of *she* to refer to ships. This usage was first noted by Ben Jonson in his *English Grammar* of 1640; he names ships as an exception to the rule that *it* refers to inanimate objects, for "we say, *shee sayles well*, though the name be *Hercules*, or *Henry*, (or) the *Prince*" (1972 [1640]: 57). In 2002, it was announced that Lloyd's List, the world's best-known source of maritime business news and information, would stop using *she* in reference to ships, switching over instead to *it*. This announcement made headlines in both England and in the United States.

The classical gender hierarchy which historically informed the choice of the generic masculine surfaces in a different form in the discussion of "personification" (the label most often given to use of gendered pronouns for inanimate objects) in grammars of the nineteenth and early twentieth centuries. Alexander Bain (1879: 122) explains that the masculine is used for things "remarkable for strength, superiority, majesty, sublimity." Modern grammar books and style guides continue to address the question of using gendered pronouns in reference to inanimate objects, often to standardize such "aberrant" usage. For example, the *Associated Press Style Guide and Libel Manual* (Goldstein 1998: 96) sets down this guideline for the use of *her*: "Do not use this pronoun in reference to nations or ships, except in quoted matter. Use *it* instead." This guide only addresses feminine references (there is no similar note under *him*), but in English usage, both masculine and feminine personal pronouns can be used in reference to inanimate nouns. As discussed in Chapter One, it is just these "exceptional" nouns, which seem to flout natural gender concord, that have perplexed descriptive linguists, required notes in grammar books, and created difficulties in defining the nature of the Modern English gender system.

Historical context

In Old English, the use of masculine and feminine anaphoric pronouns to refer to inanimate objects was the norm – the way in which the grammatical gender system played out in the personal pronouns. The use of neuter pronouns to refer to some inanimate nouns was the exception, because if these nouns were of masculine or feminine grammatical gender, to refer to them with the neuter pronoun *hit* was to break grammatical gender agreement. The examination of the question of when it became the exception rather than the norm to refer to inanimate objects with gendered pronouns is, in fact, part of an examination of the larger shift between gender systems in the history of English, from grammatical to natural gender.

As Chapter Three makes clear, most animate nouns were already following patterns of natural gender agreement with anaphoric personal pronouns as early as Old English. But when did *it* come to refer to all things (or almost all things)? And what can the behavior over time of those exceptions (the subset implied in "almost all") reveal about the variation still present in Modern English? By studying patterns of agreement between inanimate object antecedents and anaphoric personal pronouns in earlier stages of English, during the critical transition period, we can see the gender shift in the pronouns in progress and benefit from the historical context that this perspective provides on the Modern English gender system.

Focus of this historical linguistic study

This chapter examines the transition from the grammatical gender system of Old English to the semantic or natural gender system of Modern English, looking specifically at anaphoric personal pronoun reference to inanimate objects, in order to provide new details about the progression of the gender shift and to explore how this historical context can inform our understanding of the variation still present in the language today. This study of reference to inanimate objects in texts from the early periods in the Helsinki Corpus (OE II–ME I) indicates that the major gender shift for inanimate nouns in written texts occurs in late Old English/early Middle English, but that the seeds of change are already present in Old English before 1000 AD. Importantly, in addition to clarifying chronology, the examination of the diffusion of the gender shift through the lexicon made possible by this study provides some insight into the gender system of early Modern English as well as Modern English. It may, for example, help to explain the prevalence of feminine pronouns used in reference to inanimate objects. And it may provide a framework for understanding which nouns have taken on conventionalized gender references (e.g., *sun*, *moon*, *nation*). For historical linguists, it also provides a case study for mechanisms of syntactic change such as reanalysis and extension, as well as evidence arguing against Middle English creole hypotheses. (See Appendix 2 for a list of the specific texts used in the Old and early Middle English sections of the Corpus as well as an explanation of the study's methodology.)

The empirical investigation of agreement patterns in Old and Middle English presented in this chapter examines mechanisms in the language's grammar to uncover the gender variation and patterns of change. All the evidence presented here comes from written texts, and it is critical to remember that change undoubtedly occurred first in the spoken language, then was reflected in the written language. The variation in pronoun use witnessed throughout the early periods of English discussed here was probably happening primarily below the level of consciousness in the spoken language. In other words, speakers at this time were probably not fully aware (if aware at all) of the extent of variation or of the syntactic change in progress. (A useful analogy may be the current variation between *who* and *whom*, which many speakers do not notice in their own or in others' speech, but in retrospect will be framed as variation characteristic of language change in progress – in this case, part of the loss of distinction between subject and object case in the pronouns.)[1] Whenever possible, the discussion works to address more sociolinguistic considerations and implications of the material. By highlighting the most consequential results of this study of the Helsinki Corpus, the following sections aim to capture a relatively coherent story of the gender shift in the personal pronouns, while recognizing its complexity and the "messiness" of the details, and to spin out the implications of this story for our understanding of Modern English gender.[2]

4.2   Historical syntax and previous research on the gender shift

The gender shift in English raises interesting questions in theoretical syntax and in the history of English syntax specifically. To begin with the latter, the traditional and inherently artificial chronological "blocking" of the early history of English

---

[1] Some speakers are, of course, highly aware of what they see as the "corruption" of the language in the confusion of *who* and *whom*, but we live in an age of English prescription that is foreign to medieval culture. We have no evidence in medieval written commentary that everyday speakers or scholars were particularly aware of the gender shift or other syntactic changes occurring during the period. It may be that this conversation, if it was happening, is simply not recorded given the scarcity and nature of vernacular texts during the period. It seems to be natural within speech communities for speakers to evaluate and attempt to control the speech of others ("verbal hygiene," to invoke a valuable coinage by Deborah Cameron [1995]), but most variation occurs below the level of consciousness and only a few features rise to prominence and become the source of public commentary or censure. The personal pronouns may eventually lose the distinction between subject and object as well, although predictions of this scenario have a reasonably long history and the distinction has so far been tenacious. There is clear confusion and variation between subject and object pronouns for many speakers of English – some dialectal and some resulting from hypercorrection, among other causes. The final result – whether the paradigm will be reduced to only one nonpossessive form as is the case for other nouns or whether it will become more word order dependent rather than grammatical function-dependent – is unclear at this point.

[2] For a full technical account of all the details of the Helsinki Corpus study's results, including factors and parameters determined to be inconsequential in explaining the gender shift, see Curzan 1998. All statistical results determined to be critical to understanding the overall findings of the study have been included here.

into Old English and Middle English (with the break anywhere within fifty years on either side of 1100 AD) would be easier to dismiss if so many linguistic innovations did not coincide at this particular breaking point, including the gender shift. The conservative nature of the Old English, West Saxon manuscript tradition and the almost complete break in text production with the coming of the Normans contribute to the seeming "naturalness" of this division in the history of the language: they distort the record to make the linguistic changes between the two periods appear more sudden and dramatic than they undoubtedly were. It is beyond question, however, that the syntax – as well as the phonology, morphology, and lexicon – of available Old English records and of most early Middle English records demonstrates a significant leap in the structural development of English.

The proposal that English anaphoric pronouns shifted to natural gender as early as the Old English period opens the possibility of an exception: an innovative, modern syntactic feature flourishing before the Middle English period. But the results of the more comprehensive study presented in this chapter confirm earlier findings that grammatical gender remained healthy in the personal pronouns through late Old English; it is not until early Middle English that the balance of gender concord in the pronouns tips towards natural gender, at least in the written language. In other words, the turning point of yet another grammatical change corresponds with this artificial division between Old and Middle English.

At the same time, this study reveals that the seeds of grammatical gender decay had already been planted in the Old English anaphoric pronouns. The natural gender system has a strong enough foothold in the overall anaphoric agreement system that inanimate nouns – the most critical and resistant class of nouns in the shift – demonstrate some instability between grammatical and natural gender agreement in anaphoric reference, with a discernible tendency for inanimate nouns to co-occur occasionally with neuter pronouns in recognition of sex and animacy distinctions. This nascent tendency towards natural gender agreement for inanimate nouns proves to be more patterned than random, and these patterns become more pronounced in the early Middle English period once the shift between gender systems is fully underway.

The two previous systematic studies of the gender shift in the pronouns came to contradictory conclusions. Moore (1921), after examining twenty "representative" Old and Middle English texts, concludes that natural gender agreement already dominated in the personal pronouns in Old English: "The fact is that in OE the use of the gender-distinctive forms of *he, heo, hit* was almost the same as our own use of them" (Moore 1921: 89).[3] For example, in *Beowulf*, of approximately 429 gender-distinctive forms of *he, heo, hit*, only eight (or less

---

[3] Thomason and Kaufman (1988: 125) seem to accept Moore's findings, stating: "The replacement of grammatical gender by natural gender in third-person pronoun reference had already occurred by 950 throughout England, and reassignment of gender to nouns on this principle was well under way by 1066." They then rely on this assumption as further proof against Old Norse influence on syntactic developments in northern dialects of English (discussed in more detail in Chapter Two).

than 2 percent) occur in conflict with natural gender. Interestingly, Moore defines natural gender according to his perceptions of naturalness in Modern English gender assignments – in other words, *it* for 'child,' *she* for 'Church,' and either *he* or *she* for animals are all categorized as natural. This decision points to the ways in which the "naturalness" of the Modern English gender system is socially and culturally constructed – to the point where its construction can be assumed as the basis for an empirical study of its origins.

Moore's general conclusion about the survival of, rather than the invention of, natural gender in Middle English proves valuable; there is general agreement in the scholarship that there is an evident tendency towards natural gender in Old English personal pronouns. However, his study is hampered by the lack of differentiation between animate and inanimate antecedents, and by the non-representative nature of these texts for the language as a whole. They are all in verse and they focus heavily on animate subjects. Moore also does not differentiate in his results between instances of *hit* as an anaphoric pronoun and *hit* as a "formal subject."

Heltveit's study (1958) offers a direct challenge to Moore's findings: the results indicate that the use of masculine and feminine pronouns to refer to grammatically gendered inanimate nouns remains regular and productive throughout the Old English period. Heltveit concedes only: "The most we can say is that there seems to have been a certain tendency for *hit* to express natural gender in conflict with the traditional system of grammatical gender already at a time when this system was, on the whole, intact" (Heltveit 1958: 366).

Heltveit's study is based on *Byrhtferth's Manual* and *Ælfric's De Temporibus Anni*, two texts that focus primarily on objects in their descriptions, and he finds that overall, anaphoric pronouns occur in conflict with natural gender (i.e., agree with grammatical gender) 63.1 percent and almost 85 percent of the time respectively. For animate nouns, the formal distinction between *he* and *heo* almost always corresponds to the semantic distinction male and female; in contrast, *hit* is almost never used in conflict with grammatical gender. The small study of anaphoric pronouns in Ælfric's Homily *Inuentio Scæ Crucis* by Mitchell (1986: §70) supports Heltveit's conclusions about the relative health of Old English grammatical gender agreement.[4] It must be noted, however, that Heltveit's texts are not representative either: they describe primarily inanimate, astrological objects and they describe many of the same objects over and over again. For example, in

As Heltveit (1958) asserts and the study in this chapter confirms, grammatical gender remained healthy in the pronouns throughout the Old English period, and the possibility of Old Norse influence on the loss of grammatical gender cannot be so easily dismissed.

[4] Mitchell justifiably criticizes the statistics in both Moore's and Heltveit's studies for their potentially misleading implications. Percentages of sex triumphing over gender or vice versa are problematic because they do not account for the coincidence of sex and gender. The methodology employed in this study avoids this problem by separating animate and inanimate antecedents, and the overall statistics that are included are also supplemented by specific information about the antecedent nouns.

Byrhtferth's Manual, of the eighty masculine nouns in the Helsinki Corpus excerpt, forty-three are the word *monað* 'month' or the names of specific months, and all forty-three take masculine anaphoric pronouns. In *Ælfric's De Temporibus Anni*, of the seventy feminine nouns, fifty-nine are the word *sunne* 'sun,' all of which take feminine pronouns. Not only do these few nouns monopolize an inordinate percentage of the token count, but they also do not seem to be representative of the wider lexicon. Nouns like *sun*, *moon*, and *star*, which are the subject of the bulk of these scientific texts, are members of the subset of resilient nouns, which seem to retain gender through Middle English and into early Modern English, as described in this chapter. For this reason, these astrological texts and the nouns they contain cannot serve as representative of the language as a whole, and they cannot tell the full story of how grammatical gender was being lost in the rest of the lexicon.

One important implication of Heltveit's study is that putting a later date on the shift to natural gender in the personal pronouns emphasizes the link between the loss of formal gender distinctions in the noun phrase and the loss of grammatical gender in the personal pronouns. In other words, as long as adjectives and demonstrative pronouns differentiate for gender and agree with the grammatical gender of nouns in the noun phrase, then personal pronouns also tend to follow grammatical gender outside the noun phrase. A subsequent study by Dekeyser (1980) of Dutch substantiates Heltveit's claims that the anaphoric pronouns retained the corresponding grammatical gender for inanimate nouns, as long as the gender-distinctive forms of the demonstrative pronoun *se*, *seo* and *þæt* were in use (367).[5] The consensus then, reaffirmed by Naomi Baron (1971) and Howe (1996), dates the gender shift in the pronouns decisively in the early Middle English period, a dating confirmed by this study as well.

This study addresses some of the remaining questions about the processes involved in the transformation of the English gender system, to explain not

---

[5] In Standard Dutch, there are two determiners for inanimates: *de* (for masculine and feminine nouns) and *het* (for neuter nouns). As Dekeyser (1980) describes, there has been a shift to the masculine pronoun *hij* for all *de*-nouns, even historically feminine ones, to correlate with the adnominal distinction. In the regional dialects of Belgium, however, there are three forms of the definite article which correlate with grammatical gender, and the anaphoric pronouns follow the same pattern (except for neuter [+HUMAN] nouns, where sex may override gender). It is the Standard Dutch spoken by educated speakers in northern Belgium (Flanders) which sheds the most light on the transition between systems; in this dialect, there is the binary contrast between *de*- and *het*-nouns, but the anaphoric pronouns maintain the tripartite grammatical gender distribution. Most of these speakers also speak a regional dialect, so "their competence in the field of historical PRO forms is nurtured by their dialect" (Dekeyser 1980: 108), even though these nouns are no longer necessarily distinctively marked for gender in the noun phrase. The shift to the Standard Dutch pattern of parallel binary forms is, according to Dekeyser, incipient in this variety as regional dialects lose ground among educated speakers. In Heltveit's view, the Old English grammatical gender system was particularly weak compared to other Germanic languages because the indefinite article lacked the neuter suffix -*t* (Old English had *an* for all three genders), so there was no indefinite article distinction to bolster the distinction maintained by the definite articles *se*, *seo*, *þæt*. Heltveit considers pronominal -*t* to be the "mainstay of grammatical gender" in Scandinavian languages.

just when the gender shift happened but also *how* it happened. For example, in Old English, how occasional are the *hit* references to masculine and feminine inanimate nouns? Are there any patterns? When does natural gender agreement become the norm, rather than the exception? What grammatical, lexical, or dialectal factors are involved in the shift? What are the implications for our understanding of Modern English? And, at the most fundamental level, can the progression of the shift be shown to follow more general principles of historical syntactic change?

The last question points to a long-standing weakness in historical syntax: the fairly rare linkage of general historical principles to individual case studies of syntactic change. Compared with the extensive work in historical phonology and even morphology, historical syntax – much like historical semantics – represents a surprisingly neglected field. Most scholarship in diachronic syntax has focused on specific changes in a given language or on a specific kind of change across languages. The theoretical gaps, however, are being filled. Recent work by Harris and Campbell (1995) on historical syntax in cross-linguistic perspectives provides an important, more general theoretical framework in which to view language-specific changes.[6] Two of the three major mechanisms of change they propose – grammatical reanalysis and extension – effectively help to explain the progression of the gender shift in English personal pronouns. Although English is unusual within its own language family in having lost grammatical gender, it adheres to more universal patterns of syntactic change.

The three major mechanisms of syntactic change proposed by Harris and Campbell can be summarized as follows: (a) reanalysis, or the reinterpretation of an underlying syntactic structure without necessarily the modification of surface

---

[6] Harris and Campbell sidestep one of the traditional stumbling blocks in diachronic syntax by emphasizing their goal of understanding the mechanisms of syntactic change, not predicting syntactic change. As a justification for this kind of explanation, they draw an apt comparison with theoretical biology:

> [A]bsolute prediction of change is not, as sometimes suggested, an appropriate goal for diachronic syntax, or indeed for any retrospective science. Evolution by natural selection is recognized as scientifically legitimate explanation in spite of the fact that it does not predict the evolutionary changes it is almost universally acknowledged to explain. Predicting that any particular evolutionary change will occur at any particular time is not an important goal of the study of biological evolution . . . [Language] is likewise affected by the presence in some instances of similarly random innovations and by a social environment which changes in ways that are at present mostly unpredictable. (Harris and Campbell 1995: 325)

Their general theoretical framework also effectively undercuts the traditional dichotomy between abrupt and gradual change: reanalysis can be a discrete phenomenon but its actualization, involving processes such as extension and lexical diffusion, is more gradual. It also accounts for synchronic syntactic variation: when rule extension occurs, the new rule and the rule it is displacing can coexist for a significant period of time in that linguistic domain, resulting in variation in surface manifestations. One set of variants may be marked, but the two sets of forms may also be interchangeable alternatives, at least until the older forms come to be seen as archaic – the progress of this replacement process often follows the traditional "S-curve" model for linguistic change.

manifestations; (b) extension, or changes in the surface manifestation of a syntactic pattern without the immediate modification of the underlying structure; (c) borrowing, or the replication of a syntactic pattern from another language (language contact can also be a catalyst in change that then occurs through reanalysis or extension). Reanalysis, the major mechanism of syntactic evolution, requires ambiguity in surface structure (but not necessarily opacity): a subset of surface manifestations of a particular construction must be open to the possibility of multiple analyses; one potential analysis (the old one) is applicable to all manifestations of the construction, and the other (the new one) is applicable to the subset (Harris and Campbell 1995: 72). The actualization of syntactic reanalysis – the repercussions of the formation of a new set of underlying relationships and rules – often involves extension, as previously nonconforming syntactic surface structures are made to conform to a syntactic pattern that already exists in the language; reanalysis and extension are not, however, coextensive (*ibid*.: 81). Extension, in short, is the removal of a condition from a rule; extensions of a rule generalize to a natural class based on already relevant categories for the syntactic rule (*ibid*.: 102). It is important to note that ambiguity, or the possibility of multiple analyses, does not necessitate language change; language and language speakers can tolerate (and often exploit) healthy levels of ambiguity (see J. Milroy 1992: 39–42).

Reanalysis, ranked by Harris and Campbell as the most basic mechanism involved in syntactic change, plays a critical part in the shift from grammatical to natural gender in English, as the results of this study demonstrate. In this case, the surface structure open to multiple analyses is anaphoric agreement between masculine inanimate nouns and the two pronouns *his* and *him*. These two forms, originally masculine in such constructions with masculine nouns in accordance with the Old English grammatical gender agreement system, have the potential to be reinterpreted as neuter, given that the singular genitive and dative third-person pronoun forms for the masculine and neuter are identical. In other words, if, for example, *his* refers back to the Old English grammatically masculine noun *stan* 'stone,' it could be interpreted as either masculine (in accordance with grammatical gender) or neuter (in accordance with natural gender). This reanalysis of grammatical gender concord as natural gender rests on analogy with the natural gender agreement system already firmly in place with animate antecedent nouns, as described in Chapter Three. In other words, the actualization of this reanalysis seems to involve the extension of the natural gender agreement system from animate antecedent nouns to inanimate ones – a form of preservative reanalysis, in which an older structure is reanalyzed as conforming in a new way to already existing elements of the language (Harris and Campbell 1995: 89).

4.3   Gender agreement patterns in Old English

The previous chapter established an important context for the pronoun gender shift: the strong pattern of natural gender agreement between nouns referring to humans and personal pronouns as early as Old English. In contrast, grammatical gender agreement remains strong for inanimate nouns in Old English – as it does with nouns for animals[7] – with only some variation that strays from the older, grammatical system of concord. An examination of texts in the Old English part of the Helsinki Corpus reveals no significant decrease in grammatical gender agreement from 750 to 1150 AD, indicating that the transition point in written material occurs in the early Middle English period, as traditionally defined.[8] At the same time, the variation that does occur within this overall picture of robust health for grammatical gender agreement with inanimate nouns demonstrates the nascent rise of natural gender agreement in the pronouns.

Unlike the dominance of the masculine in the distribution of human antecedent nouns, the gender of inanimate antecedent nouns in the Old English part of this study is fairly well distributed among the three major gender categories – masculine (31.7 percent), feminine (24.8 percent), and neuter (27.6 percent) – with

---

[7] On a hypothetical scale of animacy, nouns referring to animals would seem to lie somewhere between nouns referring to humans beings and those referring to inanimate objects. Unlike nouns for humans, for which natural gender and grammatical gender almost always correspond, the grammatical gender of animals is more arbitrary: for example, *hræfn* 'raven' is masculine and *culfer* 'dove' is feminine; *earwicga* 'earwig' is masculine, *nædre* 'snake' is feminine, and *swin* 'pig' is neuter. In fact, the assignment of feminine gender is less arbitrary than the others: the majority of the feminine nouns refer to female animals (e.g., *byren* 'she-bear,' *henn* 'hen'). But the assignment of the masculine and of the neuter for other animals shows no such semantic basis; the only observable pattern is that the masculine once again appears more often in the study than any other gender. In Modern English, animals are quite often the object of affective or culturally determined gender reference. As the biological sex of animals is often difficult to determine by appearance, the gender of pronoun references to animals of unknown sex is determined by the speaker's attitude and by characteristics of the animal, with the default gender being the neuter. Reference to Old English nouns for animals, however, demonstrates no such flexibility: the gender of the anaphoric pronouns corresponds in almost all instances with the grammatical gender of the noun in this study of pronouns in the Helsinki Corpus. And the predominance of grammatical gender agreement for animal antecedents continues into the early Middle English period. See Curzan 1998: 85–87, 148–49 for more details. Interestingly, one statistic about gender agreement for animal antecedents supports the theory that there is a growing distinction in the language between animate and inanimate objects during the early Middle English period. The higher frequency of masculine-neuter pronouns in reference to animals (39 percent) is comparable to the use of these pronouns with human antecedents (37.4 percent). Inanimate objects, on the other hand, witness a dramatic drop in the use of *his* and *him* (down to 5.5 percent) as they are increasingly referred to with *there*-pronouns, as is discussed later in this chapter.

[8] For all of the Old English Corpus study results presented in this chapter, OE I (texts before 850 AD) has not been included because the results can be summarized briefly in a paragraph and illuminate little about the status of grammatical gender in Old English. The very short texts of *Cædmon's Hymn* and the *Leiden Riddle* contain no anaphoric pronoun references. In *Documents 1*, there are seventy-three anaphoric pronoun references, sixty-two of which have human antecedents, and eleven of which have inanimate antecedents. Of the sixty-two animate antecedents, the gender of all the anaphoric pronouns corresponds with the grammatical gender of the noun except for the seventeen instances of the neuter noun *wif* 'woman,' all of which take feminine pronouns. All eleven of the anaphoric pronoun references to inanimate objects involve neuter pronouns referring to neuter nouns.

the masculine being the most common and with a small percentage of antecedent nouns being of multiple gender, foreign, or plural. However, there are more neuter anaphoric pronouns referring to inanimate nouns than masculine or feminine (29.6 percent, compared to 28.1 percent for both masculine and feminine), with 14.1 percent of the pronouns being masculine-neuter (i.e., either *him* or *his*). These numbers for the anaphoric pronouns reflect in part the fact that many multiple-gender and plural antecedent nouns occur with neuter pronouns and in part that the variation from the grammatical gender system that occurs in Old English tends towards the neuter (i.e., natural gender). If the numbers for neuter pronouns used as "general reference" (see Appendix 2) in all three periods are included, the majority status of the neuter pronouns becomes more dramatic; including both general references and formal subjects, neuter pronouns exceed masculine ones by from 24 percent (OE III) to 40 percent (OE IV).[9] This majority status of neuter anaphoric pronouns with nouns referring to inanimate objects points to the seeds of the emerging independence of the gender system controlling the anaphoric pronouns from the gender system controlling attributive forms inside the noun phrase. In other words, the neuter is already becoming a commonly used pronoun to refer back to specific objects as well as less specifically defined ideas mentioned in the discourse. There is also limited but interesting evidence that the neuter is becoming the default pronoun for inanimate nouns as early as Old English; for example, in the excerpt from *Lacnunga*, there appears one made-up, nonsense noun *lilumenne*, which is referred back to as *hit*, suggesting that the neuter has become, at least in some cases, the pronoun for nouns of unknown or unknowable gender.[10]

The "healthiest" inanimate nouns in Old English, the ones demonstrating the highest percentage of grammatical gender agreement, are the feminine inanimate antecedent nouns: 86.5 percent in OE II, 82.1 percent in OE III, and 86.3 percent in OE IV (see Table 4.1).[11] Almost all the remaining anaphoric references

---

[9] In the Old English parts of the Corpus, the number of neuter pronouns used as formal subjects and as general references respectively totals: 73 and 141 in OE II; 90 and 114 in OE III; 41 and 62 in OE IV.

[10] The evidence with borrowed, foreign nouns in the Old English texts is too limited to draw any significant conclusions.

[11] Both Heltveit (1958) and Moore (1921) present numbers for how many of the anaphoric pronouns disagree with the natural gender of the antecedent, but as described in Chapter One, *natural gender* is a slippery term. (As a case in point, Moore defines *she* for the church and for ships as natural.) In addition, these statistics do not differentiate between, for example, a "grammatical" feminine reference to a feminine inanimate noun and an "ungrammatical" masculine reference to that noun: both disagree with the "natural" gender of the noun. This study instead presents statistics for the number of anaphoric pronouns whose gender conflicts with the grammatical gender of the antecedent noun; these statistics show both the number of neuter references and the number of ungrammatical gendered references. The statistics include a token count rather than a normalization of the count per thousand words because the most interesting number for this study is the percentage of each type of agreement, as opposed to its frequency per thousand words.

involve the neuter form *hit* and, significantly less frequently, the masculine-neuter forms *his* and *him*. With feminine antecedent nouns, there is no reason to exclude these masculine-neuter pronouns from the overall agreement statistics: whether they represent masculine or neuter forms, they still violate grammatical gender concord. In other words, if the pronoun *him* is used to refer back to the feminine noun *lind* 'shield,' it is not clear whether it represents a masculine or neuter reference, but in either case it violates grammatical gender agreement, which should be feminine (i.e., *hire*). And, in fact, irregular, clearly masculine references to feminine nouns (i.e., *he* or *hine* used to refer to a feminine noun) are extremely rare; in other words, there is no evidence in this study to support a trend towards masculinization in the anaphoric pronouns, as suggested in Clark 1957.

The "health" of grammatical gender agreement with masculine inanimate antecedent nouns is more difficult to determine given the ambiguous status of the masculine-neuter forms. Therefore, two sets of agreement statistics are included here: Table 4.1 provides the figures (token and percentage) for the co-occurrence of nouns of all genders (the leftmost vertical column) with singular pronouns of all genders; Table 4.2 provides figures for the co-occurrence of masculine, feminine, and neuter nouns with distinctively masculine, feminine, and neuter pronouns.

Excluding the forms *his* and *him*, masculine nouns occur with distinctively masculine pronouns (i.e., forms of *he* and *hine*) with strikingly high frequency: 87.8 percent in OE II, 82.8 percent in OE III, and 79.5 percent in OE IV. These figures are even higher than those in Heltveit 1958, undoubtedly because they count only inanimate nouns. (Heltveit's figures encompass both human and non-human antecedents.) These numbers clearly demonstrate that grammatical gender agreement remains strong through late Old English written texts, although the frequency of grammatical gender agreement with masculine nouns shows a slight drop over the three periods. The figures for grammatical gender agreement with the masculine-neuter forms included do not show the same drop (60.3, 66.3, and 64.8 percent respectively); but, importantly, they co-occur with a decline in the use of masculine-neuter pronoun forms, from 31.3 percent in OE II to 19.5 percent in OE III, and down to 18.5 percent in OE IV. OE IV witnesses a drop in the use of neuter pronouns and a rise in the use of feminine ones; but it should be noted that OE IV is the smallest data set and the feminine pronominal references all occur in the text *Prognostications* in an odd series of passages referring to the masculine noun *mona*.

Elsewhere in the Old English part of the study, there are intriguing examples of feminine pronouns referring to masculine nouns. All such examples in this study occur in less canonical texts (e.g., medical treatises and recipe books). Examples (1) and (2) concern remedies for how to treat a patient for an ape or human bite (Old English *bite*, a masculine noun) and how to rid a patient of a *pocc* 'pock, blister' (a masculine Old English noun) in the eye – two remedies not necessarily endorsed in the Modern English-speaking world:

Table 4.1: *Anaphoric agreement patterns between Old English nouns and anaphoric personal pronouns, with the number of occurrences and the percentage of that agreement pattern for nouns of that gender*

	OE II (850–950 AD)				OE III (950–1050 AD)				OE IV (1050–1150 AD)			
Noun	m	f	n	m-n	m	f	n	m-n	m	f	n	m-n
m	79 60.3%	—	11 8.4%	41 31.3%	197 66.3%	3 1%	38 12.8%	58 19.5%	35 64.8%	5 9.3%	4 7.4%	10 18.5%
f	3 2.1%	122 86.5%	15 10.6%	1 .7%	1 .5%	151 82.1%	29 15.8%	3 1.6%	1 2%	44 86.3%	6 11.8%	—
n	22 11.3%	1 .5%	132 68%	39 20.1%	3 1.9%	—	134 84.3%	22 13.8%	3 4.6%	1 1.5%	60 92.3%	1 1.5%
mf	1		1	1	3	16	1	1	1	1	1	1
mn	2		1		5		1					
mfn	2			1								
fm		3		1		1						
fn		8				16	3	1		4		
fmn		2		3		8						
nf							5					
nm		1	3		3		8	2			1	
nmf					1							
for					1	4	2		26			
unkn.	3				4			2				
pl	3	3	19	7	—	3	22	1		1	22	3

Table 4.2: *Anaphoric agreement patterns between Old English masculine, feminine, and neuter nouns and anaphoric personal pronouns (excluding masculine-neuter pronouns), with the number of occurrences and the percentage of that agreement pattern for nouns of that gender*

	OE II (850–950 AD)			OE III (950–1050 AD)			OE IV (1050–1150 AD)		
Noun	m	f	n	m	f	n	m	f	n
m	87.8%	—	12.2%	82.8%	1.3%	16%	79.5%	11.4%	9.1%
f	2.1%	87.1%	10.7%	.6%	83.4%	16%	2%	86.3%	11.8%
n	14.2%	.6%	85.2%	2.2%	—	97.8%	4.7%	1.6%	93.8%

(1)   Wið apan **bite** oððe mannes smyre mid fearres geallan. Sona **heo** bið hal. (*Quadrupedibus* 55)

'For the **bite** of an ape or of a man, smear with a bull's gall; soon **it (she)** will be whole (healthy).'

(2)   Gif **poc** sy on eagan, nim mearhsapan & hinde meoluc, mæng tosomne & swyng, læt standan oð hit sy gluttor, nim þonne þæt hluttre, do on ða eagan, mid godes fultume **heo** sceal aweg. (*Lacnunga* 112)

'If there be a **pock** on the eye(s), take marrow-soap, and a hind's milk, mingle together, and whip, let stand till it be clear, then take the clear [mixture], put it on the eyes; with God's help **it (she)** will [go] away.'

In example (2), the feminine pronoun occurs at a significant distance from the antecedent noun with two intervening feminine nouns (*sapa* 'soap' and *meolc* 'milk'); in example (1), however, the feminine pronoun occurs in close proximity to the masculine noun *bite* with no intervening feminine nouns (*gealla* 'gall' is a masculine noun).

The pattern of agreement for inanimate neuter antecedent nouns and their anaphoric pronouns seems to show a surprising amount of variation in the gender of the anaphoric pronouns – surprising, that is, until we consider the nouns in question. The number of neuter nouns occurring with masculine pronouns rises as high as 11.3 percent in OE II (the number taking feminine pronouns remains low: from 0.5 to 1.5 percent). But almost all of this instability centers on the word *mod* 'mind, soul,' which shifts between neuter *hit* and masculine *he*, reflecting the semantic slipperiness between an individual's mind or soul and the individual himself (the pronoun *himself* is used here deliberately because the generic mind- or soul-bearer is always masculine). The individual's mind, as a thinking and active entity, commonly loses its neuter status when it is referred back to and transforms in subsequent references into the generic individual, who always takes masculine anaphoric pronouns (as demonstrated in the previous chapter).[12] One example from the *Cura Pastoralis* with the noun *mod* perfectly illustrates this fluctuation in gender as well as the potential effects of the grammatical ambiguity of the pronoun *him*. The first reference back to *mod* is the neuter pronoun *hit*, followed quickly by the reflexive form *him*; the ambiguity and possible reinterpretation of this form as masculine may facilitate the subsequent masculine reference *hine* back to *mod*.

(3)   Wietodlice se il hæfð his holh on ðæs unnyttan monnes heortan, forðæm
        ðæt yfelwillende **mod** gefielt hit self twiefald oninnan **him** selfum, & gehyt
        hine on ðæm ðiestran mid ðære ladunge, sua se iil hine selfne gehyt on
        him selfum. (*Alfred's Cura Pastoralis* 243)

        'Indeed, the hedgehog has his hole in the useless man's heart, because the
        vicious (evil-desiring) **mind** winds **itself** double inside **itself (himself)**,
        and hides **itself (himself)** in the darkness with excuses, like the hedgehog
        hides himself inside himself.'

With most inanimate antecedent nouns, this kind of pronoun reanalysis works in exactly the opposite direction: a masculine use of *his* or *him* is reinterpreted as neuter, facilitating subsequent neuter anaphoric references. The overall effects of this kind of reanalysis reveal themselves clearly in early Middle English personal pronoun agreement.

Such examples with the word *mod*, which help to explain the grammatical gender agreement statistics for neuter inanimate nouns, highlight the fact that overall statistics tell only part of the story of the gender shift. The overall figures for gender agreement speak to the general health of grammatical gender throughout the Old English period, but it is the individual words in question that provide the crucial insight into the mechanics of anaphoric gender agreement both as it functions regularly and as it begins to fluctuate. The individual words show how the system works when it works and where it begins to break down – that is, where gender variation first occurs in the anaphoric pronouns – as early as Old English.

The typical grammatical gender agreement pattern for inanimate nouns is exemplified by the following sentence from the *Old English Vision of Leofric*, in

---

[12] In contrast, the feminine noun *sawol* 'soul,' which arises often in Old English religious texts, occurs almost invariably with feminine anaphoric pronouns. The sole exception, a passage in which *sawol* occurs with two masculine pronouns, illustrates the effect of distance on anaphoric agreement, as the reference reverts from the feminine soul to the generic (and therefore masculine) soul-bearer:

> forðæm sio **saul**, ðonne **hio hire** unðonces gebædd wierð ðæt yfel to forlætanne ðæt **hio**
> ær longe on woh **hire** agnes ðonces gedyde, secð ðonne ða forlorenan hælo, & wilnað ðære,
> suelce **he** ðonne wel & nytwyrðlice libban wolde, gif **he** forð moste. (*Alfred's Cura Pastoralis*
> 251)

> 'Because the **soul**, when **it (she)** is unwillingly commanded to surrender the evil that **it**
> **(she)** formerly long in error of **its (her)** own will performed, seeks then the abandoned
> health/prosperity, and desires it, as if **he** would live well and profitably, if **he** thenceforth
> could.'

which the feminine noun *duru* 'door' (the object Leofric is trying to open) is referred back to with the feminine accusative pronoun *hi*:

(4)   ða þa he to þære **dura** com & þær langsumlice swyðe cnucede & georne cunnode, hwæðer he **hi** on ænige wisan undon mihte. (*Old English Vision of Leofric* 182)

     'Then he came to the **door** and there knocked a long time, and eagerly tested whether he **it (her)** in any way could open.'

Masculine antecedent nouns adhere to the same rules of gender agreement, and the following example – selected from many possible examples for its inherent interest – proves instructive not simply about the mechanics of grammatical gender concord (with the masculine noun *ðost* 'dung') but also about medieval treatments of swelling or other *ablawunʒe* 'upblowing' in the neck using fresh *ðost*:

(5)   Sceal þeah se hund ban gnagan ær, þy biþ se **þost** hwit & micel. Gif þu **hine** nimest & gaderast æt fylne þonne ne biþ **he** to unswete to gestincanne. (*Læceboc* 48)

     'The hound must gnaw a bone beforehand; this way the **dung** will be white and great; if you take and gather **it (him)** at [its] fall, then **it (he)** will not be too unsweet to smell.'

With some mass nouns, such as the masculine nouns *hired* 'household,' *here* 'troop, army,' or *dæl* 'portion,' grammatically gendered anaphoric reference can demonstrate agreement in both gender and number, or these nouns can take plural pronouns in more notional concord. For example, the noun *here* often appears with singular masculine anaphoric pronouns, as in the following example from the *Anglo-Saxon Chronicle*:

(6)   Her for se **here** on Norþhymbre, & **he** nam wintersetl on Lindesse . . . (*Chronicle MS A Early* 72)

     'Here went the **army** to Northumberland, and **it (he)** took up winter-residence in Lindesse . . .'

The noun also appears at times with plural pronouns to refer to the soldiers in the *here*. This variation between singular and plural agreement with mass nouns, familiar to Modern English speakers with nouns such as *group* or *jury*, is effectively captured in one passage from *Boethius* with the word *dæl* 'part,' used to refer in this case to two groups of evil sinners (one less evil than the other). The first reference back to *oðer dæl* in example (7) is the plural pronoun *hi*, triggered perhaps by the plural genitive construction *þara yflena* 'of the evil [ones]' in the antecedent noun phrase; the second reference back to *oðer dæl* is the masculine singular pronoun *he*.

(7)   Ac ic wille dælan þa yflan þam yfelum nu on twua; forðæm þe oðer **dæl** þara yflena hæfð ece wite, forðæm **hi** nane mildheortnesse ne geearnodon;

oðer dæl sceal beon geclæsnod, & þa amered on ðæm heofonlican fyre, swa her bið seolfor, forðæm he hæfð sume geearnungæ sumre mildheortnesse. forðæm he mot cuman æfter ðæn earfiðum to ecre are. (*Alfred's Boethius* 120)

'But I will divide the evil from the evil now in two; owing to the fact that the one **part** of the evil will have eternal punishment, because **they** have not earned any mercy (mild-heartedness); the other **part** will be cleansed and then purified in the heavenly fire, as silver is here, because **it (he)** has [gotten] some consideration of some mercy (mild-heartedness), on that account **it (he)** may come after these hardships to eternal grace.'

This example demonstrates semantic gender agreement in the first sentence with *dæl* giving way to grammatical gender agreement in the second sentence. Another passage from *Alfred's Boethius* involving the noun *dæl*, this time in reference to part of a tree, illustrates a different kind of fluctuation between grammatical and natural gender agreement – here between the masculine singular and the neuter singular – with a different motivation. The first reference back to *se dæl* in this passage is the masculine pronoun *he*, followed several clauses later by the neuter pronoun *hit*:

(8)   þæt eall se **dæl** se ðe þæs treowes on twelf monðum gewexð, þæt **he** onginð of þæm wyrtrumum & swa upweardes grewð oð ðone stemn, & siððan andlang þæs piðan, & andlang þære rinde oð ðone helm, & siððan æfer þæm bogum, oððæt **hit** ut aspringeð on leafum & on blostmum & on bledum. (*Alfred's Boethius* 91–92)

'That all the **part** of the tree that grows in twelve months, that **it (he)** begins from the roots and so grows upwards to the stem (trunk), and afterwards along the pith and along the rind (bark) to the top and afterwards over the boughs, until **it** springs out into leaves and into blossoms and into branches.'

The explicit reference in the passage to *treow* 'tree,' a neuter noun, could explain the neuter pronoun, but the mention of the tree occurs before the initial masculine pronoun *he*. The more significant factor in the shift to natural gender in example (8) is probably the distance of the pronoun from the antecedent noun.

The importance of distance between the anaphoric pronoun and the antecedent for the retention of grammatical gender has long been assumed in scholarship on gender agreement but never proven (Heltveit 1958, Mitchell 1986, Corbett 1991). It seems only logical that the farther the pronoun occurs from the antecedent noun, the more likely the pronoun is to take semantic (i.e., "natural," in this case) gender rather than grammatical gender. As Heltveit (1958: 368) generalizes, "To judge from the material available there is reason to believe that the farther removed the pronoun was from its antecedent the more easily did it express natural gender in conflict with grammatical gender." This study involved a straightforward word count to capture distance (as opposed to analyzing clausal structure); and these results confirm the previously intuitive hypothesis about the effect of distance on Old English grammatical gender agreement.

For masculine and feminine nouns (i.e., not including any nouns of multiple gender), the mean distance from the antecedent noun to a pronoun of the corresponding grammatical gender is consistently smaller than the mean for the distance to a neuter pronoun. The mean distance for all inanimate nouns is 6.7 words for OE II, 7.5 words for OE III, and 6.5 words for OE IV. For masculine nouns, the mean distance ratio for masculine pronouns versus neuter pronouns is 5.8 : 7.5 words; in OE III, 7.1 : 8.8 words; and in OE IV, 8.0 : 9.8 words. For feminine nouns, the mean distance ratio for feminine pronouns to non-feminine pronouns is 6.2 : 16.1 words in OE II; in OE III, 7.3 : 10.4 words; and in OE IV, 7.7 : 16.5 words.

Generally speaking, then, the farther the pronoun from the antecedent noun or from the preceding anaphoric pronoun in a string of pronoun references, the higher the odds that it will follow natural gender agreement. A passage from the *Old English Vision of Leofric*, in which Leofric is praying and is visited by the vision of a hand, perfectly exemplifies this grammatical phenomenon:

(9)   & wæs seo bletsiende **hand** styriende & wendende upward. þa forhtode
        he & tweonode him hweðer hit swa wære, swa him þuhte. ða mid þæs
        modes tweonunge þa æteowde **heo** him swa swutole swa he his agene geseon
        mihte; & wæron fægere fingras smale & lange, & þæra nægla toscead & se
        greata lira beneoðan þam þuman eall wæs gesyne & fram þam littlan fingre
        toweard þæs earmes, & sumne dæl of þære slyfe. ða ne dorste he **hit** na
        leng behealdan, ac heng þæt heafod adun, & **hit** þa geswac þæra bletsunga.
        (*Old English Vision of Leofric* 185)

'And the consecrating **hand** was stirred and moved upwards. Then he was afraid and doubted whether it were so as it seemed to him. Then with doubt in [his] mind, then **it** (**she**) showed [itself/herself] to him as clearly as he could see his own; and the fair fingers were slender and long, and the distinction of the nails and the great muscle beneath the thumb all was perceptible, and from the little finger to the arm, and some part of the sleeve. Then he dared no longer behold it, but hung the (his) head down, and **it** then ceased from the blessings.'

The feminine noun *hand* that Leofric sees is first referred to with the anaphoric pronoun *heo* due to the noun's grammatical gender. Several clauses later, when Leofric dares not look at the hand any longer but hangs his head instead, it is a naturally gendered *hit* at which he fears to stare.[13]

---

[13] Conjoined or disjoined noun phrases referred back to with singular pronouns provide interesting evidence about the effect of distance as well. In the Old English part of this study, if the antecedent noun phrase combines nouns of different genders, one of which is neuter, the anaphoric pronoun is always neuter (or masculine–neuter); with all other plural noun phrases of mixed gender, the anaphoric pronoun, if singular, is almost always neuter, with only a few exceptions. In these

At least one subset of nouns, which I call *resilient nouns*, appears to be fairly impervious to the effects of distance: these nouns seem to follow grammatical gender concord almost no matter how far the pronoun is from the antecedent noun. These nouns represent a semantic category, one that is difficult to define with any exactitude. They are often common words, sometimes the natural world objects of myth and folklore. Terrestrial bodies seem to be resilient nouns, including the feminine nouns *eorðe* 'earth' and *woruld* 'world,' and the masculine noun *middangeard* 'middle-land, earth.' For example:

(10)   Drihtnes is **eorðe** and eall þæt **heo** mid gefyld is. (*Paris Psalter* 48)

'The **earth** is the Lord's and all that **it (she)** is filled with.'

(11)   & oncnawan be þyses **middangeardes** fruman, þa **he** ærest gesceapen wæs, þa wæs **he** ealre fægernesse full, & **he** wæs blowende on **him** sylfum. (*Blickling Homilies* 115)

'And to know about the creation of this **world**, when **it (he)** was first shaped, then **it (he)** was full of all fairness (beauty), and **it (he)** was flourishing within **itself (himself)**.'

In Old English, words for the earth appear resiliently with both masculine and feminine anaphoric pronouns, depending on the grammatical gender of the noun. The early Middle English results may help explain why the feminine references prove more resilient in the long run than the masculine ones.

Certain terrestrial landmarks and temporal phenomena seem to be resilient nouns, including the masculine nouns *stream* 'stream,' *monað* 'month,' and *dæg* 'day,' and the feminine nouns *ea* 'river,' *burg* 'city,' and *cirice* 'church' (which is often still referred to with the feminine in Modern English). Several of these nouns are basic-level terms within that particular lexical or semantic field, and their grammatical gender may influence the gender of specific terms within the field, many of which are borrowings from Latin or other languages. For example, all names for specific months (e.g., *Februarius*, *Iunius*) are masculine, as are names for specific days such as *Ephiphanus* and *bissextus* (a particularly useful term for the extra day in a leap year). All specific cities are feminine, even when the city names maintain their foreign suffixes (e.g., *Bizantium* in an excerpt from *Orosius*).

Nouns referring to various celestial bodies often prove to be resilient,[14] particularly the sun and moon, which often co-occur in contexts that highlight their contrasting genders:

exceptional cases, the gender of the anaphoric pronoun corresponds with the grammatical gender of the closer (or second) noun: for example, a masculine pronoun to refer to feminine *stefn* 'voice' and masculine *sang* 'song,' and feminine pronouns to refer to masculine *fefer* 'fever' and feminine-neuter *adl* 'disease.'

[14]   The multiple-gender noun *heofon* (mf) appears with both masculine and feminine pronouns in the included Old English texts, but it never appears with a neuter pronoun; it seems to be "resiliently gendered," even if with two genders.

(12) Symble ðonne se **mona** gangeþ æfter ðære **sunnan**, ðonne weaxeð **his** leoht, þonne **he** byð beforan **hyre**, þonne wanað **hys** leoht. Ond swa **he** bið þære **sunnan** near swa bið **his** leoht læsse, ond swa **he** bið **hire** fyrr swa bið **his** leoht mare, ond hwæðre **he** bið symble þurh þa sunnan onlyhted. (*Martyrology* 38–39)

'Always when the **moon** comes after the **sun**, then **its (his)** light waxes; when **it (he)** is in front of **it (her)** [the sun], then **its (his)** light wanes. And the nearer **it (he)** is to the **sun**, so is **its (his)** light less; and the farther **it (he)** is from **it (her)** [the sun], so is **its (his)** light more/greater, and yet, **it (he)** is always by the sun illuminated.'

The one exception to the rule in this study with the noun *sunne* – when it occurs with a neuter rather than a feminine pronoun – comes on the heels of six feminine anaphoric references and is probably semantically motivated. After a series of questions in *Adrian and Ritheus* about the location and behavior of the sun, Adrian asks about the composition of the sun and receives the following reply:

(13) Saga me hwilc sy seo **sunne**. Ic þe secge, Astriges se dry sæde þæt **hit** wære byrnende stan. (*Adrian and Ritheus* 36)

'Tell me what the **sun** be. I tell you, Astriges the sorcerer said that **it** were burning stone.'

In this passage, the one time in the Old English part of the study when grammatical gender concord breaks down with the word *sunne*, the neuter pronoun refers to a deconstructed entity, stripped down to its essential parts.[15] A similar use of the neuter pronoun *hit* for a deconstructed (and gendered) entity occurs in a passage from *Boethius* about the composition of a *mann* 'man, human':

---

[15] Given the resiliency of the feminine noun *sunne*, the passage in the *Vespasian Psalter* about the sun in which it consistently takes masculine pronouns most likely involves the masculine noun *sunna*, which is a rare but possible form:

in **sunnan** he sette geteld his & **he** swe swe brydguma forðgande of brydbure his . . . (*Vespasian Psalter* 15)

'In the **sun**, he [God] set his tent, and **it (he)** goes forth like a bridegroom from his bride-chamber . . .'

The same biblical passage is translated in the *Paris Psalter* with the feminine:

seo **sunne** arist swiðe ær on morgen up, swa swa brydguma of his brydbure. And **heo** yrnð swa egeslice on **hyre** weg . . . (*Paris Psalter* 39)

'The **sun** arises up so early in the morning, like a bridegroom from his bride-chamber. And **it (she)** hastens so awfully on **its (her)** way . . .'

The references in both passages are consistent enough to suggest different antecedent nouns of different genders referring to the same celestial body.

(14)   ða cwæð he: Wast þu hwæt **mon** sie? ða cwæð ic: Ic wat þæt **hit** bið sawl & lichoma. (*Alfred's Boethius* 90)

'Then he said, Do you know what a **man** is? Then said I, "I know that **it** is a soul and a body.'

When a person is broken down into body and soul, even the noun *mann* (a very resiliently gendered noun otherwise) can become neuter.

Many of these resilient nouns occur with high relative frequency throughout the texts in the study, which raises the question of whether frequency (as opposed to semantics) is the determining feature of resilient nouns. Given that the data from these written texts cannot be taken as representative of the spoken language, the most frequent antecedent nouns in the study may or may not correspond to the most frequently used nouns in everyday speech. Many of the resilient nouns are, however, common and familiar terms describing features of the natural world. Of the ten most frequently referred to masculine and feminine nouns in each Old English period in this study, many consistently follow grammatical gender agreement and many of them fall into the general categories of resilient nouns outlined above: the masculine nouns *dæg, mona, monað, middangeard*; and the feminine nouns *burg, cirice, ea, eorðe, sawol, sunne*. But such is not always the case: a few frequently occurring antecedent nouns demonstrate significant instability in the gender of their anaphoric pronouns. For example, the noun *hand* occurs with relatively high frequency in OE IV and demonstrates the fluctuation between the feminine and neuter anaphoric pronouns discussed above with respect to the influence of distance.

In individual cases of natural gender reference, it is often possible to hypothesize specific reasons for the innovative gender agreement. They include syntactic factors such as distance, and lexical field considerations such as the gender of basic-level terms. The proximity of semantically similar but differently gendered nouns in a given segment of discourse may also cause unconventional – but not necessarily natural – gender reference. A clear example occurs in *Prognostications*, a passage in which the feminine noun *ðunorrade* 'thunder' is referred back to with a masculine pronoun, probably because it directly follows a passage about *ðunor* 'thunder,' a masculine noun:

(15)   Gif **þunor** cumeð on forantniht, se cyðeð hwylcehwegu deaðlicnesse towearde. Gif **he** cymð on middeniht, se becnað halie saule ofer worulde farende . . . Gif **þunorrade** bið hlynende of eastdæle, se becnað cyninges deað oðð biscopes oððe mycle gefeoht. Gif **he** bið suð gehered, se becnað cininges wifes cwealm. (*Prognostications* 47)

'If **thunder** comes at dusk, this shows someone facing deadliness. If **it (he)** comes at midnight, this means a holy soul is traveling over the world . . . If **thunder** resounds from the east, this signifies the death of a king or of a bishop or a great battle. If **it (he)** is heard [from] the south, this signifies the death of a king's wife.'

As Mausch (1986) has argued with respect to gender fluctuation in late Middle English pronouns, the context of the reference is often critical to understanding the motivation for unconventional gendered anaphoric pronouns (e.g., the gender of nearby nouns), and the same holds true as early as Old English.

Certain nominal suffixes, particularly the strong feminine suffixes *-nes* and *-ung*, appear to demonstrate an early tendency towards natural gender agreement in the anaphoric pronouns. The *Peterborough Chronicle* provides a prototypical example with a neuter reference to *ungeðhwærnes* 'disturbance, quarrel,' which is even modified by a feminine demonstrative pronoun:

(16) On þisum geare aras seo **ungehwærnes** on Glæstingabyrig betwyx þam abbode þurstane. & his munecan. ærest **hit** come of þæs abbotes unwisdome . . . (*Chronicle MS E* 214)

'In this year, the **quarrel** arose in Glastonbury between the abbot Thurstan and his monks. First **it** came from the abbot's imprudence (unwisdom) . . .'

However, as example (27) from Middle English indicates, it is unclear how consistent this pattern is. Nouns with the masculine suffixes *-dom* and *-scipe* are too infrequent to allow meaningful conclusions, although the few instances in the study include neuter anaphoric references. The abstract nature of these nouns, as well as the productivity of these suffixes in the creation of new words, may contribute to the gender instability of these suffixes – as discussed above, *hit* appears to be becoming the default pronoun for new nouns as early as the Old English period.

This discussion of various factors involved in the early appearance of natural gender agreement in the anaphoric pronouns as early as Old English captures at least some of the complexity of the grammatical process. The dialectal spread of the change is undoubtedly similarly complex during the period, but the Old English record provides almost no evidence for it: the bulk of texts are in West Saxon dialect and the non-West Saxon texts provide few examples of anaphoric references to inanimate objects. In addition, many of the available Old English texts are conservative dialectically and rhetorically, due in part to the West Saxon scribal tradition and in part to the nature of the material (e.g., homilies, biblical translation, religious instruction). It is not until the early Middle English texts that it becomes possible to chart the dialectal spread to any extent.

Without question, many of these examples are arguable: other readers may interpret the anaphoric pronouns as having different antecedents or as "general reference." In fact, this "interpretability" should be seen as only a strength, rather than a weakness, of the data. The point is that anaphoric reference is confusing, as discussed at some length in Appendix 2. So the fact that a particular neuter pronoun could refer to a specific antecedent or to the more general idea expressed in the passage is exactly the kind of ambiguity that can lead to syntactic change.

We do not have access to the spoken language and how colloquial variation may have played out. Non-canonical Old English texts such as scientific, medical, and recipe texts provide, at least, more variation in some of their content and language than many of the canonical texts. These materials are also particularly valuable for this study given their focus on inanimate objects and, hence, the high frequency of anaphoric references to them. In the astrological texts *Byrhtferth's Manual*, *Ælfric's De Temporibus Anni*, and *Prognostications*, there is a particularly high frequency of resilient nouns, given the concentration on terrestrial and extraterrestrial entities. These texts confirm the consistent grammatical gender agreement patterns with these nouns, but they shed a dimmer light on the status of the grammatical gender system in the language as a whole because these nouns are not representative of inanimate nouns in general. The medical and recipe texts *Quadrupedibus*, *Læceboc*, and *Lacnunga* also show a high frequency of anaphoric reference to inanimate nouns, and in these texts, to a wider range of nouns. They also all demonstrate a high rate of gender fluctuation in the anaphoric pronouns. These three texts prove the most difficult to analyze in the Old English part of the corpus with respect to anaphoric agreement, and they may well be the most enlightening about the ways in which grammatical gender agreement gives way to natural gender agreement. Translation from Latin undoubtedly has the potential to influence reference in texts as well, but even so, readers would still be faced with the resulting inconsistency in pronoun reference as syntactic structures to be interpreted. It is, therefore, worth examining a few examples from *Quadrupedibus* in more detail.

The description of complex remedies for various illnesses naturally lends itself to a large number of vague anaphoric pronoun references. The text often lists many ingredients that should be mixed, boiled, and applied, and it concludes most recipes by endorsing the effectiveness of "it." The pronoun clearly refers to the remedy, but often it is impossible to identify one particular antecedent noun, as in the following remedy for dizziness:

(17)   ðam mannum þe swinclunge þrowiað, haran lungen & seo lifer somod
        gemencged & feower penega gewæge myrran & ðreora befores & anes
        huniges, þis sceal beon awylled on godum ecede & syþþan mid geswetton
        wine gewesed. & æfter þam drince sona hyt hæleþ. (*Quadrupedibus* 23)

        'For the man who suffers dizziness, a hare's lung and the liver mixed
        together and four pennies' weight of myrrh and of three of beaver and
        of one of honey; this must be boiled in good vinegar and afterwards, in
        sweetened wine soaked. And after that drink, immediately/soon it heals.'

All such references to lists and processes with no identifiable antecedent noun have been categorized as "general reference." The obvious data-collection solution to the difficulties posed by the text in this respect seems to be the classification of all anaphoric references to remedies as general references. But in other passages describing remedies, there appear masculine and feminine anaphoric pronouns more clearly referring to one specific antecedent noun, usually a general descriptive term for the mixture or the crucial ingredient in the therapeutic mixture.

For example, the remedy for pimples includes a masculine pronoun referring to *gealla* 'gall,' rather than a neuter pronoun referring to the smearing of the gall on the face:

(18)   Wið nebcorn þe wexað on þam andwlatan, smyre mid gate **geallan**. Ealle þa nebcorn **he** of þam andwlitan aclænsað & ealne þone wom **he** geðynnað. (*Quadrupedibus* 31)

'For pimples that grow on the face, smear with a goat's **gall**; **it (he)** will cleanse all the pimples from the face, and **it (he)** will lessen all the terror/alarm.'

A comparison of this syntactic construction – with one antecedent noun in the remedy and a gendered pronoun referring to it – with a similar passage involving the feminine noun *sealf* 'salve' suggests that the neuter pronoun in the latter case represents an instance of natural gender concord rather than general reference.

(19)   Wið earena sare, eft gelice þon þe her bufan gecweden is, genim þa ylcan **sealfe** hluttre, drype on þæt eare. Wundorlice **hyt** hæleþ. (*Quadrupedibus* 19)

'For sore of the ears, again, like that which is said here above, take the same clear **salve**, drip into the ear. Wondrously **it** heals.'

It could be argued that the verb *hælan* 'to heal' encourages neuter pronoun subjects, creating an almost impersonal construction. This verb does often appear with the neuter in what appears to be a "rote" phrase; there are, however, also instances in which grammatical gender prevails for the subject pronoun, as in the remedy for swelling of the gums, a remedy that involves the application of the masculine noun *tusc* 'tusk':

(20)   Wið toþreomena geswelle, hundes **tux** gebærned & gegniden & seted on, **he** wel hæleþ. (*Quadrupedibus* 61)

'For swelling of the gums, a hound's **tusk** burned and ground together and set on, **it (he)** heals well.'

The confusion and contradictory evidence involved in identifying the antecedents in so many of these passages from *Quadrupedibus* has implications far beyond the methodological difficulties it poses for this study. The more important, underlying point is that speakers of this early variety of English would have been faced with exactly the same ambiguity about the antecedent of any given anaphoric pronoun. Given the prevalent use of neuter pronouns to refer to descriptions of mixtures that often involve specific nouns, there may be good reason why many of these particular nouns (e.g., *sealf* 'salve,' *gealla* 'gall,' *drenc* 'drink') show a tendency towards neuter anaphoric references throughout the text. The use of the neuter in reference to mixtures and in "stock" phrases such as *hit hæleð* could be reanalyzed as reference to one specific antecedent noun – a reference that would follow natural gender agreement. This apparent instance of natural gender in these contexts could, in turn, potentially affect other instances of these nouns in the text. The remedies in this medieval text are fascinating purely as historical artifacts in the progression of medical practices; they also may be notably revealing about some of the more colloquial grammatical constructs in the language that could have fostered the reanalysis of grammatical gender agreement as natural gender.

In this way, the evidence from texts like *Quadrupedibus* nicely counterbalances the evidence from more conservative, often religious, West Saxon texts. The linguistic details available in such texts help to illuminate some of the factors involved in the very early stages of the diffusion of the gender shift. These factors include grammatical considerations such as the distance of the pronoun from the antecedent noun and the proximity of semantically similar but differently gendered nouns within a segment of discourse. Nascent patterns in the lexical diffusion of natural gender agreement are also apparent at this early stage: for example, the resilient nouns, many of which appear with high frequency, demonstrate quite stable grammatical gender agreement, while many suffixed nouns show comparably high instability between grammatical and natural gender agreement. Establishing the approximate date of these "early stages," however, is difficult. The analysis of almost all Old English linguistic evidence must rest on the assumption that change in the written language lags behind change in the spoken language. In these texts, the historical linguist can catch only a glimpse of the more frequent and perhaps less orderly gender variation which was undoubtedly flourishing to an even greater extent in the spoken dialects of Old English and which does not manifest itself with any regularity in the written language until the early Middle English period.

4.4   Gender agreement patterns in early Middle English

The written texts in the Helsinki Corpus dated between 1150 and 1250 AD seem to provide the critical snapshot of the shift from grammatical to natural gender. (The adjective "written" in that statement is a reminder that the written language does not necessarily perfectly represent the spoken language of the time.) Before this period, grammatical gender agreement appears robust in the anaphoric pronouns, and after this period, grammatical gender agreement appears infrequently and mostly with resilient nouns. The written language of this 100-year period in this study uniquely records the mechanisms at work in the shift to natural gender in the anaphoric pronouns: the effects of reanalysis and extension (i.e., analogy) on the structure of the agreement system; the lexical diffusion of this syntactic change; and the dialectal spread of the innovation from north to south.

In a study of shifts in the gender systems of Dutch dialects, Dekeyser (1980) proposes that changes in the grammatical gender agreement system of the anaphoric pronouns are directly linked to changes in the grammatical gender agreement system of the demonstrative pronouns in the noun phrase. Sandström (1999), in a study of changes in the gender systems of Swedish dialects in Nyland,

Finland, concludes that speakers with distinctions between masculine and feminine in pronouns also have distinctive masculine and feminine inflections in the use of the definite article. In Old English, if the health of grammatical gender in the anaphoric pronouns is linked to the maintenance of gender-distinctive demonstrative pronouns and adjective inflectional endings, it seems possible that the presence of gender-distinctive forms in the antecedent noun phrase could encourage the maintenance of corresponding grammatical gender in the anaphoric pronouns. Or if natural gender in the anaphoric pronouns arises from a language user's confusing or forgetting the antecedent noun's grammatical gender, the presence of gender distinctions in the noun phrase should prevent such a lapse. Charles Jones (1988) examines the breakdown of grammatical gender agreement in the noun phrase before 1250, and the study presented here indicates that the breakdown of grammatical gender inside and outside the noun phrase occur roughly simultaneously, as Dekeyser predicted.

As the natural gender agreement system gradually extends from animate nouns to inanimate ones in early Middle English, it is the masculine inanimate nouns as a whole that are affected first, before feminine nouns. This important general finding from the study makes intuitive sense: it represents a logical consequence of the grammatical reanalysis that triggered the extension process. With the reinterpretation of the pronouns *his* and *him* as possible neuter forms in reference to masculine inanimate antecedents, the underlying syntactic construction can be reinterpreted as natural gender concord. In other words, if a speaker sees or hears *him* used to refer to a masculine noun, this speaker can easily interpret this pronoun as neuter instead of masculine (i.e., natural gender reference instead of grammatical gender), particularly if the gender system demonstrates instability; the speaker is simply extending the system of natural gender reference already in place with animate nouns.

As in the Old English part of the study, inanimate antecedent nouns in the early Middle English texts demonstrate more balance among gender categories than the overall antecedent noun statistics: masculine nouns make up 18.5 percent of the inanimate antecedents; feminine nouns 35.6 percent; and neuter 33.7 percent. Distinctively masculine pronouns (i.e., *he* and *hine*), however, constitute only 6.7 percent of the anaphoric references to inanimate objects in the texts, a significant drop from Old English statistics. This large drop is not paralleled by the feminine pronouns, at 26.2 percent or the neuter pronouns, which rise significantly to 61.6 percent. The discrepancy between the number of masculine nouns (18.5 percent) and the number of masculine pronouns (6.7 percent), as well as between the number of feminine nouns (35.6 percent) and the number of feminine pronouns (26.2 percent), reveals in and of itself, without examining specific examples, that the natural gender system has strengthened in anaphoric reference to inanimate nouns. In other words, to reverse the perspective on the statistics, the number of neuter pronouns dramatically exceeds the number of grammatically gendered neuter nouns, indicating that neuter pronouns are being used to refer to grammatically gendered masculine and feminine

Table 4.3: *Anaphoric agreement patterns between early Middle English nouns and anaphoric personal pronouns (1150–1250 AD), with the number of occurrences and the percentage of that agreement pattern for nouns of that gender*

Noun gender	m	f	n	m–n
m	47 (33.1%)	18 (12.7%)	66 (46.5%)	11 (7.7%)
f	3 (1.1%)	151 (55.3%)	104 (38.1%)	15 (5.5%)
n	—	13 (5.0%)	236 (91.5%)	9 (3.5%)
mf	—	10	1	—
mn	—	—	5	2
fn	—	—	8	—
nf	—	—	1	
nmf	—	1	—	—
foreign	—	3	11	—
plural	1	2	34	5
unknown/new	—	3	6	—

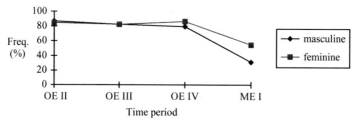

Figure 4.1 *Grammatical gender agreement between masculine and feminine inanimate nouns and their anaphoric pronouns from Old English through early Middle English*

nouns. Even assuming all the masculine-neuter references to masculine nouns (i.e., *his* and *him*) were intended as masculine pronouns, there would remain a significant discrepancy.

The numbers in Table 4.3 strongly suggest that the anaphoric agreement system for masculine inanimate nouns shifts to natural gender earlier than that for feminine inanimate nouns. It seems to become ungrammatical, or at least in some way linguistically undesirable, to use masculine pronouns to refer to inanimate objects before it becomes unacceptable, or at least grammatically marked, to use feminine pronouns in this way (see Figure 4.1). For masculine nouns in ME I, the balance between grammatical and natural gender agreement has shifted in favor of the latter: masculine nouns occur with distinctively masculine pronouns 33.1 percent of the time (down from Old English 60.3 percent to 66.3 percent) and with distinctively neuter pronouns 46.5 percent of the time;

masculine-neuter pronouns comprise only 7.7 percent of the references (see Table 4.3).[16] This last number is strikingly low, a continuation of the decline in use of these forms first witnessed in Old English probably because of their ambiguity; neuter inanimate nouns show a similar drop in the use of masculine-neuter forms, a trend explored in more detail below.

Examples of this linguistically innovative natural-gender construction in the early Middle English texts, in which neuter anaphoric pronouns refer to masculine inanimate nouns, appear "normal" to the modern eye. In the following two passages, all the anaphoric references to the masculine nouns *neorxenewang* 'paradise' and *tur* 'tower' follow natural gender:

(21)   & **neorxenewang** is feowrtig fedme herre þone Noes flod wæs, & **hit** hangeð betwonen heofone & eorðen wunderlice, swa **hit** se Eallwealdene ȝescop, & **hit** is eall efenlang & efenbrad. (*Vespasian Homilies* 145)

'And **paradise** is forty fathoms higher than Noah's flood was, and **it** hangs between heaven and earth wondrously, as the Almighty created **it**, and **it** is all equally long and equally broad.'

(22)   [þe deofles here of helle] weorrið & warpeð eauer towart tis **tur** forte keasten **hit** adun & drahen into þeowdom. þt stont se hehe **þerin.** (*Hali Meidhad* 129)

'[The devil's army from hell] constantly attacks and throws toward this **tower** in order to cast **it** down and drag into slavery [the one] who stands so high **therein.**'

For feminine antecedent nouns, the balance between gender systems has yet to tilt towards natural gender in the early Middle English part of the study. They follow grammatical gender agreement with feminine pronouns in 55.3 percent of the instances in ME I; they follow natural agreement with neuter pronouns in 38.1 percent of the instances, and with masculine-neuter pronouns in 5.5 percent. These numbers are significantly higher for grammatical gender concord and lower for natural gender concord than those for masculine nouns, but they still demonstrate a fairly dramatic change from Old English: almost a 30 percent drop in the use of feminine pronouns with feminine antecedents and a 20–30 percent rise in the use of neuter pronouns. As is the case with masculine nouns, instances such as example (23), in which the feminine noun *byrðen* 'burden' is referred to with neuter pronouns, appear grammatically modern and unmarked – the norm rather than the exception, as they still are for feminine nouns in many early Middle English dialects.

---

[16] The agreement percentages for inanimate antecedents that exclude the masculine-neuter pronouns *his* and *him* also clearly demonstrate the inroads of the natural gender system. Grammatical gender agreement for masculine nouns has dropped to 35.9 percent, as neuter pronouns appear with 50.4 percent of the masculine antecedent nouns.

(23)   Hwen two beoreð a **burðerne**. & te oþer leaueð **hit**; þenne mei þe þe up
       haldeð **hit** felen hu **hit** weieð. (*Ancrene Wisse* 119)

       'When two bear a **burden** and the one leaves **it**, then the one who holds **it**
       up can feel how **it** weighs.'

The agreement statistics for feminine nouns also witness a slight rise in the use
of masculine-neuter pronouns – up to 5.5 percent, from Old English numbers
under 2 percent – but this number is not surprising given the higher percentage
of natural agreement during the period. The feminine nouns display very little
grammatical gender confusion with masculine pronouns.

   Interestingly, the numbers could be read to suggest "anaphoric feminization"
during the transitional period. The statistics for ungrammatical feminine pronouns used to refer to both masculine nouns (12.7 percent) and to neuter nouns
(5.0 percent) are strikingly high. Two passages in which the masculine nouns *stenc*
'smell, stink' and *mæg* 'way' are referred to with feminine pronouns effectively
exemplify this grammatical phenomenon.

(24)   þe seofeþe ful **stunch**. heo wes wurse to þolien þenne efreni of all þa oðre
       pine. (*Lambeth Homilies* 43)

       'the seventh foul **stink**, **it (she)** was worse to endure than each of all the
       other torments.'

(25)   bituhhe muchel & lutel is in euch worldlich þing þe middel **wei** guldene.
       ʒef we **hire** haldeð þenne ga we sikerliche. (*Sawles Warde* 176)

       'between great and small is, in each worldly thing, the middle **way** golden.
       If we maintain **it (her)**, then we will go surely.'

The form *heo* is a documented dialectal variant of the masculine singular pronoun,
but there is little evidence in the *Lambeth Homilies* to suggest *heo* is serving as a
masculine form in example (24): in the excerpts of the text in the Helsinki Corpus,
there are numerous instances of *he* referring to masculine animate antecedents
and no instances of *heo*.

   The increased use of feminine pronouns with masculine antecedent nouns
appears to be more than gender confusion with masculine nouns undergoing
"anaphoric agreement flux"; it could be a more widespread consequence of the
earlier shift of masculine inanimate nouns to natural gender agreement in the
anaphoric pronouns. Interestingly, while neuter antecedent nouns also occasionally appear with feminine anaphoric pronouns, this part of the study records no
instances of clearly masculine pronouns referring to neuter nouns.

   The fact that anaphoric pronouns referring to feminine inanimate antecedents
shift to natural gender later than those referring to masculine antecedents means
that it is generally grammatically acceptable to refer to inanimate nouns with
feminine pronouns longer than it is generally acceptable to do so with masculine
pronouns. It is conceivable that Modern English may still be experiencing the
repercussions of this fact. In scholarship on Modern English gender, it has been

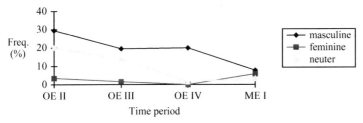

Figure 4.2 *Percentage of masculine-neuter anaphoric pronouns used to refer to masculine, feminine, and neuter inanimate nouns from Old English through early Middle English*

noted that the majority of gendered references to inanimate nouns in Modern English are feminine (Svartengren 1927, 1954; Malone 1985). And while some of these references are undoubtedly meaningful and semantically or emotively driven, others are more conventionalized (for example, "let her rip" or *she* for *ship*).

The reanalysis of gender agreement with masculine inanimate nouns effectively exemplifies the general principle that syntactic change is often triggered by structural ambiguity, and it moves in a direction to avoid ambiguity. The multiple analyses rendered possible by the ambiguous anaphoric pronouns *his* and *him* allow the reanalysis of the grammatical gender agreement system with masculine inanimate nouns and the subsequent extension of natural gender agreement to this class. These two forms remain available and ambiguous during the gender shift: the neuter dative form *him* is only gradually replaced by the objective form *hit* (for accusative and dative functions) during Middle English; the neuter genitive form *his* remains in use through early Modern English as the possessive form *its* does not come into general use until the seventeenth century (Nevalainen and Raumolin-Brunberg 1994: 177–78). Ambiguity with the masculine form undoubtedly plays a role in the replacement of dative *him* by accusative *hit* with reference to neuter nouns; this ambiguity also seems to drive the "culprit" ambiguous forms *his* and *him* out of use for both masculine and neuter inanimate nouns.[17]

The numbers are dramatic (see Figure 4.2). From OE II to OE IV, the overall use of masculine-neuter pronouns to refer to inanimate nouns drops from 17.8 percent in OE II to 12.1 percent in OE III, down to 6.4 percent in OE IV; by ME I, the number has fallen to 5.5 percent. For masculine antecedent nouns, the number of masculine-neuter pronouns drops from 31.3 percent to 18.5 percent of the anaphoric references from OE II to IV, and down to 7.7 percent in ME I. For neuter antecedent nouns, the pronouns *his* and *him* almost completely

---

[17] Avoidance of ambiguity in this case helps to explain why the accusative form *hit* is selected for the neuter "objective" pronoun, while the dative forms *him* and *hire* are selected for the objective pronouns for the masculine and feminine respectively. It is structurally asymmetrical but it adheres to the transparency (or uniqueness) principle of "one form–one meaning."

fall out of use in the Old English part of the study (20.1 percent in OE II, down to 1.5 percent in OE IV), and the number remains low in ME I at 3.5 percent. The numbers for feminine antecedent nouns rise slightly from the Old English part of the study to the early Middle English part, and there are at least two possible explanations: as the natural gender agreement system becomes established, the likelihood of potentially neuter forms (including *his* and *him*) used in reference to feminine nouns rises; the forms *his* and *him* are also less grammatically ambiguous with feminine antecedent nouns because in this syntactic construction, they are logically neuter. (As discussed above, there is no proof for masculinization in anaphoric reference.) There is no parallel drop in the overall frequency of the pronouns *his* and *him* for all classes of antecedents: 37.8 percent in OE II and 37.4 percent in OE III, 41.5 percent in OE IV, and 36.8 percent in ME I. For animate nouns, for which natural gender and grammatical gender correspond, these forms are not ambiguous; for inanimate nouns, however, at a time when many anaphoric pronouns follow grammatical gender but some follow natural gender, these forms are highly ambiguous because they could represent either kind of agreement. They prove to be the pivotal forms that are reanalyzed during the gender shift and that simultaneously drop dramatically in use in such constructions.

As these results imply, the extension of natural gender to inanimate nouns seems to coincide with a strengthening of the distinction between animate and inanimate nouns (e.g., the growing opposition of *who* and *what/that*; see Markus 1995).[18] The ambiguity surrounding the forms *his* and *him* crosses just this animacy line. In other words, the use of *hit* to refer to inanimate nouns distinguishes them from animate nouns grammatically in a natural gender system, whereas *his* and *him* are not distinctive between masculine and neuter, and therefore not distinctive between animate and inanimate. And it is these forms, *his* and *him*, that drop out of use for inanimate antecedents, while they continue to be used in large numbers to refer to animate nouns. It seems logical that as the animate-inanimate distinction strengthens in the grammar, the distinctive masculine pronominal forms should come to be restricted to animate referents before the ambiguous masculine-neuter ones. The numbers show, however, that

---

[18] Early Middle English also witnesses grammatical reinforcement of biological sex distinctions with the introduction of the feminine pronoun *she*, as described in Appendix 1. The nominative forms of the masculine and feminine third-person singular pronouns, *he* and *heo*, appear to have been merging in many dialects to *he* (although whether the spelling merger represents a phonological merger is an open question). The rise in use of the variant feminine form *she* insured the retention of a grammatical distinction between masculine and feminine (and hence between male and female) in English personal pronouns; this distinction is not a *necessary* grammatical feature, but ambiguity in the gender of references to animate nouns seems to have been a type of ambiguity that English (or its speakers) avoided. The distinction in the relative pronouns between animate and inanimate is not maintained in all dialects or registers of Modern English, and the lack of an inanimate possessive relative pronoun is a notable asymmetry in English (e.g., "I sold the car whose engine died").

the distinctive masculine forms continue to refer to both inanimate and animate nouns after the masculine-neuter pronouns come to refer almost exclusively to animate antecedents.[19]

The dramatic drop in the use of *his* and *him* to refer to inanimate nouns coincides with the rise in use of *there-* forms (e.g., *thereof*, *thereon*, *therein*), sometimes called prepositional adverbs (Mustanoja 1960: 424–25) or pronominal adverbs (Nevalainen and Raumolin-Brunberg 1994: 177–78). These forms occur with increasing frequency in the early Middle English section of the study, both as general references (instead of *it*) and as anaphoric-like references back to inanimate objects. Mustanoja and Nevalainen and Raumolin-Brunberg agree that *there-* forms often substitute for constructions with a preposition followed by the neuter pronoun *it*.[20] For example, in the passage from the *Ancrene Wisse* in example (26), the form *þrof* appears after the masculine pronoun *hine*, all in reference to the masculine noun *æppel* 'apple,' and could quite conceivably be a substitute for a phrase such as *of him*.

(26)   Eue biheold o þe forboden **eappel**. & seh **hine** feier & feng to delitin i þe bihaldunge. & toc hire lust þer toward. & nom & et **þrof**. (*Ancrene Wisse* 31)

'Eve looked at the forbidden **apple** and saw it **(him)** to be fair and [she] began to delight in the beholding, and took her desire there towards, and took and ate **thereof**.'

Whether or not *there-* forms should be considered a type of adverb or a type of pronoun is too complex a question to be addressed in this study. These forms have not been included in the overall agreement statistics in this study; given their potential as substitutes for prepositional phrases including the neuter anaphoric pronoun *it*, this fact means that the overall statistics for the frequency of natural gender agreement in this part of the study probably underestimate the extent to which the natural gender system has become established by early Middle English.

---

[19] The continued use of distinctively masculine pronominal forms in reference to some inanimate nouns, specifically resilient nouns – particularly as the inanimate–animate distinction strengthens in the grammar and less referential ambiguity in this area is tolerated – supports the idea that these nouns may be culturally gendered. Their grammatical similarities with animate nouns with respect to anaphoric gender agreement suggests possible semantic similarities based on perceived animacy and/or gender.

[20] Nevalainen and Raumolin-Brunberg (1994: 177–78) note that *thereof* became a popular alternative for 'of it' in Middle English, perhaps due to its flexibility in reference. It had two distinct advantages over other pronominal forms: it was not marked for gender and it was not marked for number. Their study proves *thereof* to be the most frequently used neuter possessive form – more popular than *of it* or *his* – from 1500 to 1640, then dropping out of usage dramatically from 1640 to 1710, as the form *its* became a possible alternative. The period studied here, 1150 to 1250, seems to witness the beginnings of the rise in use of *thereof*, as *his* becomes less acceptable for reference to inanimate nouns of all genders, long before the advent of the pronoun *its*.

4.5   Lexical diffusion of the gender shift in early Middle English

There is general agreement that some syntactic changes involve lexical diffusion – in other words, they spread gradually through the lexicon, affecting some words before others (as opposed to the entire language undergoing the syntactic change simultaneously). It is a logical consequence of the fact that some rules and patterns in synchronic syntax are lexically governed (Harris and Campbell 1995: 113). The statistics described above for anaphoric gender agreement with inanimate antecedent nouns paint a picture of significant variation during the transition period between systems, both across dialects and through the lexicon. The question is whether it is possible to make sense of this variation – of its patterns and implications – in terms of how this syntactic change is happening in the language of the period. And the evidence suggests that the picture these details draw – the story of the gender shift – is one of lexical diffusion, as some nouns shift to natural gender before others.

One passage from *Sawles Warde*, a West Midland text that records the shift in progress, effectively captures many aspects of the variation involved in the lexical diffusion of natural gender agreement. In the description of hell in example (27), the masculine noun *stenc* 'smell, stink' and the feminine noun *sorg* 'sorrow' are both referred back to with neuter pronouns, in accordance with their natural gender. In both sentences, the parallel between the adjectives describing the stink and the sorrow (*unþolelich* 'unbearable' and *untalelich* 'inexplicable') and the subsequent verbs (*þolien* 'to bear' and *tellen* 'to relate') confirm these two specific nouns as the antecedents, rather than a more general reference to hell. In the third sentence, the feminine noun *hell* is referred back to with the form *þrinne* 'therein,' and the feminine noun *þosternes* 'darkness,' modified by the relatively new gender-neutral article *þe*, takes the feminine pronoun *hire*, adhering to grammatical gender concord.

(27)   ... ful of **stench** unþolelich. for ne mahte in eorðe na cwic þing **hit** þolien. ful of **sorhe** untalelich. for ne mei na muð for wreccedom ne for wa; rikenin **hit** ne tellen. Se þicke is **þrinne** [helle] þe þosternesse; þt me **hire** mei grapin. (*Sawles Warde* 171)

'... full of an unbearable **stink** for no living thing on earth could bear **it**; full of inexplicable **sorrow** for no mouth can for misery or for woe rightly relate **it**. So thick is the **darkness therein** [in hell] that one can touch **it (her)**.'

The two feminine nouns *sorg* and *þosternes* in this passage comply with two different anaphoric agreement systems: the first natural and the second grammatical. This kind of evidence argues for the lexical diffusion of this particular syntactic change. As described in Harris and Campbell's general framework for grammatical change, the extension of natural gender to inanimate nouns in early Middle English proceeds according to natural classes already relevant in the structure of the language: first masculine nouns and then feminine ones. Within both subsets of inanimate nouns – masculine and feminine – the effects of lexical diffusion are also apparent as some nouns shift before others.

As was true in the Old English part of the study, high frequency of occurrence and retention of grammatical gender do not necessarily correspond for either masculine or feminine nouns in early Middle English. The five most frequent masculine nouns in ME I are *lichama* 'body,' *mægðhad* 'virginity,' *cla∂* 'cloth,' *hired* 'household,' and *Sunnandæg* 'Sunday.' All of these nouns appear with at least one neuter reference, and several of them display high gender variation in the anaphoric pronouns. The noun *lichama* is an exceptional inanimate noun with respect to anaphoric reference, much like *mod* 'mind,' because reference often slips between the body and the person who lives in the body. Some of the masculine pronouns and all of the feminine ones used to refer to *lichama* seem to refer to the body as a person rather than a thing, while the "ungrammatical" neuter references refer to the body as an object (similar to the variation in anaphoric reference with the neuter noun *bodig*). Two passages in the *History of the Holy Rood-Tree* illustrate the tension between grammatical and natural gender when *lichama* refers to a woman's body (echoing the example with Juliana in Chapter Three). In a description of the tortures done to Sibilla, grammatical gender triumphs over natural gender:

(28)   o∂ ∂et hiræ **licame** wear∂ swa swi∂lice iswungon swulce he mid sexum
       tosnædod wære. (*History of the Holy Rood-Tree* 28)

       'until her **body** was so severely beaten as though **it (he)** were cut to pieces
       with knives.'

Shortly thereafter, however, in the description of the fire which destroys Sibilla's coffin, natural gender prevails:

(29)   þt hus þt þe hal3æ **lichame** inne biburi3ed wæs wear∂ al innan on brune
       of ∂are þruh ∂e **heo** on læ3 & þe læ3 on ælce healfe ut ræsde . . . (*History
       of the Holy Rood-Tree* 30).

       'the building that the holy **body** was buried in became all within on fire
       from the chest in which **she** lay, and the fire rushed out on every side . . .'

The noun *mægðhad* 'virginity' also proves interesting because, despite its masculine suffix, it seems to have acquired feminine gender in the corpus texts in which it appears, probably influenced by the feminine Latin synonym *virginitas*, as well as semantic factors. A typical passage occurs in *Hali Meidhad*:

(30)   for i þe menske of **mei∂had** & in **hire** mihte ne muhten ne nane folhin him.
       ne þt eadi meiden. (*Hali Meidhad* 143–44)

       'in the honor of **virginity** and in **her** power, none can follow him [God]
       but that blessed maiden.'

Of the six references to *mægðhad* with no clear personification in ME I, four occur with feminine pronouns and two with neuter. (The noun is always personified as feminine, which undoubtedly also affects its gender in other contexts.) The two neuter references occur together in a description of virginity's importance, shown in example (31). If anything, discourse considerations seem conducive to feminine gender concord as the noun is thematized and referred to as heaven's queen. The first neuter pronoun may reflect the effect of distance on gender concord; the second neuter pronoun agrees in gender with the first (the effect of anaphoric pronoun strings) and with the description of *mægðhad* as "se heh þing."

(31)   for **meiðhad** is heouene cwen. & worldes alesendnesse. þurh hwam we beoð iborhen. Mihte ouer alle mihtes. & cwemest crist of alle. for-þi þu. Ahest meiden se deorliche witen **hit**. for **hit** is se heh þing ... (*Hali Meidhad* 134–35)

'for **maidenhead** is heaven's queen and the world's redemption through which we are saved. Power over all powers and most pleasing to Christ of all. Therefore, raise up, maiden, to guard **it** so dearly for **it** is so high a thing ...'

The five most frequent feminine nouns – *synn* 'sin,' *lar* 'learning,' *heorte* 'heart,' *sawol* 'soul,' *ælmesse* 'alms' – do not manifest a higher percentage of grammatical gender agreement either. The noun *synn* appears with neuter pronouns over 65 percent of the time, and *lar* appears with neuter pronouns in all twenty-two instances (although these all occur in the *Ormulum*, the text in the study with the highest percentage of natural gender agreement). The noun *heorte* shows a fairly high degree of variation, with twelve feminine pronouns and five non-feminine ones, and *ælmesse* slightly less variation, with twelve feminine and two neuter pronouns. Only *sawol* appears with only feminine pronouns, and it appears to be a resilient noun (a striking contrast with *mod* 'mind' and *lichama* 'body,' two nouns that demonstrate significant gender variation).

The early Middle English results with nouns such as *sawol* continue to support the contention that there exists a subset of nouns, the resilient nouns, that more tenaciously retain their grammatical gender, some as late as Early Modern English, as noted in the earliest English grammars (see Chapter One). The regularity of syntactic change does not mean that it proceeds without exception; these exceptions, or the "residue" of the change, can result from at least two developments of a syntactic change: not all sentence patterns necessarily undergo the reanalysis of an underlying construction; as the new general pattern and the conventional forms coexist during the transition, the former is stronger in most contexts, but the latter may be strong in syntax governed by frequently occurring words, kinship terms, sacred terms, and fixed expressions (Harris and Campbell 1995: 328–29). This second cause of residue proves helpful in explaining some of the variation witnessed in the shift to natural gender in English. It has been noted in previous scholarship that these common, sacred, or fixed terms may fail to undergo regular phonological or morphological change; the syntactic patterns they govern, such as anaphoric agreement, may also be exceptional. It would be difficult to create a definitive list of such exceptional nouns in this shift – the resilient nouns – but it is possible to identify some of the most obvious ones, such as *sun, moon, wind, city, soul*. It is also not necessarily desirable to attempt to create a definitive list. Theoretical explanations of English gender invariably break down as soon as they attempt to pinpoint binary or definitive features for exceptional gender references or lists of exceptional nouns. One crucial aspect of creating the connection between linguistic gender and social gender in English is accepting the flexibility of social constructions of gender and of the semantic categories employed to describe them.

Several of the resilient masculine nouns discussed in the Old English section do not appear in this part of the study: such as *monað* 'month,' *mona* 'moon.' The noun *dæg* 'day' appears only with masculine pronouns, *deað* 'death' with four masculine and one neuter pronoun, and *wind* 'wind' with one masculine-neuter pronoun. *Steorra* 'star' shows fluctuation between the feminine and neuter: the two feminine appear in *Hali Meidhad* and the one neuter in the *Ormulum*. The resilient feminine nouns continue to display tenacity in the retention of grammatical gender. The nouns *burg* 'city,' *eorðe* 'earth,' and *sawol* 'soul' appear with only feminine pronouns, *sunne* 'sun' with six feminine and two non-feminine. *Cirice* 'church' takes two feminine and two neuter pronouns, the latter two both appearing in the *Peterborough Chronicle*, an east midland text whose dialect is notably advanced in the progression of natural gender agreement. The noun *woruld* 'world' displays higher variation than *eorðe* in the early Middle English period, but feminine pronouns still predominate. Interestingly, the masculine noun *middangeard* 'earth' also retains grammatical gender in this period, although in the long run, feminine references will prevail for 'earth,' perhaps in part because feminine nouns shift to natural gender later and perhaps for semantic reasons. In this way, the agreement patterns of the resilient nouns seem to parallel those of other nouns in the study. While generally speaking, they all show higher percentages of grammatical gender agreement than most other nouns, the masculine resilient nouns display more variation in this period than the feminine ones. Importantly, I am not arguing that these resilient nouns are personified in the sense that they are given personalities and treated as human characters. Instead, it seems that they may be categorized as in some way animate, and/or gendered, in a way foreign to Modern English speakers but corresponding to contemporaneous constructions of animacy and gender.

Some nouns, such as those referring to vices and virtues, sometimes teeter on the brink of personification in the descriptive passages from *Vices and Virtues*: they do not appear with verbs that require personification, but they are often depicted as active entities, as exemplified by the sin *asokelnes* 'laziness' (a feminine noun) in the following passage:

(32)   accidia, ðat is, **asolkenesse**, ðe me haueð ðurh mire ȝemeleaste maniȝe
          siðes beswiken. **Hie** me haueð imaked heuy and slaw on godes weorkes
          ðurh idelnesse; **hie** me haueð ofte idon eten oðermannes sare swink all
          un-of-earned. Ofte **hie** me haueð idon slæpen . . . (*Vices and Virtues* 3)

'Accidia, that is **laziness**, which has through my negligence many times deceived me. **It (she)** has made me heavy and slow in God's works through idleness; **it (she)** has often made me eat another's sore labor all unearned. Often **it (she)** has made me sleep . . .'

Virtues and sins are also sometimes personified, almost always as feminine entities, which may reinforce the use of feminine pronouns to refer to them in other contexts. But the gender of personified nouns – most often character traits and abstract notions like wisdom used allegorically – does not always correspond to the grammatical gender of the noun. Personified gender seems to constitute its own gender system, distinct from grammatical gender. It is remarkably stable and may result from the conventions of allegory or classical influence.

The text *Sawles Warde* includes a wide array of personified nouns, both those whose gender corresponds and those whose gender does not correspond with the grammatical gender of the noun: the feminine nouns *strengð* 'strength' and *mæð* 'ambition' are both personified as feminine, as is the masculine noun *wærscipe* 'cunning'; masculine *fær* 'fear' is personified as masculine, as is the neuter *witt* 'intellect.'

In the description of the mysterious and powerful Phoenix in the *Vespasian Homilies*, the bird is personified as masculine: all the references to *Fenix* are masculine, as are those to *fugel*, a grammatically masculine noun. All the references, that is, except one. At the end of the descriptive passage, the writer notes that no one knows the sex of the bird, and in this one reference, the writer uses a neuter pronoun:

(33)   **He hine** forbærnð & eft edʒung upp ariseð, & næfð **he** nænne ʒemaca, & nan mann ne wat, hweðer **hit** is þe karlfugel, þe cwenefugel, bute God ane. þes halge fugel is Fenix ʒehaten, wlitiʒ & wynsym, swa **hine** God ʒescop . . . (*Vespasian Homilies* 148)

'**He** burns up (himself) and rises up young again, and **he** has no mate and no one knows whether **it** is a male-bird, or a female-bird, except God alone. This holy bird is called the Phoenix, blessed and joyful, as God shaped **him** . . .'

The neuter pronoun is preceded and followed by masculine pronouns in reference to the same bird, which could be used to argue both that the masculine pronoun is generic (the bird is truly of unknown sex, as the narrator has stated) and that the masculine is not generic (the narrator must use the neuter pronoun in order to be truly generic).

4.6   Grammatical and discursive factors in the diffusion of the gender shift

In the complex progression of the gender shift, there is interplay between the lexical diffusion of the change and syntactic factors such as distance. In the Old

English part of the study, when the gender shift is just beginning, distance appears to be a critical factor in the tendency towards natural gender in the anaphoric pronouns. As the shift progresses, however, the influence of distance seems to wane, as other factors (semantic, lexical, and discursive) become more prominent. The patterns for masculine and feminine nouns, already seen to be affected differently in the diffusion of natural gender through the agreement system, also diverge in the correlation of the distance between the antecedent and the anaphoric pronoun and anaphoric gender agreement. Feminine nouns continue the pattern described in Old English where pronouns manifesting natural gender agreement are, on average, farther from the antecedent noun than pronouns manifesting grammatical gender agreement. Masculine nouns, however, which show a much higher percentage of natural gender agreement in the pronouns during this period, break the pattern and distance no longer appears to be an influential factor in the gender of anaphoric pronouns with masculine antecedents.

The Old English part of the study provides mixed results about the importance of gender-distinctive marking in the noun phrase for grammatical gender concord in the anaphoric personal pronouns. In sum, demonstrative pronouns such as *se* and *seo* in the antecedent noun phrase seem to facilitate grammatical gender concord outside the noun phrase but not require it, as other factors can override the presence of gender markers in the noun phrase. In the late Old English and early Middle English periods, it is argued that certain nominal inflectional endings come to mark case across all three genders (e.g., *-ne* for the accusative) and inflected forms of the demonstrative pronouns begin to function as discourse markers rather than as case and gender markers (C. Jones 1988). The correlation between distinctive gender markings in the antecedent noun phrase and grammatical gender agreement in the anaphoric pronoun, therefore, becomes difficult to track, if not irrelevant. In these early Middle English texts, the demonstrative pronoun *þe* 'the' modifies nouns of all three genders, as well as borrowed foreign nouns; and the formerly neuter demonstrative pronouns *þis* 'this' and *þæt* (*þat*) 'that' appear also with masculine and feminine nouns, as well as borrowed ones. As Charles Jones (1988) argues, these uses of the neuter demonstrative pronouns should not be taken to represent gender confusion or changes in nominal gender because they are no longer functioning only as gender markers. For the gender-distinctive inflectional endings which do remain, it is possible to see if there is any correlation between grammatical gender in the antecedent noun phrase and in the anaphoric pronoun. Even if they have taken on wider case-marking or discourse functions, they may still carry enough gender-distinctiveness to influence the anaphoric pronouns.

The demonstrative pronouns *þis*, *þæt*, and *þes* 'these' have been excluded from the following statistics; the demonstrative pronouns *se* and *þone* 'the' have been included as masculine (nominative and accusative), *seo* and *þeos* as feminine. The inflectional endings *-ne* and *-es* have been included as masculine and masculine-neuter respectively, the ending *-re* as feminine. The results indicate that when a distinctively masculine or feminine inflectional marker appears in the noun phrase, there is a higher probability that the anaphoric pronoun will reflect the grammatical gender of the noun. Of the seventeen antecedent noun phrases with distinctive masculine forms, twelve take masculine pronouns (70.6 percent), two feminine, two neuter, and one masculine-neuter. Of the thirty-four antecedent noun phrases with distinctively feminine forms, twenty-four (64.6 percent) take feminine pronouns and ten non-feminine ones. Both of these numbers are significantly higher than the overall frequency of grammatical gender concord for masculine and feminine nouns.

In sum, these numbers could be used to support the hypothesis in Heltveit (1958) that grammatical gender continues to control concord in the anaphoric pronouns as long as the gender-distinctive forms of the demonstrative pronouns remain productive in the grammar. Once these forms decay, as witnessed in many of the antecedent noun phrases with *þis*, *þæt*, *þe*, or other non-distinctive forms, grammatical gender concord loses syntactic support and the tendency toward natural gender in the anaphoric pronouns becomes stronger.

These grammatical factors may well interact with discursive factors. As discussed in Chapter Three, Newman (1997: 94) argues that anaphoric pronouns in Modern English carry discursive meaning and affect how the referent is to be viewed. This observation seems to hold true in earlier periods of English for antecedent nouns referring to humans; and a similar argument could be made for inanimate antecedents. With a subset of antecedent nouns in this study, which demonstrates fluctuation between grammatical and natural gender reference during the period, there are patterns that suggest possible discourse motivations for the appearance of one gender as opposed to the other. Thematic prominence is probably the most obvious factor.[21] The highlighting of an inanimate object as the focus of the sentence or longer segment of discourse seems to favor the use of grammatical gender in anaphoric pronouns, while other "background nouns" may be more likely to take the neuter. In the following passage from *Vices and Virtues*, the masculine noun *pott* 'pot' is the grammatical and rhetorical subject and all the anaphoric references to it are masculine. The masculine noun *ofen* 'oven' into which the pot is put is rhetorically secondary and the anaphoric reference to it is the neuter *þar inne* (as opposed to *in him*).

---

[21] A passage from the *Ancrene Wisse* involving the masculine noun *hund* 'dog' also supports this theory of the effect of discursive prominence:

> þe **hund** þe fret leðer oðer awurið ahte. me **hit** beat ananriht þt **he** understonde for hwi **he** is ibeaten. (*Ancrene Wisse* 167)

> 'The **dog** that chews leather or worries cattle, one beats **it** right away, so that **he** understands why **he** is beaten.'

In this instance, discourse considerations may be a contributing factor in anaphoric pronoun choice: when the anaphoric pronoun referring to the animal is in subject position (when the animal is more semantically animate), it takes a gendered pronoun, whereas it is referred to with the neuter in object position (when the animal is a recipient rather than an actor).

(34)   al swo is þe **pott** ðe is idon on ðe barnende **ofne**. Gif **he ðar inne**
bersteð and brekð, **he** is forloren and sone utȝeworpen; ȝif **he** belæfð
hal and ȝesund, ðe pottere **hine** deð ðar to ðe **he** iscapen was. (*Vices and*
Virtues 73)

'as is the **pot** that is put in the burning **oven**. If **it (he)** bursts **therein** and
breaks, **it (he)** is abandoned and soon thrown out; if **it (he)** remains whole
and sound, the potter puts **it (him)** there to which **it (he)** was made.'

In a sentence from the *Lambeth Homilies* in which the noun *ofen* reappears, it
is referred to first with a masculine pronoun (and then subsequently with a
masculine-neuter pronoun); the syntactic distance between the antecedent noun
and the anaphoric pronoun in both example passages is comparable, but in the
second, *ofen* is rhetorically prominent – the subject of discourse.[22]

(35)   Seoððan **he him** sceaude an **ouen** on berninde fure **he** warp ut of **him**
seofe leies. (*Lambeth Homilies* 41)

'Afterwards he showed him an **oven** in burning fire, **it (he)** threw seven
flames out of **it (him)**.'

Another possible discourse factor is more difficult to describe with precision:
it can be summarized as the event-entity distinction. Some inanimate nouns (e.g.,
deað 'death,' *tima* 'time') can represent either entities that carry perceived power
or as discrete events; the former situation seems to favor grammatical gender
reference and the latter natural gender. The noun *deað* almost always takes the
masculine (it is often almost personified), as in example (36), but in an example
in *Vices and Virtues*, where death is more of an event than an entity, it takes the
neuter:

(36)   Ne ondræd þu þe **deað** to swyðe for nanre wite, þeh **he** þe full god ne þyncce,
he byþ ælces yfeles ænde ne cumð **he** næfre ma. (*Vespasian Homilies* 5)

'Do not fear **death** too greatly for any punishment; although **it (he)** does
not seem fully good to you, it is the end of all evil and **it (he)** never comes
again.'

(37)   For ðan he was hersum his fader anon to ðe **deaðe**, swa swa he him self
hit ne hadde noht ofearned. (*Vices and Virtues* 119)

'For he was obedient to his father all the way to the **death**, howeverso he
himself had not earned **it**.'

It is important to note that the "entity" description is not the same as personification: it does not involve the attribution of human characteristics to the object.

---

[22] The theory of discourse prominence affecting anaphoric gender agreement dovetails nicely with
similar discourse factors proposed by C. Jones (1988) to explain gender shifts within the noun
phrase. At the same time, the fact that the noun in this case is appearing in two different texts
means there are multiple other possible factors affecting pronoun choice.

The discourse factors that seem to influence anaphoric pronoun gender are undeniably easier to identify when they apply than when they do not. There are certainly instances in which discourse considerations could arguably encourage grammatical gender, but natural gender occurs instead, such as example (38).

(38)   þu steorest þe **seastrem**. þt **hit** flede ne mot fir þen þu merkest. (*Margarete* 70)

'You steer the **sea-water** that **it** cannot flood farther than you mark.'

In another example, the feminine noun *synn* 'sin,' which often appears with feminine pronouns, takes a neuter pronoun in a context where even personification seems possible:

(39)   Schrift scahl beon on hihðe imaket. ȝef **sunne** timeð be niht; anan oðer in marhen. ȝef **hit** timeð be dei; ear þen me slepe. (*Ancrene Wisse* 166)

'Confession must be made in haste. If **sin** comes at night, [make confession] at once or in the morning. If **it** comes during the day, then before one sleeps.'

In example (39), taken from the *Ancrene Wisse*, the factor determining the natural gender reference to *synn*, as to many other inanimate nouns in the text, which overrides any discursive or grammatical factors, is probably the dialect of the scribe.

4.7   Dialectal spread of the gender shift in early Middle English

The frequency of natural gender concord for inanimate antecedents witnessed in each ME I text creates a snapshot of the dialectal spread of this syntactic change. Similar to other types of syntactic simplification during this period, this grammatical change spreads from the north and east midland areas toward the south. The results of this corpus study allow for only general conclusions about the dialectal spread, but they suggest intriguing patterns worthy of further research.

Three of the four east midland texts in the study – the *Ormulum*, the *Trinity Homilies*, and the *Peterborough Chronicle* – record the highest frequencies of natural gender in the anaphoric pronouns. The *Ormulum* and the *Peterborough Chronicle* show natural gender concord with all inanimate antecedents and the *Trinity Homilies* contain only one exception. The other two texts which show high natural gender concord are the *Ancrene Wisse* and *Katherine* (both west midland texts), with over 80 percent natural gender concord for masculine nouns and over 70 percent for feminine nouns. The fourth text categorized as east midland in the Corpus, *Vices and Virtues*, has also been localized to Essex, which helps explain why it is more conservative in this feature (and the high concentration of personified inanimate nouns may reinforce traditional forms of grammatical gender agreement).

The three southern texts are notably conservative in this feature, demonstrating a high degree of grammatical gender agreement. The feminine nouns in the *Bodley Homilies* take feminine pronouns in 95.5 percent of the instances and 83.3 percent in the *History of the Holy Rood-Tree*. *Peri Didaxeon* records over 65 percent grammatical gender agreement for both masculine and feminine nouns, high numbers for a scientific text. The one Kentish text, the *Vespasian Homilies*, is similarly conservative, with over 50 percent grammatical gender for masculine nouns and 80 percent for feminine ones.

The west midland texts appear to be more transitional in nature. The percentage of natural gender concord is generally higher than that of Southern or Kentish texts, but not as high as east midland texts. (Layamon's *Brut* is the exception, with grammatical gender agreement reminiscent of Old English patterns.) The most striking feature which these transitional texts share is the use of feminine pronouns for both masculine and neuter inanimate nouns. The transitional period may be characterized by a rise in both neuter and feminine pronouns used in reference to masculine antecedent nouns, and a related upswing in the use of feminine pronouns with neuter antecedent nouns.

As discussed in Chapter Two, the dialectal spread of the gender shift in anaphoric pronoun agreement to a semantic system suggests the importance of contact with Old Norse speakers in the northern and east midland areas of England. Whether or not confusion over inflectional endings or gender between Old English and Old Norse speakers was a cause of the grammatical change in English is a matter of speculation; but the evidence supports theories that language contact can and will speed changes incipient in one language. At the same time, the evidence presented here refutes Middle English creole theories, which push the impact of Old Norse on English to its extreme. The diffusion of natural gender seems to follow patterns of historical syntactic change such as reanalysis and extension without a cataclysmic disruption in this diffusion. In addition, the seeds of change (i.e., gender variation) appear early in the language and the residue of the change linger in later stages of the language.

To sum up this section, by the middle of the thirteenth century, in written texts, the natural gender system seems to have generally taken hold. One passage from the *Ancrene Wisse* nicely captures what looks "normal" or "natural" in terms of gender reference to the modern eye but is, in fact, grammatically complex. The passage involves a disjoined pair of clauses, one which includes the feminine noun *nædl* 'needle' and one the masculine noun *æl* 'awl.' In Old English, this construction might have elicited a masculine pronoun due to the proximity of the masculine antecedent noun; in early Middle English it occurs with the neuter pronoun *hit* instead:

(40)   A wummon þe haueð ilosed hire **nede**. oðer a sutere his **eal**. secheð **hit** ananriht & towent euch strea aþet **hit** beo ifunden. (*Ancrene Wisse* 166)

'A woman who has lost her **needle**, or a shoemaker his **awl**, searches for **it** immediately and turns over every straw until **it** is found.'

To tell the story in an anecdotal way, no matter whether the antecedent noun be a grammatically feminine needle or a grammatically masculine awl or both, by early Middle English, it is more likely to be a neuter *hit* by the time it is found.

4.8   Gender agreement patterns in later Middle English

If the shift to a semantic gender system in English anaphoric personal pronouns follows the typical "S-curve" for linguistic change, the dramatic incline of change in the written language appears to flatten after 1250 AD, as the shift enters its final stages. A few nouns still retain grammatical gender or are in flux between the two gender systems, particularly in the southern dialects, but for the most part, natural gender has taken hold in anaphoric pronoun agreement. These final stages of the gender shift, however, do not proceed according to a "pure" S-curve, unaffected by other linguistic and extralinguistic factors. Instead, the final stages of the syntactic diffusion take some unexpected directions, creating patterns new to the language, but familiar to speakers of Modern English. Of particular importance is foreign influence, specifically of French and Latin, which distinctively manifests itself in the gender of nouns in later Middle English, as do allegory and symbolism.

Mustanoja (1960: 45, 48), in one of the best surveys of Middle English syntax available, summarizes that the influence of French and Latin "plays a considerable role" in the development of gender of Middle English nouns; in addition, during the twelfth and thirteenth centuries, "symbolism and allegory developed into a complete and intricate system embracing all phenomena of life and nature," a fact reflected in the language. The foreign influence to which Mustanoja refers is focused primarily on the literary language, and some of the patterns of gender reference may reflect a divergence of the written language from the spoken or ways in which the written language may have come to influence the spoken.

A brief examination of four later Middle English texts in the Corpus highlights some of the notable features of the late stages of the gender shift – both the expected and unexpected – and points to areas in need of further research. Given the southward spread of many linguistic changes in English, including the demise of grammatical gender, the Kentish dialect proves particularly conservative in many linguistic features; the *Kentish Sermons*, therefore, prove to be one good benchmark for how far natural gender has progressed by the end of the thirteenth century around the country. (The shift is already practically complete in the north by early Middle English, as described in the previous section.) In the Corpus excerpts from the sermons, natural gender concord fully controls the anaphoric pronouns. Animate antecedent nouns overwhelm inanimate ones – as they do in every religious text in the study – and all the inanimate nouns are referred to with neuter pronouns, including foreign nouns. For example, in the following passage, the Old French loanword *miracle*, a masculine noun in French, is referred to with the neuter pronoun *hit*:

(41)　Nu ye habbet iherd þe **miracle** and wet **hit** betokned (*Kentish Sermons* 219)

'Now you have heard the **miracle** and what **it** signified.'

The *Ayenbite of Inwyt*, also a Kentish text but of a later date – dating to the mid-fourteenth century – proves slightly more conservative with respect to this particular grammatical feature. Neuter references to Old English masculine and feminine nouns (e.g., masculine *uayrhede* 'beauty,' feminine *tonge* 'tongue') appear throughout the text. Other nouns demonstrate variation between grammatical and natural gender agreement in the pronouns, as exemplified by the masculine noun *mete* 'meat, food':

(42)　Me zayþ þet **mete** is þe miȝt-uoller þanne **he** heþ ynoȝ of myȝte. and of norissinge. and þe more þet **he** is norissinde: me zayþ þet **he** is þe substancieler. (*Ayenbite of Inwyt* I, 112)

'It is said that **food** is the more powerful when **it** (**he**) has enough of might and of nourishing; and the more that **it** (**he**) is nourishing, it is said that **it** (**he**) is the more substantial.'

(43)　þet is to zigge þet þou sselt nyme þerne **mete** mid greate wylle of herte and mid grat lost. And þou **hit** sselt ase **hit** be uorzuelȝe wyþ-oute chewynge. (*Ayenbite of Inwyt* I, 111)

'That is to say that you must take the **food** with great desire of heart and with great appetite. And you must swallow **it** as **it** be without chewing.'

Natural gender agreement occurs in example (43) despite the grammatically masculine(-looking) demonstrative pronoun *þerne* in the antecedent noun phrase. Discourse factors are a possible explanation for the variation here. The feminine noun *bene* 'prayer' appears in the excerpts from the *Ayenbite of Inwyt* with anaphoric pronouns of all three genders:

(44)　þe **bene** þe more þet **hi** is commun: þe more **hy** is worþ. (*Ayenbite of Inwyt* I, 102)

'The **prayer**, the more that **it** (**she**) is common, the more **it** (**she**) is worth.'

(45)　þis **bene** paseþ alle oþre ine þri þinges. ine digneté in ssorthede. an ine guodnesse. þe digneté is ine þan þet godessone **hit** made. (*Ayenbite of Inwyt* I, 99)

'This **prayer** passes all others in three things: in dignity, in shortness, and in goodness. The dignity is in [the fact] that God's son made **it**.'

(46)　þe worþ and þe profit of þise **bene**: is zuo grat þet **he** beloukþ ine ssorte wordes al þet me may wylny of herte. (*Ayenbite of Inwyt* I, 99)

'The worth and the benefit of this **prayer** is so great because **it** (**he**) embodies in short words all that one can wish for from/in [the] heart.'

The neuter reference to *bene* in example (45) could be influenced by the specific reference in surrounding text to the *pater noster*, which is always referred to with neuter pronouns. This type of influence would run counter to theories that the gender of a basic-level term is more likely to affect the gender of specific nouns in the lexical field, much as the gender of a species may affect the gender of individual members of the species; however, it also seems clear that nearby nouns in a segment of discourse, if semantically similar, can have a similar effect on gender agreement. The feminine reference in example (44) reflects the retention of grammatical gender in the anaphoric pronouns through the fourteenth century in southern dialects; the masculine in example (46) may represent a grammatical tendency in Middle English, noted by Mustanoja (1960: 51), to use masculine pronouns to refer to nouns of all genders. The trend towards masculinization described in Mustanoja (1960: 51) stands in striking contrast to the early Middle English results of this study. Interestingly, if it is the case, this trend seems to occur after the establishment of the semantic gender system for the majority of English nouns, animate and inanimate. It may, therefore, represent an extension of the use of the masculine as a default pronoun for animate nouns. The extended use of the feminine in early Middle English appears to be a grammatical, rather than a semantic, phenomenon. There are still more feminine nouns that retain grammatical gender than masculine nouns in the *Ayenbite of Inwyt* excerpts, including *wiell* 'well,' *sawol* 'soul,' and *heorte* 'heart.' In sum, grammatical gender agreement in the anaphoric pronouns is still apparent in written southern dialects of English through the fourteenth century.

The feminine noun *sawol*, which appears consistently with feminine anaphoric pronouns, is the only inanimate noun in the *Bestiary* not to take neuter pronouns in accordance with natural gender; given the pattern of resilient feminine gender with this noun from Old English through early Middle English, however, such grammatical gender agreement appears far from exceptional. The *Bestiary* is of far greater interest for its record of gender agreement with animal antecedents. This text perfectly captures the growing independence of agreement patterns for animals, as they move away from strict grammatical gender concord to a more speaker-dependent model, similar to Modern English. Gender is no longer marked in the attributive forms within the noun phrase in the *Bestiary*, which facilitates new patterns of agreement in the pronouns. Some animals retain their Old English grammatical gender: *culfer* 'dove' and *turtle* 'turtle dove' are both feminine; *heorot* 'hart' and *pandher* 'panther' are both masculine. Other nouns referring to animals, however, demonstrate nontraditional patterns of gender agreement in this text, and they do so with notable consistency. For example, the word *fox* 'fox,' an Old English masculine noun, appears with all feminine pronouns. On the other hand, the noun *nædre* 'serpent, adder,' feminine in Old English, takes masculine pronouns in the descriptive passages of the *Bestiary* devoted to it. In the first of these passages, the gender of *nædre* is arguably influenced by the masculine gender of *wyrm* 'snake,' a noun that names its species and that precedes it in the segment of text:

(47) An **wirm** is o werlde,
      wel man it knoweþ,
      Neddre is te name:
      ðus **he** **him** neweð,
      ðanne **he** is forbroken and forbroiden,
      and in **his** elde al forwurden. (*Bestiary* 5)

      'There is a **snake** in the world, man knows it well – **adder** is the name;
      Thus **he** renews **himself** when he is crushed and torn, and in **his** old age
      completely deteriorated.'

In the subsequent passage concerning *nædre*, the word *wyrm* does not appear, and
yet the noun remains masculine. It is possible that the gender can be attributed
to foreign influence through translation from the Latin word *serpentis*; it is also
possible that, as Mustanoja (1960: 52) describes for gender variation in references
to birds in Middle English, the writer simply views this animal as male or female,
possibly due to its characteristics, or the writer has a particular sex of the animal
in mind. These patterns of gender reference to animals parallel those in Modern
English.

    In a later passage in the *Bestiary* describing the behavior of the *heorot* 'hart,'
the word *nædre* reappears, but this time in the background, as nourishment for
the hart. As such, the noun *nædre* is no longer grammatically masculine, but
rather neuter:

(48) He [ðe hert] drageð ðe **neddre** of ðe ston
      ðurg his nese up on-on,
      of ðe stoc er of ðe ston,
      for **it** wile ðerunder gon;
      and sweleð **it** wel swiþe . . . (*Bestiary* 10)

      'He [the hart] drags the **adder** from the stone up through his nose, from
      the stump or from the stone, for **it** will go under there, and quite fiercely
      swallows **it** . . .'

The pattern of gender variation exemplified by examples (47) and (48) mir-
rors discourse-dependent patterns discernible with inanimate objects discussed
earlier in this chapter – patterns of reference dependent on whether or not the
antecedent noun is thematized in the segment of discourse. As the thematic focus,
animal antecedents are more likely to take gendered pronouns; in the background
of another thematized object or animal, they are more likely to take the neuter.
This pattern does not always hold, but it can explain many instances of variation,
as can the proximity of differently gendered nouns (see also Mausch 1986).

    Some gender variation allows for no such grammatical or discursive expla-
nation – it appears more random, perhaps a realistic reflection of variation in
spoken discourse. For example, in the following two sentences from the *Bestiary*
describing a *fisc* 'fish,' an Old English masculine noun, the fish first takes a neuter
pronoun and then a masculine one:

(49)   ðis **fis** wuneð wiþ ðe se grund,
    and liueð þer eure heil and sund,
    til it cumeð ðe time
    ðat storm stireð al ðe se,
    ðanne sumer and winter winnen;
    ne mai **it** wunen ðer-inne,
    So droui is te sees grund,
    ne mai **he** wunen ðer ðat stund,
    oc stireð up and houeð stille . . . (*Bestiary* 16–17)

'This **fish** dwells above the sea bottom, and lives there always healthy and sound, until the time comes that a storm stirs all the sea, when summer and winter prevail; **it** cannot remain therein; so troubled is the sea's floor, **it** (**he**) cannot dwell there at that time, but moves up and rises silently . . .'

The two pronouns appear in parallel syntactic structures, and the pronoun farther from the antecedent noun is gendered, while the closer one is not, defying the effects of distance witnessed in the patterns of variation in Old English gender concord. Mustanoja (1960: 52) creates a list of genders for animals in Middle English, but the high possibility for variation, much like Modern English, makes such a list of limited use. The underlying point is that anaphoric reference to animal antecedents has been freed from grammatical gender by later Middle English and has become dependent on linguistic context, speaker attitude, and social constructions of masculine and feminine.

As mentioned earlier, French and Latin influence is traditionally seen as having a significant impact on gender variation in Middle English. The various effects of foreign influence on the diffusion of the gender shift with respect to resilient nouns, especially the celestial bodies, in later Middle English are particularly well captured in Chaucer's *Astrolabe*.[23] Throughout this text, neuter pronouns are used for most inanimate nouns, such as *label* 'brass rule' and *almury* 'pointer' in the following passages:

(50)   Than hast thou a **label** that is shapen like a reule, save that **it** is streit and hath no plates on iether ende with holes. (*Astrolabe* 669)

(51)   This same **almury** sitt fix in the heved of Capricorne, and **it** serveth of many a necessarie conclusioun in equacions of thinges as shal be shewid. (*Astrolabe* 669)

The latitudes and altitudes of celestial bodies are all neuter, as are the instruments used to measure them. The neuter is clearly the default gender for inanimate nouns, as the following sentence concerning a half of a number suggests:

---

[23] Due to the high frequency of resilient nouns in the *Astrolabe* and the relative brevity of the text, the entire text (not only the Corpus excerpts), available in Benson 1987, was examined for the study.

(52) Tak than the half of 8 and adde it to 48 that was his secunde altitude, and than hast thou 52. (*Astrolabe* 675)

While the neuter prevails for most inanimate nouns in the *Astrolabe*, the text is still full of gendered pronouns referring to inanimate objects, particularly masculine ones, due to the text's focus on heavenly bodies, which are, for the most part, resilient nouns.[24] While these nouns are still referred to with gendered pronouns as they were in Old and early Middle English, they are often referred to with differently gendered pronouns in later Middle English. For example, the sun quite consistently takes masculine pronouns instead of feminine ones, a pattern that continues into Early Modern English literature[25]:

(53) . . . or ellis for whan the sonne entrith in eny of tho signes he takith the propirte of suche bestes . . . (*Astrolabe* 668)

Maintaining the same gender opposition witnessed in earlier English texts, albeit reversed, the moon appears with feminine pronouns:

(54) And yif thou wilt pleye this craft with the arisyng of the mone, loke thou rekne wel hir cours houre by houre, for she ne dwellith not in a degre of hir longitude but litel while, as thow wel knowist. But natheles yf thou rekne hir verrey moevyng by thy tables houre after houre . . . (*Astrolabe* 681)

The stars and planets are generally masculine, as they were in Old English. When the planets are named, however, their gender becomes variable; the following two sentences are syntactically parallel and the planet Venus takes a feminine pronoun, while the planet Jupiter takes a masculine-neuter one:

(55) than saw I wel that the body of Venus in hir latitude of 4 degrees septemtrionals ascendid . . . (*Astrolabe* 680)

(56) Than say I wel that the body of Jupiter in his latitude of 2 degrees meriodional ascendid . . . (*Astrolabe* 681)

As Mustanoja (1960: 45–48) explains, the new genders of these celestial bodies, particularly the sun and moon, in later Middle English can be ascribed directly to foreign influence, as these new pronoun references correspond to the gender of the Latin and French synonyms.[26] The few exceptions with resilient nouns in

[24] The large number of references to masculine resilient nouns helps to account for the relatively high frequency of the pronouns *his* and *him* in reference to inanimate nouns in the text (as opposed to *there*- forms). Most of these pronouns refer to the sun, planets, or stars, and probably represent masculine forms rather than neuter ones.

[25] There are only two exceptions with neuter pronouns referring to the sun in this text, and they occur in almost identical constructions: *fro sonne arisying tyl it go to reste* (*Astrolabe* 672); *fro the arisyng of the sonne til it go to reste* (*Astrolabe* 673).

[26] Lass (1992: 108) strongly disagrees with the description of gendered pronoun references to the sun and moon in Middle English as a kind of grammatical gender, or as a structurally "linguistic"

the *Astrolabe* reflect patterns evident in the earlier diffusion of the gender shift. First of all, these nouns occasionally appear with neuter pronouns, in accordance with their inanimate status, as in the following two passages concerning planets and stars:

(57)   . . . so that the **planete** arise in that same signe with eny degre of the forseide face in which **his** longitude is rekend, that yit is the **planete** *in horoscopo*, be **it** in nativyte or in eleccion, etc. (*Astrolabe* 671)

(58)   This is to seyn that whan eny **sterre** fix is passid the lyne meridional, than begynneth **it** to descende; and so doth the sonne. (*Astrolabe* 673)

As the neuter comes to be used with almost all inanimate nouns, it is not surprising to see it used occasionally in reference to such resilient nouns also. The occasional feminine references to these resilient masculine nouns in the *Astrolabe* might seem more surprising, but they also mirror patterns already discerned in early Middle English – in this case, the extended use of feminine pronouns to refer to inanimate nouns of all genders, after masculine inanimate nouns shift to natural gender earlier. The following two passages show feminine pronouns referring to a planet and a star:

(59)   Loke whan that a **planete** is in the lyne meridional, yf that **hir** altitude be of the same height that is the degre of the sonne for that day . . . (*Astrolabe* 678)

(60)   Awayte wel than whan that thy **sterre** fixe is in the same altitude that **she** was whan thou toke **hir** firste altitude. (*Astrolabe* 679)

The feminine reference to star could be attributed to foreign influence (Mustanoja 1960: 46), but no such foreign synonym can account for the feminine gender of planet in this case.

In a footnote about the gender of celestial bodies in Middle English, Mustanoja writes: "The fact that even in later Middle English (14th century) sun is not infrequently feminine and moon and star are occasionally masculine is difficult to account for. It is hard to think of it simply as a survival of grammatical gender" (*ibid.*: 46). More likely, these pronoun references probably reflect patterns in the loss of the grammatical gender system: these nouns are exceptional in the demise of grammatical gender and in the rise of natural gender. They comprise one of the last subsets of inanimate nouns to retain grammatical gender

phenomenon at all. He argues that these masculine and feminine references are "quite predictable personifications with clear extralinguistic models," available to any "educated medieval speaker with the usual knowledge of classical mythology." But the pervasiveness of gendered references to these entities through Middle and Early Modern English suggests a grammatical phenomenon that goes beyond personification and beyond speakers educated in mythology. In addition, the grounding of linguistic categories in extralinguistic models does not necessarily make them less linguistic, especially in a semantic system.

concord in the anaphoric pronouns and they are the nouns most susceptible to foreign influence, which serves to perpetuate the use of gendered pronouns in reference to them. Somehow these nouns are seen as gendered at a time in the language when the distinction between animate and inanimate is strengthening and the masculine and feminine pronouns are coming to be associated solely with animate, gendered beings. In other words, their exceptional status as resilient nouns, which may have been seen as animate (and gendered) in ways foreign for Modern English speakers, could help to explain why they are the nouns to be influenced by French and Latin gender. In this way, studying the development of natural gender in the history of English helps redefine the meaning of natural gender in Early Modern and Modern English so that it corresponds in some ways to contemporaneous constructions of culturally determined animacy and gender.

4.9   Conclusion

In his 1832 grammar book, *A Grammar of the English Language*, William Cobbett begins his discussion of gender by stating "it is hardly possible to make a mistake" (Cobbett 1986 [1832]: 89). He explains:

> There are no terminations to denote gender, except in the third person singular, *he, she,* or *it*. We do, however, often *personify* things. Speaking of a *nation*, we often say *she*; of the *sun*, we say *he*; of the *moon*, we say *she*. We may personify things at our pleasure; but, we must take care to be consistent, and not call a thing *he*, or *she*, in one part of a sentence, and *it* in another part. (*Ibid.*: 89)

The results of this study suggest that the variation in gender reference to inanimate nouns in modern varieties of English is not simply "personification." Some of the variation may represent residue from patterns of diffusion of the gender shift in the personal pronouns; some of the variation reflects contemporaneous constructions of gender in the culture. Some of the variation is certainly personification and some of it is conventional; even in some of these conventional gender references, however, it is possible to discern the history of foreign influence on particular subsets of words in English. And the fact is that Modern English speakers are not necessarily consistent in the non-conventional uses of gender to refer to inanimate objects, echoing the variation witnessed in the early English texts discussed throughout this chapter as the grammatical gender system breaks down.

With the loss of grammatical gender, as Cobbett notes, there are no inflectional endings in English to mark gender: only the personal pronouns differentiate genders, and some grammarians would include a set of derivational suffixes such as *-ess* and *-ette*. These suffixes have been a source of controversy in feminist language reform movements, much like generic *he* or the noun *man*.

Debates about what kind of pronoun to use in reference to nouns such as *nation* or *ship* or *man* in English, with the replacement of grammatical gender by natural gender, highlight the ways in which the grammar of pronoun reference becomes meaningful, semantically and socially, in terms of the noun's referent (rather than the noun's morphology). So referring to ships as *she* cannot be isolated as solely a point of grammar, divorced from social construction and language prescription related to gender.

5 Gender and asymmetrical word histories: when boys could be girls

5.1 Introduction

Contemporary question

The masculine–feminine dichotomy constructed by or captured in the third-person pronouns *he* and *she* pervades the lexicon as well as the grammar of English: throughout the history of English there have been gendered pairings of words to refer to male and female human beings, both adults and children. As is often the case with open-class or content words compared to grammatical forms, the histories of words referring to men and women, boys and girls have been much less stable semantically than the pronouns over time. The appearance of the pronoun *she* and the borrowing of the plural *th-* pronoun forms are remarkable because such changes in pronouns are so rare. The appearance of *boy* and *girl* and the borrowing of numerous words such as *husband*, *bachelor*, and *damsel*, on the other hand, are more typical of the extraordinary amount of word borrowing that English speakers have done over time. What is more remarkable about these words for men and women, boys and girls, are the semantic shifts that so many of the words have undergone, from shifting between positive and negative meanings to shifting genders altogether. In fact, the gender-bending in the title of this chapter – "when boys could be girls" – highlights the opacity of many such semantic shifts for most Modern English speakers, as well as the fact that what is now a more symmetrical pairing of words in English (*boy and girl*) was not always so symmetrical. The same holds true for several other Modern English word pairs: *man and woman* ("when women could be men"), *husband and wife* ("when women could be husbands"), and *bachelor and spinster* ("when bachelors were married" or "when spinsters still spun"), and the list goes on. Many feminists argue that even these "more semantically symmetrical" pairings are often not symmetrical: for example, *man* is still often used as a generic (even if it is not necessarily interpreted this way), and *spinster* carries negative connotations that are foreign to *bachelor*.

The semantic derogation of words for women has been the focus of a significant amount of feminist attention and scholarship, as it represents one of the most obvious manifestations of sexism in the language. Another focus of attacks on sexism in the language has been the use of generic *man*, which in many ways parallels the use of generic *he* in Modern English, but has a very different history. Finally, recently some women and other "minority speech communities" have been explicitly objecting to the use of certain terms to refer to them. The specifics of the semantic development of these controversial words also raise interesting theoretical questions in historical semantics, from the nature of polysemy to the nature of pejoration, as well as the application of semantic binaries.[1]

Historical context

The lexical fields of words for adults and children in English have undergone a series of dramatic changes since Anglo-Saxon times: words have been borrowed, and words have died; words have fallen into ill repute, and words have risen in the ranks; and some words have "crossed over" and changed genders. At the earliest, the words *boy* and *girl* came to be paired as male–female counterparts in late Middle English, and while they may not be "illegitimate," both words are of unknown stock with unresolved etymologies. Before *boy* and *girl* came a succession of knights and knaves, maidens and wenches, all of whom have now left the lexical fields for children. *Man* and *woman* came to be paired by Middle English, and in some contexts were then replaced by the expression "man and wife" in subsequent centuries. Wives paired with husbands in Middle English as well, as the word *husband* became gender-specific. And along the way, some words fell in status (*wench, mistress*), some words rose in status (*boy, damsel*), and other words were lost altogether (*wer*).

Focus of this historical linguistic study

This chapter aims to tell the stories of some of these words, to explain, for example, how the history of *man* differs from that of *he* and how *boy* and *girl* came to be paired. Much like the histories of the pronouns that precede them in this book, the histories of the gendered words for humans that these pronouns can refer to are often complex – a fact which is as important as the specific details themselves. With this premise, this chapter, in the model of the newer scholarship in the field (cf. Kleparski 1997), works to complicate the relationship of gender and semantic pejoration: it addresses the history of some of the negative terms for

---

[1] This chapter can only begin to describe the interesting semantic developments of words for women and men, boys and girls, and the coverage of terms is, therefore, selective. Readers should turn to Baron 1986 and Hughes 1991 for engaging and detailed treatments of more such words as well as literary commentary; Kleparski 1996, 1997 for more theoretical semantic treatments of words for boys and girls; and feminist dictionaries such as Mills 1989 for further details about gendered terms from a feminist perspective.

women, as well as some of the negative terms for men, introducing other possible factors such as age and non-heterosexual gender. The discussion here works to contextualize all of these developments within a broader examination of historical shifts for gendered nouns referring to humans, of both/all genders, in order to create a more complex picture and understanding of their historical semantic developments. Organized around several lexical pairings, this chapter explores the implications of symmetry and asymmetry in semantic change, leading to a larger theoretical question: the justification of applying/imposing gender binaries to/on the lexicon and our analysis of it.

In weaving together the threads of these word stories into a text (a word which can be traced back to the Latin *textus*, meaning literally 'that which is woven'), this chapter works to keep the threads interwoven without becoming hopelessly tangled. The knots, however, may tell that we have reached the limits of what we can know about the history of words given the resources we have as well as when the power of words to signify and change defies our theoretical frameworks.

This chapter relies heavily on the *Oxford English Dictionary* (*OED*) and *Middle English Dictionary* (*MED*) – the two major historical lexicographic projects in English of the late nineteenth and twentieth centuries – for historical material and sense definitions, which are interpreted and intertwined to tell the stories of these words.[2] These semantic interpretations are supplemented by studies of other historical written material in the Helsinki Corpus and other text databases, as well as material from other dictionaries produced over the past three centuries.[3] In examining the use of these gendered words in texts and in the metadiscourse

---

[2] Treichler (1989) correctly points out that even the *OED* is not free from bias in some of its definitions; however, with supporting quotations provided, scholars have available material from which to draw their own conclusions. And the erudition and scope that characterizes these historical dictionaries is invaluable. In the lexical discussions in this chapter, I rely on etymologists for the etymological explorations, and I appreciate the wise caution by Liberman (1998: 162) that a convincing etymology is mostly "a matter of inspiration and good luck." In this chapter I have attempted to provide some of the most current information and/or speculations available as well as summaries of interesting etymological debates. It is also important to remember that a certain number of etymologies are speculative, and as such, are to varying extents influenced by the social constructs and belief systems within which the etymologist works. As Wolfe (1989: 90–92) notes, historical linguists must see connections among concepts as "plausible" in order to reconstruct words as cognates, and such plausibility will clearly depend at least in part on cultural assumptions.

[3] The scope of a corpus-based study of words for men and women, boys and girls, is potentially overwhelming. To take perhaps the most dramatic example, we need only look at the word *man*. In Old English, a study must sort through instances of the definite noun *man(n)* 'person, male person' and the indefinite form *mon(n)*, used in the equivalent of passive constructions. And while the noun is perhaps even more common in earlier forms of English given its generic and its indefinite use, it still occurs with overwhelming frequency in more modern forms of English. In just the Helsinki Corpus, the word occurs over 10,000 times in the selections from Old English through Early Modern English. Kleparski (1997: 19–20) notes the overwhelming nature of trying to analyze the conceptual macrocategory FEMALE HUMAN BEING, as the investigation could easily spin to include related conceptual microcategories such as FEMALE RELATIVE, FEMALE SERVANT, PROSTITUTE. As discussed in the next section, the fuzzy nature of semantic boundaries makes quantitative study of a "lexical field" enormously difficult.

about what these words mean in dictionaries, we can begin to speculate about what the words reveal about speakers' attitudes about gendered beings, in the past and today.

5.2   Historical semantics and previous research on gendered nouns

Historical semantics, hampered to some extent by the same "bad data" that Labov claims challenges all historical linguistics, also suffers from a historical lack of satisfactory theoretical frameworks in which to describe or explain semantic change. The recent work by Grzegorz Kleparski (1997) on the theory and practice of historical semantics is particular relevant and useful for the lexical studies in this chapter not only because he proposes new theoretical principles from which to work but also because his case studies provide the most comprehensive work to date on synonyms for 'girl, young woman' (as well as 'boy' and other words for human beings in his other works). Kleparski provides a very useful overview of selected developments in historical semantics; this more systematic account effectively supplements the briefer summary provided here.

Kleparski dates the revitalization of historical semantics to developments in cognitive linguistics, particularly prototype semantics as developed by scholars such as Eleanor Rosch and cognitive grammar developed by scholars such as George Lakoff and Mark Johnson. In brief, the premise of cognitive linguistics is that human reason or thought is embodied, and that the categories of language impose structure on the world, rather than the world being objectively reflected in language. Lakoff (1987) posits that our conceptual systems are grounded in perception, experience (including culture), and imagination (e.g., metaphor and metonymy). Prototype semantics theorizes that categories are organized around prototypical members of the category (i.e., "best examples"), with a continuum in many categories from more central to more peripheral members. Work by G. Lakoff and Johnson (1980, 1999) and G. Lakoff (1987) emphasizes the importance of metaphor both as a grammatical and conceptual structuring system as well as a possible "chaining mechanism" by which a word can acquire new meanings ("metaphorical extension") and by which peripheral members of a category may be understood in relation to the prototype.

As this description should make clear, cognitive linguistics, and particularly prototype theory, draws "fuzzier" category boundaries than semantic theories such as componential analysis, which relies on binary features analysis (e.g., [±HUMAN]) in order to describe semantic categories. Many scholars have argued for the inadequacy of componential analysis in capturing the complexity of meaning and categorization (a "check-list theory of semantics," as Fillmore [1978] refers to it, quoted in Kleparski 1997: 45), and feminists have noted the ways in which traditional theories of componential analysis have been sexist in the assumption of the masculine or male as the unmarked semantic feature (e.g., 'woman' = [+HUMAN] [+ADULT] [−MALE]). Prototype theory, within a cognitive linguistics framework, offers the possibility of theorizing the fuzziness of meaning, the indeterminacy of many category boundaries, and the importance of metaphor to conceptual systems.

Dirk Geeraerts provides a very useful theoretical framework for this kind of work in historical semantics in his book *Diachronic Prototype Semantics* (1997). Geeraerts recategorizes the traditional types of semantic change – generalization (broadening), specification (narrowing), pejoration (deterioration), and amelioration – under semasiological change (i.e., when existing words take on new meanings) of (a) denotational meaning, which includes specification and generalization as well as analogy, metaphor, and metonymy; and (b) non-denotational meaning, which includes pejoration and amelioration. Non-denotational meaning (often referred to as connotation) can include: emotional meaning (expressing the speaker's attitude toward the concept), stylistic meaning (the speaker's evaluation of the word's appropriacy in a given context), and discursive or pragmatic meaning (the term's conversational function and value). Particularly relevant for the study of words for male and female human beings is Geeraert's connection of non-denotational meanings to social constructs and belief systems: "Because the emotive meaning of words involves the expression of values and evaluations, emotive meanings characteristically reflect the existence of social structures (as in cases involving euphemism), or the way in which a particular social group is stereotypically appreciated . . ." (Geeraerts 1997: 100). (And with respect to words for women in English, "appreciated" can often seem a euphemism.)

The fuzziness of meaning and categorization as well as the importance of non-denotational meanings tied to cultural values makes clear the impossibility of predicting semantic change. Perhaps the best that can be achieved is creating in retrospect some coherence accompanied by plausible explanations, accepting that we cannot possibly account for all the complexity of meaning or all the factors affecting speakers. As Geeraerts aptly summarizes, placing an appropriate emphasis on the role of speakers in semantic change: "[I]f the ultimate motivation for change consists of the expressive needs of language users, then there is an inevitable moment of freedom in the way languages develop: language users ultimately *choose* a particular solution for the expressive problems facing them" (*ibid.*: 151). As Kleparski also notes, Geeraerts sets up one of the more useful explanatory frameworks for semantic change, stating that any explanation must consist of: (1) an overview of the range of possible changes (including mechanisms of semantic change); (2) factors that cause speakers to realize one of these possibilities; and (3) an examination of how change spreads through the linguistic community.

The more speaker-oriented perspective espoused by models such as Geeraerts's is critical to conceptualizing how words change meaning over time. Given that speakers are active participants in language formation and change, the concept of "communicative need" should be included as a factor in the analysis of any semantic change. Word meaning is inextricably intertwined with the extralinguistic world and with speakers' attempts to talk about their perspective on that world; speakers' expressive needs, therefore, strongly influence new word creation and changes in use and meaning of existing words within a speech community (the realization of possibilities, as Geeraerts puts it).[4] Relying on a Gricean model in which meaning depends on a kind of relation between speaker and hearer, McConnell-Ginet (1989: 37) explains the general process of how discursive actions become conventionalized meaning: "The production of meaning designates the processes through which speakers mean something by what they say (or writers by what they write) and through which hearers (or readers) interpret what is said (or written). The reproduction of meaning refers to our dependence, in producing meanings, on previous meanings or interpretations, to our dependence in particular on one another's experience with the linguistic form being used."[5]

Importantly, as McConnell-Ginet (*ibid*.: 44–46) notes, semantic pejoration relies on common, shared stereotypes so that negative meanings attached to the use of a neutral word in a given context in a negative way make sense (i.e., can be interpreted), even if they are not shared by the hearer; later this more negative connotation can become a denotation not dependent on a shared stereotype – dependent only on prior use of the word in a negative manner. In other words, a word such as *princess* can only be understood as a negative term for women given a shared stereotype that princesses (or royal women more generally) are, for example, demanding, fussy, spoiled, unable to take care of themselves, etc.

Even with a more discourse-oriented or speaker-based model of semantics, it can be easy to fall into historical semantic explanations that describe words changing meanings rather than speakers using words with a different meaning, in part because the written records that remain generally cannot recapture the dynamics of discourse. In addition, the overall systematicity of language can encourage explanations based on language structure. The histories of words often seem to lend themselves to functional explanations; in the literature written on the development of words for adults and children in English, the word *need* crops up fairly often. This "need" is often discussed in a structural framework, accompanied by ideas such as "holes" in a given semantic field "pulling in" a new word as a "slot-filler" (see, for example, Samuels 1972: 63–67). Perhaps a more useful way to think of "need" is communicative need, especially in the field of semantics, which is so closely tied to the extralinguistic world of speakers and referents; communicative need as well as avoidance of ambiguity and the

---

[4] McConnell-Ginet (1989), who has also pursued important work in prototype theory related to gender, specifically addresses the relationship of sexist discourse to sexist semantics, arguing that sexism in a community has implications for how members speak and how speech is evaluated.

[5] Wolfe (1989), within a similarly discourse-oriented framework, links child language acquisition to semantic change, noting that semantic change occurs in part when children process a lexical usage as the denotation of a word rather than an idiosyncratic usage or extension; this is also how metaphorical extensions become lexicalized to the point that the metaphor is no longer active (e.g., *crane* for the construction machinery; see Goatly 1997 for more details).

maintenance of communicative clarity can effectively explain many lexical innovations and shifts in meaning.[6]

In sum, the concept of "meaning" should be defined broadly enough to encompass both emotive (or connotative) meanings and denotative meanings. It is the emotive meanings of words that are often first affected by speakers' attitudes and expressive needs, and these subtle shifts can eventually lead to denotative changes. This explanation presents a fuzzy picture of the diachronic semantic field with near-synonyms in flux, used variably given discursive and social factors. For the same reasons, semantic change is complex and difficult to chart many centuries later. Many words are polysemous (i.e., they simultaneously carry multiple meanings) with meanings that have subtle connotations that may not be available to the historical linguist. Historical semantics is often tracing the shift of "functional weight" as some meanings become more central and others more peripheral, while simultaneously new meanings get added (e.g., through metaphorical extension) and others become obsolete (or relegated to specific registers or dialects). Speaker-based and functional approaches to semantics cannot explain why some terms remain peripheral or die, but no general theoretical approach in historical semantics has yet to be able to explain this satisfactorily.

The semantic development of words for women began to receive serious attention with the establishment of feminist linguistics in the 1970s, but historical semantic work has consistently been overshadowed by examinations of current sexist vocabulary and usage. Robin Lakoff (1975) notes the asymmetrical development of words such as *master/mistress* and *bachelor/spinster* but does not pursue this point in detail; later scholars such as Romaine (1999: 92–95) also note these patterns as part of broader discussions. Two of the most cited studies are Stanley 1977b, in which she argues for the existence of over 200 synonyms for 'female prostitute,' and Schultz 1975 on the semantic derogation of women. The overwhelming argument of feminist scholarship, given these asymmetries and lexical concentrations, has been that female-referential terms undergo pejoration more often than male-referential terms.

The prevalence of evaluative semantic developments – almost entirely negative – for words for girls and women has been much discussed in scholarship over the past few decades (cf. Gibbens 1955, Schultz 1975, Baron 1986,

---

[6] Functionalist explanations of language change are more effective at explaining the past than at predicting the future, but it can also be argued that linguistics, much like evolutionary biology, is not required to be a predictive science. The types of ambiguity or redundancy a language will and will not tolerate can be determined only in retrospect, as is also the case with the "functional needs" of a language at any given point in time. Yet, historical explanations based on the avoidance of ambiguity and the maintenance of communicative clarity often convincingly account for the direction of language change. Functional explanations should be not dismissed on general theoretical grounds, but rather should be tested against other available evidence; as Geeraerts (1997: 152) points out: "Because a language lives only through the linguistic activities or its users, linguistics deals with purposive actions rather than blind causality, and its method of explanation should be chosen accordingly."

Hughes 1991). Kleparski (1997: 100), in the most comprehensive study of historical synonyms for 'girl, young woman' available, concludes that the historical pejoration of words for women "needs neither further elaboration nor illustration." However, there is value to exploring what these semantic paths can reveal about cultural attitudes, simultaneously not oversimplifying "patriarchal influence" on or "sexism" in the language yet recognizing and analyzing the ways that derogation infects so many words referring to women and to children. As part of this process, as Kleparski also notes, scholars should work to complicate feminist understandings of such developments as the universalizing of pejoration: in fact, for example, not all words for females undergo entirely negative developments, and words for boys are not exempt from pejoration. A study by Ng, Chan, Weatherall, and Moody (1993) indicates that female-related words can be semantically upgraded if subjects demonstrate a favorable attitude toward women; at the same time, they note that semantic changes "encode not so much the attitudinal biases of the population at large but those of the more powerful groups in particular" (Ng *et al.* 1993: 78).

A second pervasive notion in feminist scholarship – that there are more derogatory terms for women than for men (see Schultz 1975, Stanley 1977b, Sutton 1995) – has recently been brought into question by some feminist scholars. Persson (1996) and James (1998) argue that there are more male-referential derogatory terms than female-referential ones – contradicting earlier feminist assertions but not completely invalidating the arguments that such feminist work has made about the negative sexualizing of women.[7] James (1998) argues that the majority of insulting terms for men focus on evaluating men by their accomplishments, particularly their competency in mental and physical abilities; derogatory terms for women often involve sexuality, focusing on women's attractiveness to men, faithfulness, availability, and objectifying them as sex objects (see James 1998, Liske 1994: 359). However, there are also many sexualized derogatory terms for men.

McConnell-Ginet (1989: 41) draws interesting connections between recent findings about gender difference in discourse and the construction of male-centered semantic spheres: if men talk more often and they more often are attended to, then they are more likely to have a chance to express their perspective and their terms have a better chance of becoming accepted and known.[8] It is interesting here to compare findings that women know men's slang but men do not know women's (Sutton 1995), and that women use male-biased terms but men do not use (and/or know?) female-biased derogatory terms for men, so that these terms are unable to act as sanctions on male behavior (James 1998: 409).

---

[7] The study by Sankis, Corbitt, and Wideiger (1999) presents the flip side of these studies: they conclude from their study that there are more "socially desirable trait terms" available in English to describe women than there are to describe men.

[8] Along similar lines, James (1998) argues that derogatory language toward women reflects a male-centered view of the world, because the insults about women's sexuality are insults only if taken from a heterosexual male perspective.

Fundamentally, Kleparski's (1997) emphasis on the "singularity of semantic change" is critical: the centrality of individual words and the individuality of semantic change. Each word, in many ways, has its own story to tell. And yet, the historical semantic patterns of words that refer to similar referents are often undeniable, so the story of one word may be revealing about more than just that word's meaning and history.

5.3   When boys could be girls

During World War II, the English words *boy* and *girl* acquired radical, even potentially deadly, new meanings: *boy* could refer to any nuclear device that exploded successfully, and *girl* to any that failed to explode. The bomb dropped on Hiroshima in 1945, in other words, was a very healthy boy. The employment of this kind of gender terminology has clear implications for the study of how gender biases manifest themselves in language. According to Jane Mills (1989: 105), whose feminist dictionary leaves the sexual symbolism of this language – the explosion of boy bombs – untouched, this innovation in bomb terminology is an example of a long-standing tradition in patriarchal societies: the higher value placed on a male child than on a female child. A boy is a success, a girl a failure; a boy bomb explodes, a girl bomb does not. The semantic shifts in a language – in this case, the extension in meaning of the words *boy* and *girl* – can reflect the cultural values of its speakers.

To begin at "the beginning" is to discover how little language historians know about the origins of the words *boy* and *girl* and that, unlike *man* and *woman*, this pair is not etymologically related. (It is worth noting that many words for 'boy' and 'girl' are of difficult or unknown etymology.) Both these words appear in English after the shift to a natural gender system, so they enter the language as semantically rather than grammatically gendered words.

The editors of the *OED* state that the word *girl* is of "obscure etymology," and Liberman (1998: 150) describes *girl* as "one of the most controversial words in English etymology." In its first appearance in thirteenth-century Middle English texts, the word (spelled variously *girle*, *gerle*, *gyrle*) means 'young child.' The *OED* suggests that *girl* may owe its origins to Old English masculine *gyrela*, feminine *gyrele* (Old Teutonic types *gurwilon-*, *-ôn-*). The editors of the *OED* add that such derivational obscurity for *girl* is not unusual: the words *boy*, *lad*, and *lass* also have difficult etymologies, and probably "arose as jocular transferred uses of words that had originally a different meaning." The *MED* presents two possible etymologies for *girl*, both with an introductory question mark to indicate the uncertainty of the information: "(1) ? OE *gyrela* (from earlier *gurw-*); (2) ? Akin to OE *gierela* (from *garw-*), 'a garment.'"

Robinson (1968: 233–40) collects evidence to support the second etymology proposed in the *MED* (OE *gierela*) in conjunction with the *OED* suggestion of "jocular transference." Trends in various European vocabularies suggest that often the "clothes" quite literally become the "person": that is, a term referring to apparel comes to designate the wearer of the apparel. Robinson argues that the word *gyrela* (also *gerela*, *gi(e)rela*), which is documented in Old English with the meaning 'dress, apparel (worn by either sex),' extended its meaning from 'dress' to 'young person' during the Old English period.

Liberman (1998), who has produced an impressive amount of valuable scholarship to tracing the etymologies of words with unknown origins, provides a very useful survey of scholarship on the etymology of *girl*, and he dismisses Robinson's argument as unfounded. Liberman supports the hypothesis (proposed earlier by Hensleigh Wedgwood and Walter W. Skeat) that *girl* represents a borrowing of the Low German *Gör* 'girl' with a diminutive suffix -*l* in the thirteenth century – a relatively late coinage with a "humble" etymon (i.e., one that cannot be traced back to Indo-European). In both Low German and English, *Gör(e)/girl(e)* appears more often in the plural as the gender-unspecified 'children,' and Liberman argues that even this early "'young female' must have been one of its well-realized senses" (Liberman 1998: 160).

The etymological origins of *boy* are as difficult to trace as those of *girl*. Labeling the word as "of obscure etymology," the *OED* presents the traditional hypothesis of West Germanic origins for *boy*, citing in support similar words in East Frisian (*boi*, *boy*) and Dutch (*boef*), the latter probably adopted from Middle High German *buobe*. The *MED* includes subsequent scholarship on the subject, offering an Old French etymology rather than a Germanic one: *(em)buié*, *(em)boié* 'fettered, shackled' (past participle of *embuiier*). Dobson (1940: 121–54) was early to advance the theory of the word's Romance roots: he maintains that the word has its origins in Anglo-Norman *un embuié* (*emboié*) 'a man in fetters, a slave, serf' – derived from the Old French verb *embuiier* 'to fetter.' Diensberg (1981: 79–87), who has studied the etymology of 'child' words extensively, criticizes some of Dobson's phonological evidence as well as his failure to adequately explain the loss of the Old French prefix *em-* or of the ending -*é* in the Middle English form of the word; he suggests instead that the word stems from Old French *baiasse/-esse* 'woman servant,' a term documented at the end of the twelfth century. But Diensberg, in turn, cannot provide sufficient reasons why this word did not enter English as *baiesse* 'female servant,' but rather as the back-formation *boi-*, with the native masculine suffix -*e* added.

A more recent piece by Liberman (2000), part of his ongoing research on words of unknown etymology, returns to the theory of Germanic origins, and in his well-documented proposal he also provides an interesting possible linguistic explanation of the phrase "oh boy." Liberman hypothesizes a prehistorical blend of two different roots: *boi(a)* 'younger brother' and *bo-* 'devil.' This etymology, he argues, helps to explain the apparently contradictory meanings of *boy* in Middle English of 'male servant, attendant' and 'ruffian.' In addition, the expression "oh boy!" may be a last trace of the meaning 'devil' – that we are invoking the devil rather than a young child in moments of frustration or wonder. (However, the existence of other male-referential exclamations such as "Man!" and "Oh brother!" raises the question of whether the more generic use of certain male-referential terms has allowed them to infiltrate vocative and exclamatory constructions; see Clancy 1999: 287.) Liberman's discussion emphasizes how perplexing it seems that such a derogatory meaning ('scoundrel') could have co-existed with an affectionate one ('boy'). Yet, if one looks at the history of words for girls and women, this kind of semantic coexistence does not seem so surprising. Samuel Johnson, in his dictionary, defines *wench* as 'a young woman' or 'a young woman in contempt; a strumpet.' He then defines *trull* with the fairly neutral 'a girl, a lass, a wench,' whereas a *hussy* is 'a bad woman, a worthless wench,' a *doxy* is a 'whore, a loose wench,' and a *malkin* is a 'dirty wench' (a term derived from the mop used to clean ovens). It is either entirely perplexing or entirely possible that words for both males and females can maintain both more neutral and more derogatory meanings simultaneously, at least for some period of time within one speech community.

Whatever its origins, when the word *boy* (spelled *boie*) first appears in English during the latter half of the thirteenth century, it means 'male servant, attendant' and 'worthless fellow,' according to the *OED*. Dobson (1940: 133), citing evidence from the morality and miracle plays, attests that this latter use of the word, as a term of contempt or abuse, was more common in the medieval period. By the first half of the fifteenth century, the word *boy* had acquired the familiar meaning of 'male child,' which seems in some ways to defy the negative connotations associated with its earlier recorded meanings. In other words, while pejorative meanings often seem to become more central for words, forcing more neutral or positive meanings to become peripheral or obsolete, in this case, pejorative meanings do not seem to have been determinative of the direction of the word's semantic changes. Dobson (1940) posits for the word *boy* transitional meanings of 'male servant child' and 'man,' meanings possible because indiscriminate use of *boy* as an abusive term led to a reduction in the word's semantic power. This is certainly a viable scenario for the word's semantic development, but it must be noted that most other 'child' words, once they have acquired negative denotations or connotations, have undergone only further pejoration. What seems clear is that the written record is insufficient for capturing the motivations of change and the transitional meanings or connotations of *boy*, leaving scholars to hypothesize about the word's discursive meaning in speech during the period. What written records for this period do indicate is that *girl* could still be used to refer to all children, hence the title of this section: "when boys could be girls."

Before the Norman Conquest and the subsequent appearance of *boy* and *girl*, Old English demonstrates a relatively stable development of words in the lexical fields for children. Bäck (1934), in the most comprehensive study of Old English words for 'child,' 'boy,' and 'girl' to date, concludes that there was a primary pair of words during the period for all three meanings: one form was more dominant in early Old English and the other form became more dominant in later Old English – perhaps slightly too simplified a picture, but nonetheless useful as a preliminary guide for categorizing the textual evidence. For 'child,' there was a gradual shift from the word *bearn* to *cild*; for 'boy,' the word *cniht* gave way to *cnapa*; and for 'girl,' the word *fæmne* was replaced by *mægden*. The coming of the French in 1066, however, shook these Old English lexical fields to their foundations. Soon there were the French *bacheler*, *squire*, *garsoun*, and *servant* mixing with the English *knight* and *knave*, not to mention the foreign *damsel* intermingling with the native *wench* and *maiden*. Then ensued the deterioration in meaning for the young *knave*, *wench*, and *maid*, as well as the linguistic death (i.e., obsolescence) of the young *cnapa* and *fæmne*.[9]

Already evident in this discussion of the historical development of words for children in English is the historically close relationship between the lexical fields for children and for servants in English (and in other European languages). The two fields are often referred to as "adjoining" due to the relatively frequent movement of words between them. But it does not appear to be a two-way street for most words, with the notable exceptions of the word *boy*, as well as *knight* and *damsel*. Words have shifted their primary meaning almost exclusively from 'child' – male or female – to 'servant,' and from there, often to a morally or sexually depraved person. One possible explanation for this tendency is the existence of numerous semantic features shared between the lexical fields for children and servants: a lower status in the home and in the family; a dependent position; lack of education. And there is evidence for many of these words that they were polysemous across these fields for extended periods of time; for example, *maid* could be used to mean both 'girl' and 'female servant' for several centuries. Semantic pejoration appears to occur more often than amelioration in the lexicon generally – negative connotations powerfully influence a word's development and are not easily cast aside – which helps explain why words referring to servants do not often move "up" to more connotationally neutral words for children. The reverse pattern of semantic change, from 'child' to 'servant,' and then possibly to someone even lower in the social hierarchy, occurs in the etymological development of many 'child' words.

According to the *OED*, in late Old English or early Middle English, the word *child* extended to encompass several other meanings in addition to 'child of either sex.' It was still carrying the meaning of 'fetus' from early Old English, and it came to refer also to 'descendant, son or daughter.' In a development of particular relevance to this study, *child* gained several gender-specific meanings during the Middle English period, all of them male (as recorded in the *MED*): (1) 'a schoolboy, choirboy'; (2) 'a young man, youth, lad; youth in service'; (3) 'a youth of noble birth, an aspirant to knighthood.' Diensberg (1985: 332–33) notes that such specification of the dimension [SEX] often coincides with a reverse development in the specification of [ADULT]; in other words, the addition of the feature [+MALE] coincides with the generalization to [±ADULT]. This kind of binary feature analysis may simplify the semantic factors involved, but evidence

---

[9] The last quotation for *knape* 'male child' in the *OED* is in 1300 and the last quotation in the *MED* is 1330; there are a few scattered references to *knape* 'servant' through the eighteenth century. The relationship of *knape* and *knave* (OE *cnafa*) is unclear. The obsolescence of *fæmne* occurs early enough that it is not recorded in the *OED* or *MED*.

clearly suggests a greater potential age range in the male references for *child* in Middle English than there was in Old English, ranging anywhere from a boy to a young man. Evidence for these sex-specific, male meanings of *child*, including 'youth in service' and 'youth aspiring to knighthood,' dies out by late Middle English – and it seems only logical to relate this development to the borrowing in Middle English of Romance words such as *bacheler*, *garsoun*, and *squire*, which became dominant in the lexical field of young men, particularly those in the service. By late Middle English, the primary meaning of *child* was 'youth of either sex.'

In terms of other words referring to boys or young men, by early Middle English, the Old English form *cnapa* had become peripheral for 'boy' and was generally used only in southern dialects. It is the nature of historical semantics that there is no explanation for why this word was not favored by speakers for survival while its predecessor *cniht* survived. The word *cniht* shifted its primary meaning to 'servant' (a shift that could be interpreted as pejoration or deterioration), and came to refer also to a military servant of the king (or other person of high rank). As the editors of the *OED* explain the ameliorative development of this word: "In the fully-developed feudal system: One raised to honourable military rank by the king or other qualified person, the distinction being usually conferred only upon one of noble birth who had served a regular apprenticeship (as page and squire) to the profession of arms, and thus being a regular step in this even for those of the highest rank." So by the sixteenth century, *knight* came to refer to a man of a certain military rank, a title conferred by the sovereign in recognition of merit or as a reward.[10]

According to *OED* evidence, by Middle English, much of the functional weight in the lexical field 'boy' had been taken on by *knaue*, which meant both 'boy' and 'servant' in Old English. By 1300, there is also evidence for *knaue* referring to a 'commoner, peasant' (in opposition with 'knight'), which seems to coincide with a lowering of the word's meaning in the lexical field 'servant' to 'low-ranking servant, stable-boy' (the emotive meanings associated with the first meaning likely affected the second). By late Middle English, not only had *knaue* become peripheral in the lexical field 'boy,' but it was also becoming peripheral in the lexical field 'servant,' as it was developing the more pejorative meaning of 'rascal, ruffian' (Bäck 1934: 329). This negative specification of *knaue* to 'rascal,' which seems to have made the word less frequently used for 'boy,' coincides with late Middle English evidence that much of the functional weight for the meaning 'boy' shifts to the word *boy*. Again, for no known or apparent reason, the words *grome*, *ladde*, and *felaue*, also available to late Middle English speakers, did not successfully compete with *boy*; they either remained restricted to certain dialect areas or developed pejorative meanings similar to *knaue*.

[10] Noah Webster (1864), in his American dictionary, attributes this shift in meaning to the pugnacious pastimes of previous generations: "Originally, a knight was a youth, and young men being employed as servants, hence it came to signify a servant. But among our warlike ancestors, the word was particularly applied to a young man after he was admitted to the privilege of bearing arms."

How and/or why did the word *boy*, which first appears in the language meaning 'servant' and 'ruffian,' shift to refer to a male child in general? Diensberg (1985: 331) proposes that the word was redundant in the lexical field 'servant,' which encompassed numerous native and romance (near-)synonyms. Such redundancy cannot explain, however, why *boy* was not pushed in the same direction as *knaue*, towards 'worthless fellow.' *Boy* is one of the few words in English to defy the 'child' > 'servant' pattern of semantic shift. Diensberg proposes that dropping the semantic feature of serving is similar to adding it, but this hypothesis begs the question of why dropping the feature does not happen more often. It seems that the negative connotations associated with the meaning 'male servant' allow this word the possibility of reprieve and semantic amelioration in a way that the negative connotations associated with other 'servant' words (both male and female) do not. Cases such as this one may highlight how much of the nuance of words' denotations, connotations, and discourse implications is lost in text-based historical semantics. With the word *knight*, which also refers to 'male servant' in Middle English and then undergoes subsequent amelioration, the editors of the *OED* provide some conjecture about how use in the context of military service may have fostered this extension and eventual shift in primary meaning. With *boy*, we are left to speculate, as Dobson has, on possible weakening of negative connotations or the extension of playful or slang uses of the word. These places where patterns break down and the singularity of semantic change becomes evident should emphasize for speakers and scholars the complexity of explaining semantic change, let alone predicting it. We create patterns in retrospect, in the same ways that we weave narratives, imposing structure and linearity on the workings of language. This fact does not necessarily invalidate the patterns that we find – they often correspond with social structures and belief systems. But it is important to remember that the patterns often do not feel like patterns to the speakers of any particular historical moment as they use these words in conversation or writing, and if they notice semantic change, it may only be to critique the slang or informal usage of the younger generation – the young people to whom the words *boy* and *knight*, *girl* and *maiden* refer – or the lexical features of less familiar language varieties.

Words referring to female children seem to demonstrate an even stronger tendency to follow the apparent 'child' > 'servant' pattern in early English. In all of Middle English data presented in Kleparski (1997) on synonyms for 'girl, young woman,' there is perhaps only one word, the Romance borrowing *damsel*, which seems an exception: its earliest recorded meaning in English is 'female servant' and it is later employed to mean 'girl, young woman' (see Kleparski 1997: 143–48). By early Middle English, the Old English form *mægden* had both lost its neuter gender in the grammatical gender system to become semantically and (consistently) grammatically feminine and it had split into two forms: *maiden* and *maide*. Both *maid* and *maiden* came to be used in Middle English to mean not only 'female child' but also 'virgin' and 'female servant.' Kleparski argues for 'virgin' as the prototypical meaning for *maiden* because it serves as the basis for extension of the word to refer to males in the period (i.e., 'male virgin,' available through the sixteenth century) and this meaning is still evident in the modern adjective (e.g., *maiden voyage*). The word *maiden*, unlike other terms for female children, may never have undergone significant pejoration in later centuries (and it came to be obsolete in reference to servants) because it carried religious implications, in particular to the Virgin Mary.

Diensberg argues that by the end of the thirteenth century, *mægden* had surrendered the meaning 'female child' to the word *wench* (spelled *wenche*), which developed from Old English *wencel* 'child' (a neuter noun, like Old English *cild*). Kleparski, however, provides convincing evidence that the three words *maid*, *maiden*, and *wench* coexisted in Middle English as near-synonyms for 'girl.' During the Middle English period, the word *wench* seems to have taken on two additional meanings: in a parallel development to *knaue*, *maid*, and *maiden*, the word extended from the more neutral meaning 'girl' to encompass reference to 'female servant,' as well as to the more negative 'mistress, prostitute.' (Moral depravity, it seems, turns knaves into rascals but turns wenches into prostitutes.) Kleparski, like other scholars before him, presents as one triggering factor of this specification etymological connection to the Middle English adjective *wankel* 'unsteady, tottery': its connotations of 'weakness,' often associated with women, could have infected the development of *wench* – although Wolfe's caution about bias in etymologies (see note 2) seems appropriate in this context. Early dictionaries find many euphemistic ways to describe this new meaning – "woman of ill fame," "a bold, forward girl; a young woman of loose character," "a young woman in contempt; a strumpet" – but the implications for the word *wench* and its female referents seem clear.[11] Yet, at the same time, some of these very same dictionaries also use *wench* in more neutral ways, in apposition with *girl* – demonstrating lingering polysemy for this word, at least in the minds of some speakers. And the polysemy seems to include 'girl,' 'female servant,' and 'prostitute, woman of ill repute' at least through the Early Modern English period. In 1619, Thomas Deloney can write in his novel *Jack of Newbury*: "I account the poorest wench in my house too good to be your whore" and "what woman, I haue beene a pretty wench in my dayes, and seene some fashions"; as well as use *wench* and *maiden* apparently interchangeably – "[he] at length fell in liking of one of his maidens, who was as faire as she was fond. This lustie wench hee so allured with the hope of marriage, that at length she yielded him her loue" (as cited in the Helsinki Corpus).

Kleparski (1997) provides a range of other synonyms for 'girl, young woman' in Middle English, including: *lass* (also meaning 'lady-love' and 'female servant'), *damsel*, *pucelle*, *daughter*, *may*, and *bird*, as well as a host of more peripheral

---

[11] These definitions are taken from (in order): Noah Webster's *American Dictionary of the English Language* (1828), John Ogilvie's *The Imperial Dictionary of the English Language* (1882), and Samuel Johnson's *A Dictionary of the English Language* (1822). Johnson's and Ogilvie's dictionaries also provide the definition 'young woman,' a sense Webster notes is "little used."

synonyms such as *file*, *maiden-child*, and *gill/jill*. Kleparski suggests that the use of *bird* in the Middle English period may be the earliest example of an animal synonym for 'girl.'[12] There is no known evidence for any such animal synonyms in Old English, but, as discussed in Chapter Three, men are much more the focus of discourse than women in the extant texts and the generally more formal nature of the documents may preclude the recording of many more colloquial expressions for men, women, boys, and girls. In any case, it is in late Middle English, when wenches are falling into sin and *maid* and *maiden* have taken on more specific meanings including 'virgin' and 'female servant,' that *girl* shifts to take on 'female child' as a more primary meaning, filling a functional role *wench* no longer could or did.

The exact, or even approximate, date in Middle English of the shift in meaning for the word *girl* from 'youth of either sex' to 'female child' is still a matter of debate. The *OED* and the *MED* refer to the same set of quotations, but, because they interpret the word's modified forms differently, they arrive at significantly different dates for the shift in meaning. According to the *OED*, the word *girl* carried the meaning 'child' throughout most of the Middle English period, and it had two sex-specific forms: *knaue girl* for 'boy' and *gay girl* for 'girl.'[13] The earliest text which the *OED* cites for *girl* 'girl' is from 1530, whereas the *MED* dates the meaning 'girl' back to 1375, over a century and a half earlier. The *MED* includes four quotations for the meaning 'girl,' dating from 1375 to 1450; of the four, three refer to *gay gerl* and only one (*The Pearl*) records *gyrle* standing unmodified. The dating of the shift in the *MED* seems to rest, therefore, on the interpretation of the modifier *gay*. In all four instances cited, the referent of *girl* (whether singular or plural) is female, but a female referent does not necessarily imply a gender-specific reference word; in other words, the authors could well have been using the equivalent of *child* to refer to girls. It is additionally unclear why the editors of the *MED* do not note the possible use of *gay* as a gender marker. They interpret *knaue* as a male gender marker in *knaue gerlys*, categorizing these *girl* quotations under the heading of 'child of either sex'; they do not similarly address the possibility of *gay* functioning as a female gender marker. The repeated

---

[12] At the same time in Middle English, *stot* could be used in reference to a woman and *crone* to an old woman (Kleparski 1997: 190–91). In Old and Middle English, the *OED* records *stot* referring to 'a horse (?one of an inferior kind),' 'a young castrated ox,' 'a heifer,' and by Chaucer's time 'a term of contempt for a woman.' While this term has died out of usage, *crone* has remained current. The word *crone* is borrowed from Anglo-Norman; it is cited first in the *OED* in 1386 in Chaucer, and it seems to have always been a term of abuse ('an old withered woman' as defined in the *OED*; 'an old prating woman' as defined by Robert Cawdrey in 1604). Given that *crone* is documented in reference to 'old, toothless ewe' from only the mid-sixteenth century (through the mid-nineteenth century), the *OED* editors suggest that the term was taken directly from Old Norman French *carogne* 'cantankerous or mischievous woman' – which is directly related to *carrion* 'carcass,' a connection few Modern English speakers would know or think to make.

[13] The *OED* editors' dating seems to rest on the assumption that *gay* functioned as a gender-specifier (or classifier), but in the entry for *gay*, these same quotations are categorized under 'In poetry: Applied to women, as a conventional epithet or praise.'

occurrence of *gay* as a modifier of *girl* in these quotations, however, cannot be so discounted. In some examples, its appearance can be attributed to alliteration, but *gay girl* also appears in non-alliterative texts, such as Chaucer's *Canterbury Tales*.

The *Canterbury Tales* proves, in fact, to be a useful text for examining the meaning of *girl* in later Middle English. The second quotation under 'girl' in the *MED* is from *The Miller's Tale*: "What eyleth yow? som gay gerl, God it woot, Hath broght yow thus vpon the viritoot." On the citation slips for *girl* at the *MED* offices, there are no notes explaining why the editors believe this use of *girl* is gender-specific.[14] But a note on another Chaucer citation slip proves revealing: it states that in the *Canterbury Tales*, *mægden* is used consistently to refer to girls. The only other instance of *girl* in the *Canterbury Tales* occurs in the *General Prologue*, and the word refers to children in general – a reference cited under this definition in the *MED*: "In daunger hadde he at his owne gyse The yonge gerles of the diocise, And knew hir counseil, and was al hir reid." Given the scanty evidence that the word *girl* carried a gender-specific meaning in the late fourteenth century, it seems unlikely that Chaucer is employing the term alone to mean 'female child' in *The Miller's Tale*, especially given the presence of *gay* as a possible specifier. This reading raises serious questions about the justification for dating the origins of the gender-specific use of *girl* to as far back as the fourteenth century.

By early Modern English, the prototypical meaning of the word *girl* seems to have shifted fully from 'child' to 'girl': the last citations for the meaning 'child of either sex' in both historical dictionaries are from the mid-fifteenth century. As Kleparski's study of Early Modern English synonyms for 'girl, young woman' makes clear, *girl* coexisted throughout this period with a range of other words in the field, including: *trull, pigeon, tit, slut, miss*; the less central *demoiselle, urchin, nymph, minx, baggage, filly*; and more peripheral terms such as *kitty, Gillan, tib*, and *mop*. Both *slut* and *miss* are interesting for the ways in which they seem (given written evidence) to flout the 'child' > 'servant' > 'person of questionable character' pattern: *miss* appears in the seventeenth century meaning both 'immoral woman, whore' and 'girl' (Kleparksi 1997: 221–22); *slut* first appears in the fifteenth century meaning 'dirty, slovenly woman' and 'loose woman,' and then evidence from the seventeenth to nineteenth centuries indicates that it could also mean 'girl.' Another interesting pattern during this period is the proliferation of animal metaphors for 'young female,' a topic that is discussed in more detail below.

---

[14] The process of collecting quotations for the *OED* and the *MED* (a project that developed out of the *OED*) involved readers – solicited originally by the *OED* editor James Murray through advertisements – and editors recording the sentences with the headword on notecards, which were then filed alphabetically and sorted for each word by sense and date, as the editors selected which quotations to include. This description is, obviously, highly simplified; for more details about the making of the *OED*, see Mugglestone 2000, K. M. E. Murray 1977, and Winchester 1998. The relevant *OED* slips were transferred to the *MED* offices in Ann Arbor, Michigan.

For the past five centuries, the word *girl* has maintained a prototypical meaning of 'female child,' even as it has extended to encompass several additional
meanings. In the seventeenth century, *girl* took on the meaning of 'maid servant,'
in an etymological shift reminiscent of so many of its predecessors in the lexical
fields for children. The seventeenth century also saw the word first recorded
as 'sweetheart, lady love,' polysemy similar to the word *lass*. By the early eighteenth century, evidence indicates that *girl* had also come to mean 'prostitute,'
as the word slid down the same path of pejoration as *wench*. The slang dictionary *Slang and Its Analogues*, published between 1890 and 1904, defines *girl* as
both "a prostitute" and "a mistress" (as well as, in the plural, "the sex – or
that part of it which is given to unchastity – in general"). But there is a significant difference between the development of these two words: as *wench* shifted
semantically from 'child' to 'servant' to 'prostitute,' it gradually lost its earlier
meanings as the word's functional weight shifted to new, more negative meanings; the word *girl*, by contrast, has taken on new, and sometimes pejorative,
meanings while retaining the meaning 'female child.' As mentioned earlier, this
coexistence of meanings is similar to that which strikes some scholars as so odd
for *boy*.

Geeraerts (1997: 100) is explicit that pejoration and amelioration do not necessitate the loss or retention of original or earlier meanings. However, the potential
power of new negative connotations and denotations to shift a word's prototypical meaning over time seems undeniable. The words *maid*, *wench*, *slut*, *trull*, and
a host of other words that have meant 'girl' have come to be used primarily as
low or insulting terms for women generally. The adjective *gay*, used in Middle
English as a specifier of feminine gender, seems to be currently losing the semantic sense 'happy' due to its prevalent use also to mean 'homosexual,' thereby
associating the word with a socially stigmatized group. (The extension of terms
from 'female' to 'homosexual male' is discussed in more detail below.) And the
word *bitch*, now used to refer negatively to women, can elicit discomfort when
used in its original meaning of 'female dog' except in specific contexts.[15] At the

---

[15] The word *bitch* has been in the language since Old English, originally referring to a female dog,
and cited as a derogatory reference to a woman ('lewd or sensual woman' in the words of the
OED editors; 'a malicious, spiteful, promiscuous, or otherwise despicable woman' according to
the *Random House Historical Dictionary of American Slang*) in the fifteenth century. In modern
usage, the word has come to refer more often to a difficult or disagreeable woman (as opposed to
a "loose" woman) – and by metaphorical extension, to any disagreeable thing or situation. Sutton
(1995) presents intriguing data about the possible reappropriation of *bitch* by at least some female
speakers – while at the same time it is one of the few derogatory terms women use toward other
women. Sutton points out that *bitch* has not been as fully reappropriated as, for example, *queer*,
but for some women it can serve as a signal of solidarity and represent an alternative model of a
social world in which women are strong and outspoken – and still "acting like women" (Sutton
1995: 288–90). Smitherman, in *Black Talk* (2000: 69), describes the word as a generic term for a
female used by women among themselves; she adds that men also use the term generically, but
"use of the term by males may not be accepted by all women." Like many other (particularly
derogatory) words for women, *bitch* has taken on new meanings in reference to homosexual men

same time, it is important not to oversimplify the effect on words of acquiring negative connotations, here specifically with respect to words referring to young females. For example, *maiden*, which meant both 'virgin' and 'female servant' has narrowed as a noun to an archaic or "fairy tale" reference to a young woman of noble birth, similar to *damsel*, which entered the language meaning 'servant' and seems to defy the general "path of pejoration" of many other words for women. As Kleparski and others rightly argue, each word has its own history. In addition, in tracing words from Old and Middle English into Modern English, modern scholars clearly only have part of the story. The complexity of words' connotations and discursive distribution cannot be captured in the limited corpora of texts available in the history of early English, especially in terms of the more pejorative uses, which may well have been taboo in certain contexts. The use of words such as *boy* and *girl* within particular discourse and speech communities, be they regional or social or otherwise, adds another layer of complexity; and it is only in recent decades that specialized dictionaries can provide us with some insight into words' meanings and discursive implications within such communities as well as speakers' responses to the semantic developments of particular words in reference to themselves or others.

5.4   Defining who can be women and girls

The pejorative meanings that the word *girl* has acquired over the centuries have made the word a source of indignation among many feminist language scholars, who denounce the term on grounds of sexism. In the *Handbook of Nonsexist Writing*, Miller and Swift (1980: 70–71) explain:

> What separates the women from the girls – linguistically as well as biologically – is age. A person may appropriately be called a 'girl' until her middle or late teens. After that, although her family and close friends may go on calling her a girl with impunity, most red-blooded women find the term offensive. Just as *boy* can be blatantly offensive to minority men, arousing feelings of helplessness and rage, so *girl* can have comparable patronizing and demeaning implications for women.

Because the word *girl* has not undergone the complete pejoration in meaning experienced by *maid* or *wench*, it continues to be at least superficially acceptable in reference to women in polite speech, even as a term of address, and the intent of the speaker in using it is not always clear. Referring to a woman in the workplace or elsewhere as a "girl" may reflect the categorization of women as children, or, particularly in the workplace, it may reflect the categorization of women as hired help. The term *girl* has the power to imply lower social and economic status as

in the twentieth century, including 'a male homosexual who plays the female role in copulation' and 'an ill-tempered or malicious' (or 'despicable') homosexual man (*Random House Historical Dictionary of American Slang*).

well as younger age. This already polysemous word may also have developed into a less specific term of disrespect in these contexts, stemming from negative connotations associated with its pejorative meanings.

A corpus-based study by Sigley and Holmes (2002) provides evidence that the age parameters for the term *girl* remain fluid; while there is an overall decrease in the use of *girl* to refer to adult women since the 1950s (at least in these corpora), *girl* is three times more likely to refer to an adult than *boy* (Sigley and Holmes 2002: 145). The study in Bebout 1995, replicating a 1984 study about gendered terms, similarly attests that the minimum age of *woman* and the maximum age of *girl* are lower in the 1990s. Sigley and Holmes conclude that the semantic boundaries of *girl* are a matter for "continued social negotiation": "The choice between *woman* and *girl* is therefore determined less by objective age than by a cluster of subjective connotations, including immaturity, innocence, youthful appearance, subordinate status, and financial or emotion dependence or vulnerability. Many of these can be seen as features traditionally attractive to men. Meanwhile, *girl* can also be used to invoke familiarity or solidarity (appropriately or inappropriately, depending on the situation)" (Sigley and Holmes 2002: 148–49). The use of *girl* as interchangeable with *girlfriend* could be interpreted as reflecting a view of women as an object of desire (*ibid.*: 147) or as something or someone to be taken care of and/or possessed.

The semantic shift of English words such as *girl* and *wench* to mean 'servant' and 'prostitute,' as well as to serve as general terms of contempt or reflecting subordinate status, cannot be divorced from the history of sexism in English-speaking societies. Still, it is also crucial to note the similar pejoration of 'child' words of the "other," masculine gender, such as *knave, garson, groom*, and even *boy*. Clearly the semantic feature of childishness – and the related, extralinguistic lower social status – is linked to the tendency towards pejoration; this pattern of semantic change is not entirely sex-dependent. Many of these words for children adhere to a pattern of acquiring negative emotive meanings that eventually lead to denotative shifts or shifts in functional weight. The emotive meanings that words acquire often reflect a language community's social structures and attitudes, in this case related to children and the other social groups referred to with 'child' words as well as the association of women with children and/or child-like features.

In Miller and Swift's denouncement of the use of *girl* to refer to women, they mention the use of *boy* as a condescending and offensive term used in reference to minority men. The colonial/imperialist connotations of the word are clear in the *Century Dictionary*, published at the end of the nineteenth century, which points to India, China, and Japan as places where the word is used to refer to "a native male servant, especially a personal servant; a butler or waiter, house-boy, office-boy, etc., as distinguished from a coolie or porter: in common use among foreigners" – and that final usage restriction is telling about the power dynamics at play with this word when used among men. The term *girl*, as well as *wench*, is recorded in reference to black women in nineteenth- and early twentieth-century America. Clarence Major, in *Juba to Jive: A Dictionary of African-American Slang*

(1994: 503), notes that the use of *wench* in reference to black women "originated among white speakers," and adds: "Black people have used the term ironically." The term *wench*, while sometimes used jocularly or ironically in a less pejorative way, remains a negative term for women. On the other hand, as one response to the negative uses of the word *girl*, parts of the English-speaking female community of late twentieth-century America have to varying extents reappropriated the word *girl* as a familiar and friendly way of addressing or referring to another female, particularly a female friend.[16] Smitherman (2000: 79) notes that the word *boy* can be used in some similar ways within the African-American community, with a more restricted sense and pattern of usage: Smitherman explains that while *boy* can be used to *refer* to a male friend or associate, it is rarely used to *address* any black male over eight or nine years old, even within the community.

In the late twentieth century, both the words *boy* and *girl* have also taken on specific meanings in the homosexual community. Again, some of these new uses are often a form of reappropriation – an attempt by speakers of this community to embrace and reclaim labels that had once been slapped upon its members, to deeply derogatory effect (for example, *girl* used in reference to effeminate homosexual men). It is revealing about the status of women and homosexuals in the community that female tags – words such as *girl*, *wench*, *harlot* – seem to be some of the most derogatory language that could be directed towards homosexuals. It equates homosexuals with women at the lowest or basest level, be that childhood or prostitution. Semantically speaking, this new application of female tags could be seen as extending the pejoration of words for females, particularly female children: they often pass from referring to women servants to women prostitutes to male homosexuals, who seem to be regarded as somehow similar to, if not lower than, prostitutes by a hostile heterosexual community. Kleparski advances the theory that words for young women can transfer to refer to men when they come to have meanings in the "domain of sexual activity" (e.g., *maiden*, *tart*, *queen*), which certainly seems to hold true; but importantly, it does not appear to be a transfer to 'male' in a general sense but specifically to homosexual males, no doubt in large part because this category of people has been constructed in reference solely to sexual behavior or orientation.

The word *harlot* (borrowed from Old French) first appears in English in the thirteenth century in reference to men: 'vagabond, villain, rogue, rascal,' later 'buffoon, juggler,' according to the *OED* (see Baron 1986: 42 for historical

---

[16] In this respect, Clancy's analysis (1999: 289–91) of the *guy/girl* pairing may oversimplify the situation. Clancy argues that the "problem" is not the pairing but rather that *guy* still possesses slang overtones whereas *girl* is acceptable in "literary language." However, the fact that *girl* can be used in print to refer to 'young females' and that "female college students also refer to themselves as girls" (*ibid.*: 290), does not mean that all speakers can or should refer to college-age females as *girls* or that the *guy/girl* pair is not potentially sexist. From my own observations, many female college students now refer to themselves as *women*. Bebout (1995: 169, 173) confirms that *woman* is gaining in popularity as a term for females of university age, and that the use of *guy* to refer to males has increased across multiple age groups, including university-age males.

speculations on the word's origins). By the fifteenth century, it also refers negatively to women, specifically to condemned sexual activity – which has become the word's primary meaning in the past few centuries, except that the word can now be applied to men again for condemned homosexual behavior. The word *faggot* also served as a term of abuse for women starting in the sixteenth century and then came to refer to homosexual men in the twentieth century. (The development of the word from the earlier meaning of 'a bundle of sticks' seems to involve metonymy from the specific practice of burning heretics at the stake and attendant expressions such as "to fry a faggot," according to the *OED*.) The words *queen* and *quean*, now homonyms differentiated only by spelling and sometimes used interchangeably in contemptuous reference to homosexuals, stem from two different Old English words: as defined by the *OED*, *cwen* 'a (king's) wife or consort'; and *cwene* 'a woman, a female; from early ME. a term of disparagement or abuse, hence: a bold, impudent, or ill-behaved woman.' The distinction between the two remained strong for centuries, according to *OED* evidence: Langland writes in *Piers Plowman* at the end of the fourteenth century that men should know "a queyne fro a queene," and Byron in 1823 uses the description "queen of queans." Both terms are cited in reference to homosexual men in the early decades of the twentieth century. The use of *queen* for a 'female partner' and *quean* for 'hussy' at various points in the word's histories probably both contribute to the extension of the words to refer to male homosexuals, especially given apparent confusion between the two terms themselves. All of these terms have remained fairly abusive terms referring to homosexuals; however, some previously female terms that became insults for homosexual men have been reappropriated in the gay community: the word *girl* has been taken into the homosexual lexicon to refer to or address a fellow homosexual in a positive way, and the word *boy* is used almost synonymously (Rodgers 1972), as the gay community transforms formerly patronizing and derogatory terms into terms of solidarity.[17]

The "sexualizing" of words for women, which leads to negative connotations and semantic developments as well as the extension to other groups defined by their sexuality, plays out in another clear pattern in the history of words for girls and women: the use of animal metaphors to refer to females – and the pejorative nature of such references has been the source of much modern feminist ire (as has the extension of terms for food to women; see Hines 1994). Feminist

---

[17] The first use of *gay* to refer to homosexuals cited in the *OED* is 1935. Exactly how that semantic transfer or extension occurred is a matter of speculation. The *OED* records earlier uses of the adjective, from the seventeenth century, to describe 'addicted to social pleasures and dissipations' as well as euphemistically 'of loose or immoral life.' By 1825 the *OED* can cite *gay* used specifically in reference to women to describe them as prostitutes. Horn and Kleinedler (2000) argue that the semantic development of *gay* represents R-based narrowing, similar to the development of *man*. In other words, a more general term specifies to refer to a culturally salient subset. In the case of the term *gay*, homosexuality is one culturally salient form of unconventional lifestyle (often associated with "dissipations") and male homosexuals are a salient (i.e., visible) subset of the queer community.

scholarship on animal metaphors for women has generally noted that there are animal metaphors with male referents as well (Persson 1996, Dunayer 1995); but for women these metaphors are entirely derogatory (as opposed to *stud* or *stallion* for men) and often highly sexualized (similar to *stud* and *stallion*), alluding to immorality or prostitution. Such animal metaphors for women typically involve both domestic animals – hence woman as pet or servant – and wild animals – hence woman as desired object and/or prey. As Caitlin Hines (1999: 16) describes the phenomenon: "[W]omen-considered-sexually are described not just as animals, but specifically as those which are hunted or possessed, conflating not just sex and appetite, but quite explicitly, control." Dunayer (1995) argues that references such as *hen* (first used to refer to women and/or wives in the seventeenth century), *cow* (also first recorded in reference to women in the late seventeenth century), and *bitch* emphasize the exploitation and denigration of women for their reproductive capacities as well as disrespect for them as "mindless servants."[18] And the terms that some speakers might see as positive (e.g., *bunny, kitten*) imply child-like weakness and tameability that may only seem like compliments from a male perspective (for more, see Whaley and Antonelli 1983). Kleparski (1997) provides a useful examination of this pattern in Middle English and Early Modern English – material that has been missing from much of the sexist language debate; Hughes (1991: 213–16) provides an invaluable list of such slang terms for women with dates of recorded usage over the past millennium. What becomes clear in all of this historical material, as with the words discussed above, is the complex relationship of gender, age, and semantic change for the words in question.

The use of animal metaphors as derogatory terms for men has at least as long a history as their use for women, but they tend to be derogatory in a different sense. For example, the use of *fox* in reference to a cunning man predates its use for a sexy or attractive woman by many centuries (the reference to women is not cited until 1963 in the *OED*). Sexuality becomes salient in words referring to women in a way that it usually does not in words referring to men. Another example of an animal metaphor reflects the complicated relationship of words for women and children, discussed above: both *chick* and *chicken* are recorded in reference to young children as early as the fourteenth century; by the eighteenth century, both terms could be used for 'a young inexperienced person' – hence the expression "no spring chicken." A quotation cited in the *OED* from G. D. Prentice in 1860 makes clear the potential negative connotations of *chicken* for women: "Call a lady 'a chicken', and ten to one she is angry. Tell her she is 'no chicken', and twenty to one she is still angrier." It is then perhaps not surprising that only *chick*, the term for a baby chicken, came to refer "endearingly" to a girl or young woman, first recorded in the *OED* in 1927.

---

[18] Dunayer's overarching argument is that the linguistic practice of insulting women (and men) with animal metaphors is more deeply rooted in speciesism (prejudice against animals based on a false dichotomy between humans and animals) than sexism. In other words, while calling a woman "a dog" indirectly insults the woman, it directly insults the dog (Dunayer 1995: 12).

The close relationship of words for children and for servants has been noted in previous scholarship and has been important to much of the preceding discussion. What the word histories in this chapter also make clear is the critical relationship of words for children (both human and animal) and words for women. The semantic shifts between these lexical fields may again reflect the effects of shared semantic features, as has been proposed for shifts between the lexical fields for children and servants: lower status in the home (and wider social community), capabilities that are less respected, less independence, etc. In addition, the age distinction between a "girl" and a "woman" is clearly historically contingent. The semantic factors of age, social status, and gender are intertwined; gender is one of many factors in social construction that can affect semantic development. Gender may have more social salience for speakers in many ways and, therefore, a more powerful influence on the history of words, but it should be not be privileged to the point where other semantic and social factors become forgotten or invisible. In this way, these word histories raise important theoretical questions about how most productively to think about the relationship of gender and semantic change, discussed in more detail below.

5.5   Questions of symmetry

The complex webs of meaning that these words for children, women, and men carry also complicate any notion of "symmetry" in the lexicon. Gender is only one factor on which to base pairs, and there is no reason to expect that masculine–feminine pairs will carry similar peripheral meanings and connotations, given social factors and attitudes as well as semantic histories – which allow words to take various paths toward similar prototypical meanings at a given time and thereby leave them with different lingering, peripheral historical meanings or connotations. In addition, as described in more detail below, gender is not a simple masculine–feminine binary, as the use of many of the terms both toward and within the queer community demonstrates.

Specific questions remain to be answered about the development of the lexical fields for children in English. For example, what explains the apparent anomaly that the word *girl* specified to mean 'female child' just as *wench* did? If male is the unmarked gender in English and if most gender-neutral words seem to specify to male if they are going to specify at all (e.g., *man, child*), why did these two words defy the pattern? A related question is why the words *girl* and *wench* both lost their gender-neutral meanings once they took on sex-specific ones. The most obvious, functional answer to the latter question is that for these words, the meanings 'child' and 'girl' were incompatible enough so as to create lexical ambiguity, and, therefore, one of the meanings had to become peripheral and eventually die out. If, however, the meanings 'child' and 'girl' are contradictory enough to cause a lexical shift, it is interesting that 'child' and 'boy' did not seem to have the same contradictory effect in the history of English. When *child* took on the meaning of 'boy' in Middle English, it did not lose its gender-neutral meaning, so that when the word eventually became peripheral in the lexical field for male children, it retained the meaning 'child.' It seems possible for gender-neutral and gender-specific meanings of one word to coexist for some period of time when the gender-specific reference is coming into use (as happened with *girl*, *wench*, and *child* in the Middle English period), but once the gender-specific meaning becomes dominant, the gender-neutral one must become peripheral. Perhaps *child* did not lose its gender-neutral meaning because its specification to the lexical field *boy*, and its subsequent marginalization from that same field by Romance borrowings, happened within a relatively short period of time in Middle English or it was always peripheral for the meaning 'boy.' There is also the distinct possibility that gender-neutral and specifically masculine meanings in one word were not or are not sufficiently contradictory or ambiguous in English-speaking language communities necessarily to cause semantic narrowing or shift within a prototype model of semantics.

The case of *man*, which has technically retained both a gender-neutral and a gender-specific meaning, proves an interesting case as to the extent to which these two meanings may be contradictory. The retention of both meanings for this word may be due in part to the emergence of prescriptivism in English. The gender-neutral meaning of *man* may be, to some extent, an earlier use now preserved in and promoted by dictionaries, grammars, and the "formal" writing adhering to prescriptive rules. If it were not for this form of preservation, many feminist linguists, such as Miller and Swift (1980: 13), argue: "its [*man*'s] ambiguity would have led long ago to its disuse in any but the limited sense it immediately brings to mind [that of 'male human being']." (When *man* lost its generic meaning in English is discussed in more detail in the following section.)

To return to the question of why *wench* and *girl* may have specified to refer to female children, it is possible that the pattern of semantic development exemplified by these two words represents the unmarked pattern ("the norm"), rather than the exception. Historically, there is an observable tendency to use sex-specific terms for male children in contrast to gender-neutral terms for children, which then must be assumed to refer to girls. This phenomenon is illustrated by the word *child* in an *OED* quotation from Shakespeare's *A Winter's Tale*: "A very pretty barne: A boy, or a childe I wonder?" It may be that for children, as opposed to adults, girls are the more culturally salient subset. It has been noted before that words for baby animals often come to refer to women (e.g., *chick*, *kitten*, *bunny*), and it appears that words for human children also show a tendency to specify to refer to females – of all ages. A prime example would be the recent semantic shifts in the English word *babe*, which has come to refer to women, particularly attractive women. And it may be only a short step from there for babes to fall into ill repute like the maids and wenches before them.

It could not have been predicted that nuclear bomb testers would choose *boy* and *girl* to refer to effective and defective bombs or that in mid-twentieth century street slang *boy* would come to refer to heroin and *girl* to cocaine. But there exist patterns in the semantic changes that these words, and other gender-specific terms like them, undergo in reference to humans: a fairly consistent descent on the social ladder from children to servants to outcasts; an objectification or reification of women that is reflected in animal and food metaphors; and the salience of sexuality in the connotations that words for women acquire and the semantic developments they undergo, including extension to other groups of speakers delimited by their sexuality (e.g, homosexual men). It is in the twentieth century that stigmatized or marginalized social groups have made notably successful, conscious efforts to reappropriate these words and take semantic change into their own hands.

5.6   "Man and wife"?

In the climate of heightened language awareness in the ever-increasingly egalitarian and politically correct culture of the United States, when couples take their wedding vows, some of the verbs are changing: men and women promise to love and respect each other, sometimes to honor each other, but rarely now to obey. And before the groom can kiss the bride, they are, at least in the United States, now usually pronounced "husband and wife." Only a generation ago, however, the verb *obey* remained apparently unchallenged and the bride and groom were pronounced "man and wife." This highly anecdotal example raises intriguing questions about words for men and women. When, for example, did this asymmetric pairing – "man and wife" – become established and was there ever a time when it was not semantically asymmetric? The replacement of the word *man* by *husband* clearly reflects the inroads and success of feminism, for this new, more symmetric pairing has become standard. (For example, in a web search of wedding sites, "husband and wife" is typically the only option provided in the fill-in-the-blank formulas for creating "your own" wedding vows.)

The kind of systematic semantic study that could potentially answer such questions has yet to be accomplished; the study presented in this section only scratches the surface of what we could learn if we can master the scope of the task. Similar to the examination of words for boys and girls above, this study also highlights the blurriness of binary boundaries, be they between adult and child or between masculine and feminine. The extent to which words can cross these boundaries raises questions about whether lexical fields should be framed in terms of boundaries or continua or fuzzy sets or some other model; and it requires consideration of the relationship of the social prominence of gender and the linguistic prominence of gender in the language as well as in our analysis of the language. This is not to argue that gender should not be considered a fundamental semantic factor; it is to argue that gender prominence and gender binaries should not be unquestioned assumptions in scholarship – that our understanding of the nature and role of gender should not be unanalyzed – especially when working with earlier periods of the language. We may well work within gender binaries in semantic analysis because speakers, particularly modern speakers, often work within gender binaries when they speak; but these are parameters and categories that we construct, both as speakers and as historical linguists.

Previous studies have established the importance of continuing to pursue historical semantic studies of words for men and women, to gain a better understanding of these lexical fields and their implications for debates about Modern English. Given modern interest in gender and language, it is somewhat surprising that there has not been more progress. In his 1933 study of Old English words for children, Bäck calls for an "investigation into the words for . . . 'man' and 'woman'" (Bäck 1933: 249). Almost fifty years later, Penelope and McGowan (1979), in a brief article about the semantic and social shifts of the words *woman* and *wife* in English, note that such a study of male and female terms has yet to be undertaken. Baron, in his insightful book *Grammar and Gender* (1986), addresses a wide range of issues in the field, including various fanciful etymologies of the words *man*, *woman*, and *wife* and a survey of suggestions in the politically correct language debate, with a focus on the metadiscourse by language observers over the centuries. Hughes (1991), in his book on the social history of swearing in English, compiles a useful list of words used to refer to women over the centuries; however, his categories remain general, and he concentrates primarily on interesting lexical concentrations (what he labels "the angel/whore dichotomy") and lexical gaps (e.g., neutral terms for women). Kleparski (1997) argues that Hughes's dichotomy oversimplifies the data, and he provides the most comprehensive, systematic study of synonyms for 'girl, young woman' in Middle and Early Modern English to date. Given this focus and methodology, Kleparski does not address the implications of this material for modern debates about sexism more than to note that it demonstrates how much more complex the word histories are than feminists typically recognize, and that the semantic fields of words for adult men and women remain mostly uncharted.

An important project focused on the historical study of words for men and women has been undertaken at Umeå University (see Persson and Rydén 1995), which has resulted in papers on various aspects of these lexical fields that begin to fill in the gaps. At this time, however, there still remains a dearth of systematic evidence on questions as fundamental as the timeline of semantic changes that the English word *man* has undergone; in addition, not all of these studies have been brought into dialogue with each other, or with some of the larger theoretical questions being asked in feminist linguistics.

This study of selected word pairings for men and women in the Helsinki Corpus works to pull together some of this scholarship and add at least a few critical details to our understanding of the semantic developments of this lexical set; but the scope of the questions still dwarfs the size of individual studies, even when brought into conversation. As importantly, this study, like the one above about words for boys and girls, raises theoretical questions about how to approach questions of gender in semantics – questions which can be usefully informed by current work in feminist discourse analysis if the two fields of inquiry are brought into dialogue.

The parameters of this particular study are a response to the methodological challenges of studying words for adult human beings systematically. With the

Table 5.1: *Results from a search of the Helsinki Corpus for selected collocational pairs referring to men and women from Old English through Early Modern English*

Old English (850–1150 AD)		Middle English (1150–1500 AD)		Early Modern English (1500–1710 AD)	
wer & wif	22	man & woman	62	man & woman	29
	1 (with -*had*)				
wæpnedmann & wifmann	13	wæpnedmann & wifmann	4	man & wife	9
	2 (with -*cynn*)		5 (NC)		5 (NC)
	1 (NC)				
wer & wifmann	2	carlmann & wifmann	1	husband & wife	5
	1 (NC)				9 (NC)
ceorl & wif	1	woman & husband	3 (NC)	husband & housewife	2
	3 (NC)				
mann & wif	1	husband & wife	2 (NC)	woman & husband	1
	2 (NC)				2 (NC)
mann & wifmann	1			gentleman & lady	2

scope limited to collocational pairs (i.e., pairs of words that tend to co-occur in segments of discourse, either conjoined or simply near each other), a Helsinki Corpus search pulls up a manageable number of hits, which are largely grammatically and semantically comparable, both synchronically and diachronically. The other benefit to setting the parameters in this way is that it provides a mechanism for trying to specify meaning, which is a significant problem with such words. For example, when the Old English word *wif* refers to a married woman, does it mean 'woman' or specifically 'wife'? This distinction is often easier to make when it is paired with, for example, *wer* 'man' versus *ceorl* 'layman, freeman, peasant, man' versus (later) *husband*.

Table 5.1 presents findings from a Helsinki Corpus search of word pairs. The number next to the pair of words represents the number that occur in conjoined parallel constructions: "X and Y," "X or Y," "X nor Y," etc. The table also includes a number for the examples in which the two words occur in close collocational proximity and in parallel constructions, but not conjoined (NC): for example, "If a man loves his wife, and a wife loves her husband."

The Old English results present few surprises in the most common pairings. As most Old English textbooks cite, the sex-specific terms in Old English were generally *wer* 'man' (cognate with Latin *vir*, and it survives only in the now opaque compound *werewolf*) and *wif* 'woman' or *wæpnedmann* 'man' (literally 'weaponed-person') and *wifmann* 'woman' (literally 'female-person'), as *mann* was still commonly used to refer to people generally. The noun *carlmann* was also a possible gender-specific term for males – the noun *carl* being apparently fairly synonymous with *ceorl* in Old English and as an adjective, carrying the meaning 'male.' Examples (1) and (2) provide typical occurrences of these compound phrases.

(1)　Gif mon bið acennen on sunnandæg oððe on nihte, swa wer swa wif . . . (*Prognostications* 297)

　　　'If one is born on Sunday or at night, either a man or a woman . . .'

(2)　. . . & hier folc on tu todælde, ægþer ge wifmen ge wæpnedmen, for þon þe þær wifmenn feohtað swa same swa wæpnedmen. (*Alfred's Orosius* 76)

　　　'. . . and here people divided in two, both women and men, because there women fight the same as men.'

Other example sentences with *wæpned-* and *wif-* effectively demonstrate the compound nature of the words derived from these two forms – and hence the apparent generic status of *mann* in these constructions. In example (3), the first components of the compounds are separated, appearing after the noun *mann*; and in example (4), the forms *wæpned-* and *wif-* appear with *-cynn* and appear to work in the same way, making the terms sex-specific.

(3)　. . . þæt hie woldon ælcne mon, ge wif ge wæpned . . . (*Alfred's Orosius* 108)

　　　'. . . that they wanted every person, both woman/female and man/male . . .'

(4)　Saga me hwilce wihta beoð oðre tid wif kinnes and oþre tid wæpned- kinnes . . . (*Adrian and Ritheus* 38)

　　　'Say to me which creature be sometimes of the female kind and sometimes of the male kind . . .'

The less morphologically symmetrical combination of *wer* and *wifmann* is much less common as a coordinate construction in the Helsinki Corpus results. The sentence in example (5) shows the pair in the same grammatical construction as example (2).

(5)　. . . gemartyrode manega þusenda wide into þas woruld, ægðer ge weras ge wifmen for Cristes geleafan . . . (*Ælfric's First and Second Letters to Wulfstan* 82)

　　　'. . . martyred many thousands widely in the world, both men and women for belief in Christ . . .'

The origins of the Old English neuter noun *wif* are unclear. Baron (1986: 34–37) provides an excellent survey of speculation on the topic, and notes that many scholars have looked for its origins in the supposed duties of a female spouse. As cited in Baron, Skinner (1671) proposed that the word comes from the verb *swive* 'to copulate' in Middle English (in Old English, it meant 'to move or sweep'); Wescott (1978 [1974]) suggested the Indo-European stem *wey-* 'turn, drip, sorcery, fault.' One of the more popular explanations is that it comes from the verb *wefan* 'to weave,' yet in Old English there existed the terms *webbe / webba*. Fell (Fell, Clark, and Williams 1984: 39–40) supports a connection with weaving, pointing out that the division of "weaponed" versus "weaving" makes good sense given the duties linked to the feminine role, and she cites evidence from wills and charters that use all of the following terms for women: *wifhand* 'female inheritor,' *wifhealf* 'woman's (i.e., mother's) side,' and *spinelhealf* 'female line of descent' (*spinel* meaning 'spindle'). It is also a tempting suggestion given similar words for women such as *spinster*, and it makes a pairing like *wifmann* and *wæpnedman* almost symmetric. Other proposed etymologies of *woman* can merge with folk etymologies that are not historically justified: "wife of man," "woe to man," "womb-man" (Verstegan 1605, cited in Baron 1986: 32–33).[19]

In certain contexts, the word *wife* seems to begin to specify to 'married woman' even in Old English, as some of the examples below demonstrate. Old English also witnesses the introduction of the compounded *wifmann*, and the relationship between the two words has been the cause of some speculation. Penelope and McGowan (1979), in their early and strongly feminist piece on *woman* and *wife*, offer this suggestion:

> The OE word w̄if is descended from the IE vocabulary, and it retained its original meaning, 'female human being,' well into the OE period. At the same time, the term was becoming narrower in its semantic range, and eventually it came to mean only 'female attached to a male.' Perhaps as a consequence of the narrower semantic range accorded to the word w̄if, the compound w̄ifman came to be used more and more frequently to mean 'female human being.' . . . It is possible, although there is no way that we could offer empirical evidence for the hypothesis, that both new compounds, w̄ifman and hūsbōnda are lexical items that were simply part of larger shifts in the OE vocabulary that came about as a consequence of increased patriarchal influence during that time. (Penelope and McGowan 1979: 499)

The formation of compounds in English with gender-specific and gender-neutral terms (e.g., *maidencild*, *knaue girl*, as well as *wæpnedman*) is common enough in English that a patriarchy-based explanation seems unnecessary. To what extent the co-existence of multiple lexical forms in reference to 'woman,' including *wif* and *wifmann*, allows or promotes the possible specification of one to 'married woman' is difficult to determine. In addition, in the following examples, it becomes clear that the semantic line between 'woman' and 'married woman' in some contexts is difficult to draw. The extent to which historical developments in the status of women affected semantic changes at the end of the Old English period is also difficult to determine. Fell, Clark, and Williams (1984) argue convincingly

---

[19] While many of these proposed etymologies appear in older literature, they have not entirely died: Louise Gouëffic in *Breaking the Patriarchal Code* (1996: 10), an ardent attack on the patriarchal agenda in language, seems to assume 'wife of man' as a given etymology of *woman*.

that the Norman Conquest and the subsequent imposition of a feudal system
wrested away the more equal rights that women had enjoyed in Anglo–Saxon
times, and this could well be reflected in the lexical developments of gendered
words;[20] in retrospect, however, it is difficult to determine – and probably dangerous to assume – any straightforward connection between, for example, the loss
of economic independence for women and the specification of *wife* from 'woman'
to 'married woman, homemaker.'

The compound *wifmann* also raises the question of the generic status of *mann*.
As example (3) demonstrates, it appears that the compound could still be separated into a generic and a gender-specific component in Old English: "ælcne
mon, ge wif ge wæpned." Fell (1984: 17–19) supports the traditional notion that
for Anglo–Saxons, *mann* carried the primary meaning 'human being' during the
period; Baron (1986: 138–39) notes, however, that in reference to males, *mann*
had already specified in Old English to 'adult male.' The first citation in the
OED for *man* meaning 'adult male' is from Ælfric's *Lives of Saints* (*c*.1000). To
some extent, this question clearly involves when the shift in prototypical meaning
occurred, as the generic meaning of *mann* was clearly possible throughout Old
English and into Middle English – and, of course, some would argue that it is
still possible today, as is discussed below. Example (6) highlights the use of *mann*
in Old English as possibly the most inclusive term for human beings – of both
genders, of all ages (as well as of all intelligences).

(6)   Men ða leofostan, hwæt nu anra **manna** gehwylcne ic myngie & lære,
      ge weras ge wif, ge geonge ge ealde, ge snottre ge unwise . . . (*Blickling
      Homilies* 107)

      'Dear men, what now I remind and advise every one of people [men], both
      men and women, both young and old, both wise and unwise . . .'

The next example shows a more clearly masculine reference for *mann*. It could
be argued that the term is functioning gender-neutrally here, but even so, this

[20] Norberg (1996: 120–21) provides this useful summary of some of the effects of the Norman
Conquest on women, drawing heavily on evidence collected by Fell, Clark, and Williams (1984),
a work I recommend for all readers interested in the historical status of women in medieval
England:

   An Anglo–Saxon lady was, for example, allowed to possess land and take part in public affairs.
   Land was bequeathed on equal terms to men and women in Anglo–Saxon England. Since
   the conception of marriage as a lifelong bond was alien to the Anglo–Saxons before the
   introduction of Christianity, an Anglo–Saxon woman could even leave her husband if she
   wished and get half of their common goods. Another indication of the fact that Anglo–Saxon
   women's position in society was relatively strong is that a man and a woman of the same
   social class had the same wergild ['man payment' or compensation after a wrongful death].
   A medieval great lady, on the other hand, lived in complete submission to her husband. She
   was entitled to no public duties and could not plead in court or make a will of her own.
   In a male-dominated feudal system based on military tenure a woman land-holder was an
   anomaly, unless she was a widow. Only in the absence of a male heir could she inherit land.
   Her property was in the care of her husband, who could even sell land she had inherited
   without her consent.

would exemplify the fairly common tendency in Old English prose – through Modern English prose – for a seemingly generic reference to specify gradually to male (with the appearance of descriptive phrases such as "his wife").

(7)   þæt is on Englisc, ælc man þe sceawað wifman mid luste (*Ælfric's Homilies* 535)

'that is in English, each man who looks upon a woman with lust'

More examples of gender-specific instances of *man* are discussed below in the examination of conjoined *man and woman* phrases.

The word *wif* pairs in Old English with other semantically masculine words (which, as discussed in Chapter Four, are also grammatically masculine) in addition to *wer*. And if *wer and wif* is the more "generic" masculine–feminine pairing, it may be that *ceorl and wif* implies a closer relationship, perhaps marital and/or sexual. For instance, in example (8), the pairing of *ceorl* and *wif* corresponds to the representation of these two people as a couple who together have a child.

(8)   **Gif ceorl & his wif** bearn hæbben . . . (*Alfred's Introduction to Laws* 104)

'If a man and his woman [wife?] have a child . . .'

These examples begin to capture the complicated semantic range of *wif*: whereas in earlier examples, it referred to women generally, here it seems to refer specifically to a married or otherwise "taken" woman, closer to its meaning in Modern English. In other words, the specification to 'married woman' may already be happening to some extent as early as Old English, as this meaning coexists with the more general meaning of 'woman.' But importantly, it should not be assumed that for the prototype of 'woman' in Old English, marriage and/or a woman's relationship to a man was of such salience that it required a lexical differentiation. In other words, we should be careful in our imposition of the modern categorization of women by marital status on linguistic evidence from earlier periods of the language. The collocation of the verbs *ceorlian* and *wifian* supports the idea that the nouns *ceorl* and *wif* together may imply a marital and/or sexual relationship in some instances. Example (9) provides a nicely parallel example of the verbs with *wer* and *wif*; other examples are less symmetrical and typically involve *man* and *wif* – a precursor of the later pairing *man and wife* – as shown in example (10).

(9)   Be þam man mæg witan, þæt hit eallunga riht nis, þæt **wer wifige oðþ on wif ceorlige** oftor þonne . . . (*Wulfstan's Institutes of Polity* 134)

'By that one can know, that it is entirely not right, that a man marry (take a wife) or a woman marry (take a man) after then . . .'

(10)   Ne nan preost ne mot beon æt þam brydlacum **ahwær þær man æft wifað, oððe wif eft ceorlað** . . . (*Aelfric's Letter to Wulfsige* 7)

No priest may be at the marriage at any time when a man marries again, or a woman marries again . . .'

As the use of *wer* and *ceorl* to refer to a husband in a married relationship hints, the word *husband* is a later addition to the language and it too underwent specification to refer to a married man. The word seems to be an Old Norse borrowing: *hus* + *bondi* 'peasant owning his own house/land, freeholder,' which appears in Old English as *husbonda* 'master of a house.' There appears also to have been a feminine form *husbonde* 'mistress of a house.' By Middle English, *husband* has specified to a 'married man.' The semantic complexity of Old English *wif* demonstrated in the examples above should make this specification of *husband* seem less surprising, and the modern example of *man* may prove instructive here. In certain instances, the word *man* can be used to mean 'husband,' perhaps jocularly for some speakers but less so for others (e.g., "I am going to stay home with my man tonight"). As a result, in Middle English, we find the new collocational pair *husband* and *wife*, as shown in example (11). Example (13) below, with the pairing of *woman* and *husband*, is unusual and probably demonstrates the growing distinction between *wife* ('married woman') and *woman*, as described in the *MED*. In other words, examples (12) and (13) potentially address different audiences: the first, women who have husbands; the second, possibly all women who can wish evil on ill husbands.

(11)   But aftur þe husbond eete þe wyfe, and þe wyfe eete þe husbond . . .
       (*The Siege of Jerusalem in Prose* 85)
       'But after the husband eats the wife, and the wife eats the husband . . .'

(12)   Of **wifys** that ar here, For the life that thay leyd, **Wold thare husbandys were dede** . . . (*The Wakefield Pageants in the Towneley Cycle* 24)

(13)   To the women in the audience: **We women may wary all ill husbandys** . . . (*The Wakefield Pageants in the Towneley Cycle* 19)

The word *housewife* first appears in 1225, and this compound most likely incorporates the older meaning of *wife* as 'woman' – so the woman who runs a household. This meaning of *wife* is still preserved in *midwife* and *fishwife* and *old wives' tale* – although it may well be at this point that most speakers interpret these compounds as referring to occupations of married women (and perhaps "outdated" in this sense). *Hussy* is a shortened form of *housewife*, first appearing in 1530 to mean 'woman householder' or a 'thrifty woman.' By the next century there is evidence of it used as a derogatory term for rustic or rude women, and for Modern English speakers, the connection of *hussy* and *housewife* is opaque.

The Middle English results indicate that the typical "generic" pairing for the period has become *man and woman*, of which examples (14) and (15) are typical. Clearly, the word *man* has lost its generic status in these references, and in many later Middle English examples, the spelling as well as the pronunciation of *woman* has become less transparent with respect to its compound status (the elision of /f/ in this compound is paralleled by Old English *leofman* 'dear person' > Middle English *lemman*, which appears in Modern English as *leman*); the word's compound status is also no longer relevant to its gender, as it is no longer gram-matically masculine due to the second word in the compound, *mann*, once the natural gender system is in place.

(14)   . . . that here ys wrytyn how **a man or woman** schuld be dysposyd that be born sundry days off the mone . . . (Metham, *Physiognomy* 155)

(15)   And þis is ful perelous bitwixe **man and womman**, whanne þei ben boþe þus deepli woundid with þe affeccioun of loue . . . (Hilton, *Eight Chapters on Perfection* 29)

Paul Schaffner, one of the *MED* associate editors, confirms the overwhelming use of "man and woman" pairings in Middle English, through a more comprehensive survey of evidence from *MED* quotations (unpublished paper).

In the Middle English part of the Corpus, there are a few lingering examples of the conjoined phrase *wæpmann and wifmann*; they all seem to occur in early Middle English texts (e.g., *Lambeth Homilies, Layamon, Juliane*). For example:

(16)   . . . fif hundret italt **of wepmen & of wimmen** . . . (*Juliane* 121)

'. . . five hundred total of men and of women . . .'

The last recorded instance of *wepmann* in the *MED* is in the early thirteenth century. The one example of *carlman and wifmann* in the Helsinki Corpus material comes from the final addition to the *Peterborough Chronicle*, written in the mid-twelfth century. The one example of *man and wife* occurs in the Northern Homily Cycle: "I am þe brede of lastand life þat medcyn es to man and wife."

In sum, in a highly simplified summary scheme, by the end of Middle English, *wer* has disappeared, *wife* has specified, the less symmetrical pairing of *man and woman* (given that *man* still functions as a generic and *woman* was originally a compound based on that generic meaning) is becoming standardized, and *husband* is replacing *ceorl* – to be paired still with *wife*.

By early Modern English, *man and woman* is well established as the standard male–female collocational pairing, as shown in a typical example in (17).

(17)   And by the sayd boke hath made bothe **the men and the women** to knowe more vyces, subtyltye, and crafte . . . (Fitzherbert, *The Book of Husbandry* 98)

It is this period that also witnesses the rise of the grammatically conjoined pairing *man and wife*. The references are generally to married couples and in the Corpus, the two terms appear invariably in this order. Given the specification of *wife* by this period, it would also indicate that this pairing was semantically asymmetric from its inception. It is an interesting question the extent to which prescription and cultural values encourage the use of the masculine before the feminine in such pairings in later periods and to what extent prosodic considerations (e.g., the "heavier" term comes second) allow the use of the feminine before the mas-culine in Old English phrases such as *wifmann and wæpnedmann* – for example, *ge wifmen ge wæpmen* in example (2) and *ge wif ge wæpned* in example (3). In any case, the former seems to override the latter in the modern phrase *husband and wife*. Example (18) does not specify marriage with *man and wife* but it certainly implies cohabitation. It is also interesting to note in this example the noun *householder*, necessary with the specification of *husband* to male. Example (19) nicely exemplifies the asymmetry of the pairing, not only in the two nouns but in the expectations assigned to these two gendered groups – the pairings *man* and *wife* as well as *husband* and *wife*. There is only one example in the early Modern English part of the study in which *husband* does not occur in object position in such a context.

(18) with a nother trustye **housholders**, eyther with **the good man or good wife** ... (Harman, *A Caveat or Warening for Commen Cursetors* 67)

(19) yet it hath in it this real Duty, that **the man love his wife**, and **the wife reverence her husband** ... (Taylor (Jeremy), *The Marriage Ring* 9)

In this last example, *man* is clearly gender-specific. By early Modern English, at the latest, it seems grammatically undesirable to refer to a woman as "a man" or to explicitly include "men and women" under "men" (although it can be used as a generic reference otherwise). In Middle English, this usage still occurs sporadically. One of the most striking and often cited examples comes from the *Ormulum* – a sentence which would now be cited as a textbook example of how the awkwardness of this statement proves that *man* is not generic.

(21) þatt Zacarie, Godess preost, / & ȝho þatt wass hiss macche / Wærenn rihhtwise & **gode menn** / Biforenn Godess eȝhne. (*The Ormulum* I, 10)

'That Zachary, God's priest, and she that was his mate were righteous and **good men** before God's eyes.'

Whether or not *man* functioned as a generic for all speakers of the language, Middle English also witnesses the use of the borrowed word *person* (from Old French) as a new generic reference, and it continues to appear throughout Early Modern English, alongside *man*.

(22) ... whanne it is priuely and synguleerly sett in-to ony o **persoone, man or womman** ... (Hilton, *Eight Chapters on Perfection* 32)

This study found no examples in Early Modern English of the type "men, man and woman." It seems that, in isolation, the noun *man* could be interpreted as a reference to any human, but it is not explicitly inclusive by this time – perhaps this type of construction has already become awkward and seemingly contradictory.

In terms of describing married couples in early Modern English, Thomas Thomas, in his Latin–English grammar of 1587, uses both *man* and *husband* in conjunction or collocation with *wife* (e.g., "as in wed lock the man to the wife" and "A kinde of sacrifice betwixt the husband and the wife"), as do other early Modern English lexicographers such as William Thomas in his Italian and English dictionary (1550), John Minsheu in his Spanish and English dictionary (1599) and Thomas Blount in *Glossographia* (1656).[21] Interestingly, in terms of possible connotational differences (or lack thereof), William Thomas describes divorce as the separation of *husband* and *wife*; Minsheu and Blount describe it as the separation of *man* and *wife*. The variation witnessed in these dictionaries supports the results summarized in Table 5.1, which indicate that the pairing of *husband and wife* appears not infrequently in the early Modern English part of the Helsinki Corpus compared with *man and wife*, although its use may be restricted by the growing frequency of *man and wife*. Example (23) is typical; the next example, with *woman* and *husband* – one of the rare asymmetical pairings in this order – probably results from the focus on the woman in this trial.

(23)   Let **the Husband and Wife** infinitely avoid a curious distinction of mine and thine . . . (Taylor (Jeremy), *The Marriage Ring* 16–17)

(24)   My Lord, if your Lordship please, **this Woman and her Husband** are both unwilling Witnesses . . . (*The Trial of Lady Alice Lisle* IV, 120C2)

While this last example pairs *woman* with *husband*, *wife* is the more frequent collocation with *husband*, and by this time, the nouns *woman* and *wife* have become sharply distinguished, as shown in example (25).

(24)   . . . for I knew the man well; **he had a very honest woman to his wyfe** . . . (Harman, *A Caveat or Warening for Commen Cursetors* 69)

So by early Modern English, the relationship of the word *woman* to the word *wife* is familiar to modern speakers of the language, and both could appear phrasally conjoined with *man*.

To move briefly beyond the scope of the Helsinki Corpus and of this study, the relationship of the use of the word *woman* to that of *lady* and *girl* in the eighteenth and nineteenth centuries has been the subject of interesting recent studies (Bäcklund 1996, Wallin-Ashcroft 1996).[22] Wallin-Ashcroft argues that female writers of the eighteenth century preferred *lady* to *woman*, unlike male writers, but also that *woman* occurred with more positive adjectives than it does in Modern English (according to the study in Persson 1990; see Romaine 1999: 137–40 for a more recent study of collocations). Bäcklund notes that Jane Austen

---

[21] Definitions from these early Modern English dictionaries, including Blount (1656), Minsheu (1599), Thomas (1550), Thomas (1587), are excerpted from the Early Modern English Dictionaries Databases (EMEDD), edited by Ian Lancashire and available at: http://www.chass.utoronto.ca/english/emed/emedd.html.

[22] As an etymological note, *lord* and *lady* have become opaque as to their compound origins and etymological relationship to each other. *Lord*, which appears in Old English as *hlaford*, represents the earlier *hlafweard* or 'the keeper/guardian of the bread (loaf),' to refer to the head of a household, on whom servants depended for food. The exact origins of *lady* are less clear: it has been hypothesized that it stems from *hlaf* + the stem *dig-* 'knead'; the *OED* editors note that this etymology is "not very plausible with regard to sense" but do not offer a more plausible alternative.

used the term *female* synonymously with *woman*, *lady*, and *girl* (women and ladies for Austen are either over twenty-five or married of any age), although *female* became a disfavored term later in the nineteenth century; Moe (1963) supplies examples of how *woman* potentially did not function as a synonym of *lady* in the 1880s. Mills (1989: 265–69) provides more details about the "rivalry" between *woman* and *lady*, including the stigmatization of *woman* (in contrast to the socially valued *lady*) in the nineteenth century. Persson and Rydén (1995: 147) assert: "To be labeled woman was totally unacceptable to upper- and middle-class women in the 19th century . . ."

The word *woman* has arguably undergone semantic amelioration with feminist movements, particularly in the twentieth century, as Mills explains in her dictionary entry, resulting in the word's adoption as the self-reference of choice by many (self-named) women. Sigley and Holmes (2002: 141) report that the use of the term *women* doubled since 1961 in the corpora they examined; however, the references to women as individuals still falls short of references to individual men 1:2. The study in Bebout (1995: 177–79) reveals that there is little agreement among males and females, ranging in age from seventeen to fifty, about what the other gender wants to be called; the most "progressive" groups in terms of using *woman* are males over twenty-one and females over thirty-one (or in their late teens). Bebout's study also points to the questionable status of *lady*. The word *lady* seems to be becoming more specialized, to refer to older, well-dressed, "refined" or "sophisticated" females, thereby becoming more parallel in terms of connotations with *gentleman* and less synonymous with *woman*; it seems to remain inoffensive to most in the phrase "ladies and gentlemen" (one of the few phrases where the woman proceeds the man, due in no small part to the social formality of the phrase, as well as, perhaps, the syllabic weight of *gentleman*). At the same time, Bebout's (1995: 166–67) results indicate that *lady* remains or has increased as a term used euphemistically as a marker of lower status, especially in job titles.

The potentially derogatory connotations of the word *lady* in Modern English returns to the question so often raised in current feminist scholarship about the derogation of words for women and the resulting semantic asymmetry in pairs such as *lady* and *gentleman*, *master* and *mistress*, *governor* and *governess*, or *bachelor* and *spinster*. One lesson of history, as the results of this study make clear, is that symmetry is not easy to define. Words come to be paired or unpaired in different ways, and there may be no more pure symmetry than there are pure synonyms. While prototypical meanings may correspond to established binaries such as masculine–feminine, peripheral meanings and connotations will trouble other similarities between paired words, will pull words in different directions of change, and will allow them to function differently in discourse.

The frequently cited "asymmetrical pairing" (in Modern English) of *bachelor and spinster* can serve as a case in point. Both terms first appear in the Middle English period, but their prototypical meanings are not parallel until much later and their connotations are rarely if ever symmetrical. The word *spinster* derives from the verb *spinnan* 'spin' and the suffix *-ster*, from Old English *-estre*, which is used to form feminine agent-nouns (see Baron 1986: 118–20 for more on possible origins of *-ster*); *spinster* first appears in English in the fourteenth century to refer to a woman who spins as an occupation. It comes to be used as a legal title, of occupation, by early Modern English, but it soon comes to refer to a woman's unmarried status; as Thomas Blount explains in his *Glossographia* (1656): "a term or addition in our Law-Dialect, added in Obligations, Evidences and Writings, to unmarried Women, as it were, calling them Spinners; And this onely addition is given to all unmarried women, from the Viscounts Daughter downward." This shift is difficult to interpret several centuries later and explanations that spinsters tended not to marry seem insufficient; Mills (1989: 225–28) presents a more detailed hypothesis involving the historical symbolism of spinning (including spindles and distaffs) among other factors, and she reads Blount's definition as a possible justification of the label in the face of resistance. By the eighteenth century, *spinster* seems to have taken on the more negative connotations of *old maid* (a phrase that had already undergone severe semantic pejoration) – in other words, a woman too old, unattractive, or in some other way "ineligible" for marriage. (However, it is possible to find expressions such as "bachelor and spinster sweethearts" as late as the early twentieth century.) On the flip side, the positive connotations of *bachelor* are clear in a feminist effort to call single women "bachelors" (see Mills 1989: 15; the *OED* provides one citation from Ben Jonson [1632] for the use of *bachelor* to refer to a single woman, labeling the usage obsolete and rare). And that last sentence may be telling about what seems to be happening in Modern English: the preferred use of *single woman* over the stigmatized *spinster*, a shift perhaps foreshadowed by this Middle English quotation: "When man . . . seoþ an oþer mannes wif Or a womman of sengle lyf" (a1425 *Iesu þat wolde* [LdMisc 463], as cited in the *MED*).

The word *bachelor* first appears in English in the thirteenth century to refer to a young knight, and then to someone who has achieved the lowest degree at a university – where the term still exists, although more often abbreviated to, for example, BA, and for many speakers, the two meanings of the term have become distanced if not divorced. Perhaps as a result, "Bachelor of Arts" has also not been the target of feminist language reforms to the same extent as other sexist usages. (Nor has *alma mater*, which August [1992] argues is equally sexist in the academy, but the fact that this phrase is in Latin and "unparsable" for most English speakers makes these cases less parallel.) The word *bachelor* appears in reference to an unmarried man as early as Chaucer, and it has remained a generally positive term since that time, becoming prototypical enough that a phrase such as "the younge married Bacheler" (George Whetstone, *An Heptameron of Ciuill Discourses*, 1582) would seem an oxymoron. The late nineteenth century witnesses use of the expression *bachelor girl*, defined in *Dialect Notes* as 'a maiden lady' (*OED*). Given use of both *bachelor maid* and *bachelor woman* in the same period, it is probable that these phrases carried different connotations as to the "attractiveness" of the female in question, especially given the stigmas attached to *woman* in the nineteenth century.

In sum, the histories of the words *spinster* and *bachelor* confirm the often noted tendency of words for women to take on more negative connotations or denotations than parallel words for men. They also highlight the complex nature of meaning and usage, the ways in which highly gendered words in Modern English have crossed gender lines historically, up to the present day, and the ways in which masculine–feminine pairings are not stable or necessarily symmetrical over time. (The word *spinster* returns in the discussion of feminist language reform in the next chapter, as the suffix *-ster* has also crossed gender lines in its historical development.)

The question of how parallel we can consider the pairing *man* and *woman* in Modern English rests to some extent on the ongoing question of whether or not *man* can or does still function as a generic term. Historically, *man* clearly could function generically, as this study confirms; but even by Middle English it would appear that this usage was not entirely unproblematic. Schaffner, in his study of "man and woman" pairings in Middle English, points out that these pairings occur juxtaposed with generic uses of *man*, possibly as part of an effort by authors to be more inclusive for particular audiences, if they were known to include women. This pattern is not, however, consistent. Even as early as Middle English, speakers and writers were not completely comfortable with *man* as a generic, inclusive term, and Schaffner quotes the translator of William Flete's *Remedies Against Temptation* speaking directly to this point, in that the translator feels that he must explain his usage: "lo alwey whan I speke of a 'man' in this writing, takith both for a man and woman, for so it is i-ment in al suche writings, for al is mankynde." Studies of Modern English usage over the past few decades, often inspired by feminist objections to use of generic *man*, indicate that speakers conceptualize males when they hear the term (see the studies cited in Spender 1985: 152). Clancy (1999) argues that the generic and kind meanings of *man* remain peripherally present, and Horn and Kleinedler (2000) suggest that given the traditional default of men as the prototype members of the category HUMAN, then "quasi-generic" *man* will be reasonably acceptable if a male image can fulfill the proposition (e.g., "Man is using up the energy sources on the planet"). This suggestion makes logical sense and explains some lingering usage patterns; it also raises important questions such as: "traditional default" for which speakers? and "reasonably acceptable" for which listeners? The assumption of a traditional prototype may not be based entirely on unbiased data; as the studies in this book have confirmed, men comprise the majority of recorded authors and subjects of extant texts, on which we must rely for historical evidence of prototypical meanings and the conventions of which influence early prescriptions of meaning and usage.

At a different theoretical level, generic *man* raises an interesting question: to what extent is it possible for a term to carry both a gendered and a generic meaning simultaneously? This question arises with the words *child*, *wench*, and *girl* in the discussion above. Apparently contradictory meanings can coexist with other terms in English, such as *day* to encompass *night* and *day* as well as to contrast with *night* (cited in Horn and Kleinedler 2000). But is gender of such cultural salience that lexical parallels such as *day* are not, in fact, semantically parallel? This question is fundamental to the next section, which examines the semantic changes currently underway with the modern word *guy*, as the history of gender in the English language continues in modern varieties of the language.

5.7   Generic guy(s): the lessons of history

The semantic changes in progress with the word *guy* in Modern English raise the opposite question of that with generic *man*: to what extent can a gender-specific term generalize to become generic? These changes also raise important theoretical questions about the salience of gender binaries in the semantic analysis of "gendered words." The use of the word *guy* has become more and more widespread and varied in past decades, particularly in American English. It can be used to refer to a male human being (covering a wide age range), as a plural inclusive in the vocative and second person (e.g., "hey guys" and "you guys"), and as a quasi-pronoun (e.g., "this guy over here" referring to, for example, a book). Clancy (1999) proposes that *guy*, in the singular, is also coming to serve as a generic reference noun for people, but the available evidence of this in current usage is not as of yet robust.[23] The *Random House Historical Dictionary of American Slang* contains examples of phrases such as "great guy," "real guy" and "right guy" in reference to specific women up to about 1940, and the phrase *good guy* may have more flexibility in gender reference than the word *guy* alone.

The accepted origins of *guy* date back to the effigy of Guy Fawkes, traditionally burned on the fifth of November, accompanied by a display of fireworks (*OED*, first citation in 1806). This typically grotesque figure in ragged clothes was often paraded about accompanied by similar effigies (also called *guys*). The *OED* cites the extended meaning of *guy* to 'a person of grotesque appearance, especially with reference to dress' back to 1836, and in a quotation from Trollope (1867), the possible ambiguity between the two meanings is apparent: "What are you doing there, dressed up in that way like a guy?" The use of *guy* to refer to a male human being more generally is of American origin and dates back in written usage to 1847, according to the *OED*, and may have been influenced by the negative connotations of 'person of grotesque or ridiculous appearance'

---

[23] Horn and Kleinedler (2000) cite Clancy for evidence of this generic use, and Clancy has only three examples: one is a second-hand anecdote; one is a quotation from Joan Allen on *Saturday Night Live*, which strikes me, as a native American English speaker, as odd; and one refers to a baby, which could also be explained by the lack of gendered characteristics of the child, which allow children to be referred to with *it*, as described in Chapter Three (so this could be a use of *guy* as a quasi-pronoun as well).

in its earliest uses, according to the *OED* editors. Of particular interest for this study is the coexistence of a gender-specific meaning ('male human being') and a gender-neutral meaning ('person of grotesque or ridiculous appearance') for at least part of the nineteenth century. As a case in point, in *Little Women* by Louisa May Alcott (1869), the three occurrences of *guy* all refer to Jo, the sister who tends toward the most stereotypically masculine behavior; the references, however, seem to be generic in their implications for her "frightful" appearance, for example:

> "Oh, Jo, you are not going to wear that awful hat? It's too absurd! You shall not make a guy of yourself," remonstrated Meg . . .

> "I wish I was a horse, then I could run for miles in this splendid air, and not lose my breath. It was capital, but see what a guy it's made me. Go, pick up my things, like a cherub, as you are," said Jo . . . (as cited in the Modern English Collection database)

The use of *guy* to refer to a 'man, fellow' is not recorded at the end of the nineteenth century in the *Century Dictionary* or Farmer and Henley's *Slang and Its Analogues*; these dictionaries record only the extended use of the effigy reference to a grotesque-looking or ill-dressed person. The shift of the prototypical meaning of *guy* to males seems to be a twentieth-century phenomenon.

In Modern English usage at the end of the twentieth century, the use of the plural form *guys* to encompass both male and female human beings seems to be fairly well restricted to forms of address or as a plural marker with the second-person pronoun *you*. It may also be restricted to more informal contexts. The *Dictionary of American Regional English* cites the use of *-guys* in some dialects as a suffix to form the plural of nouns, sometimes used with proper names to refer to other people associated with that person (e.g., "Anne-guys" for "Anne and her friends/colleagues/etc."). This usage raises the question of whether *guys* is becoming grammaticalized as a plural marker, with the second-person pronoun in more standard varieties of English and with other nouns as well in other varieties. Clancy (1999: 288) proposes grammaticalization in the context of the "semantic bleaching" of *guy* to be used as an indefinite or demonstrative phrasal pronoun (i.e., *this guy* or *some guy* used similarly to *this one*, *this thing*, *someone/somebody*, *something*); a similar "semantic bleaching" could be argued to have occurred in the phrasal plural pronoun *you guys*, recreating a singular/plural distinction lost in most dialects of English several centuries ago. The more grammatical nature of *guys* in this formation is supported by the fact that *we guys* is not used similarly (for example, there are no occurrences of it in the British National Corpus or the Michigan Corpus of Academic Spoken English):[24] the term would have masculine connotations in this construction because *we* is already plural

---

[24] The British National Corpus allows a simple search of the entire corpus from the website: http://www.hcu.ox.ac.uk/BNC/. The Michigan Corpus of Academic Spoken English, totaling almost 1.9 million words, is available at http://www.hti.umich.edu/m/micase/.

and so *guys*, redundant in terms of number, could logically be interpreted as a gender reference. (Languages, of course, tolerate enormous amounts of redundancy, so the use of *we guys* as a generic pronoun instead of *we* is certainly not prohibited.)

The question that has arisen in linguistic scholarship – and not, interestingly, as much in public forums – is whether or not this "generic" use of *guys* is sexist. Horn and Kleinedler (2000) argue that the extended use of *guy(s)* is an example of parasitic reference or R-based broadening in Horn's taxonomy (genericization of a culturally salient member of a given category) – in this way similar to *Kleenex* or *Xerox*. Clancy (1999) notes that there have been scattered protests against the use of *guys* as a generic, and he proposes that these responses may become more widespread once *guy* becomes more acceptable in print. It is clear that at the moment in American English usage, the word *guy* is polysemous across gender and animacy lines: it can refer to a male human being, many male human beings (in the first and third person), many human beings of mixed or unknown gender (in the second person), as well as inanimate objects in indefinite or deictic structures. Feminist scholars have been arguing for decades that *man/men* cannot carry both generic and gender-specific meanings simultaneously because they are too fundamentally contradictory, and the same premise clearly could be argued to hold true for *guy(s)*.

In approaching this question, are there facts – or even lessons – in the history of other words for men and women in English that may be instructive? Clancy (1999: 295) equates the polysemy of *guy*, *man*, and *he* – with a footnote that the path of development has not always been from masculine to generic, as Old English *man(n)* demonstrates a reverse development. Horn and Kleinedler (2000) argue convincingly that *man* should be viewed differently: it is not a case of parasitic reference because historically it is clearly a case of narrowing (to a culturally salient subset). In addition, *man* can be used to refer to kind (e.g., the species) in a way that *guy* cannot. It could be added that *guy* can be used as a grammatical marker of plurality in ways that *man* cannot, and this may affect the word's development. The parallel with generic *he* that Clancy draws is also potentially problematic. The direction of semantic development (i.e., broadening) is potentially similar, but the history of generic *he* is complicated, as described in Chapter Three. When the grammatical gender system was still in place, the masculine personal pronoun agreed *grammatically* with many generic nouns in Old English, which could only have encouraged its use as a generic once English shifted to a natural gender system – as well as the cultural salience of the male subset in such references. In other words, prior grammatical usage may well have influenced usage in the semantically based system; grammatical reference could have been reinterpreted as semantic (with the important note that grammatical usage should not be entirely divorced from cultural factors). In comparison to the cases of *man* and *he*, *guy* is strikingly new to the English language. And interestingly, its generic usage predates its gender-specific usage, given that the reference to 'grotesque-looking person' seems to have been fairly generic. In other words, there do not appear to be any entirely instructive parallels for analyzing the semantic development of *guy(s)*, when we look carefully at the details of these words' histories.

So "history does not matter" if one believes in the singularity of semantic change, and even semantic parallels will not be completely explanatory or predictive. In addition, it is critical to expose etymological fallacies: that words "mean" – in some fundamental way – what they used to mean or originally meant, and all subsequent semantic changes are corruptions or temporary "misunderstandings" of the "correct meaning." Words fundamentally mean what speakers believe that words mean and what they use words to mean. Clancy (1999: 282) notes: "The prototypical meaning of a lexical item may change its focus, but the old meanings can still remain connected peripherally." The crucial word in this observation is *can*: so by looking at history we may be able to make sense of peripheral meanings, but meanings can also be lost to a speech community. In addition, the changes of other words do not predict the changes of related words. As noted above, prediction will probably forever be in some way beyond the scope of historical linguistics.

At the same time, I want to argue that history does matter. Some of the same cultural structures and belief systems that affect the development of words in a lexical field historically often apply to new words in a lexical field – and there may well be lessons to be learned. We should not assume cultural similarity and project our own belief systems onto history; at the same time, it is possible to discover patterns that historicize cultural attitudes as well as (or within) the lexicon. More importantly, knowledge of the changes that have occurred with other words may affect the development of new words. Linguists historically have privileged language-internal explanations over language-external ones, but the fact is that speakers' attitudes about words can affect their development, and these attitudes can be consciously molded or altered by metadiscourse about language. In other words, words can become privileged or stigmatized due to usage patterns or due to a conscious effort by speakers to deem a word or usage appropriate or inappropriate (e.g., feminist campaigns against the use of *girl* for adult women, which has altered patterns of usage and, therefore, "the meaning" of the word). McConnell-Ginet (1989) makes the important observation that the debate about generic *he* may at this point be moot (in the newer sense of *moot* as 'no longer relevant'): it may be that generic *he* can no longer mean 'he or she' at the turn of the millennium if for no other reason than because of the controversy around the usage, which has affected interpretation by the hearer/reader, no matter what the intention of the speaker/writer. In other words, *he* cannot "mean" 'he or she' anymore, if it ever did, in a straightforward signifying relationship because that usage has been so heavily problematized; and there is no separating "real meaning" from "perceived meaning." They are all part of the discursive semantics of any given word.

History also matters in that it makes clear that in English, there are no clear parallels for the semantic development of *guy*. While the polysemy of *guy* is similar to that of *man* and *he* in some senses (i.e., they all can be male-referential and generic to some extent), the historical differences among them are critical. *Man* develops in the opposite direction; and *he* not only has a much longer history, embedded in a grammatical gender system, but it is also a grammatical form. The word *guy*, on the other hand, without as extended a history, shows indications that it is becoming grammaticalized in some uses, and its use as a generic plural grammatical marker may or may not be affecting its use as a generic plural noun. It is also arguable that *guy* may be making English language history in its use to refer to inanimate objects, which grammaticalizes a masculine term for inanimate object reference – contrary to the patterns noted by earlier scholars and in Chapter Four that the feminine is more common in reference to inanimate objects. The goal of this description is not to compile evidence that *guy* is necessarily generic and/or not sexist in current English usage; the point is that while we can use history to understand better the semantic status of *guy*, we cannot use history to predict necessarily what will happen to it.

The development of *guy* raises fascinating theoretical questions about the semantics of words for male and female human beings. In the history of English, we have evidence of generic terms narrowing to refer to one sex or the other: *wench* and *girl* specifying to mean 'young female human being'; *man* specifying to mean 'male human being.' And for at least some period of time, these words can be polysemous, encompassing both the generic and gender-specific meaning. Can gender-specific terms generalize to become "truly generic," at least at this point in English? Can words carry both meanings and not be sexist? Female-referential terms may be restricted from generalization to generic status because their female referents are not the most culturally salient or highest status subset, and because there is social resistance to the use of female-referential terms for men in anything other than a derogatory sense. Male-referential terms seem able to generalize given the cultural salience or high status of their referents, but at this point, will social resistance affect their semantic development in this direction? Much semantic change occurs below the level of consciousness, but not all – and feminist resistance does seem to have the power to affect semantics and/or usage (which are critically intertwined). The question with *guy* is whether it will remain polysemous across gender lines, or whether its grammaticalization will make its generic meanings prototypical to the point where other meanings are lost – and as importantly, whether its use as a generic will be embraced or protested, which could well affect its semantic development.[25] Or perhaps the question is not whether *guy* will be polysemous in reference to men and women – perhaps it is simply that gender will no longer be highly salient for this term. In this case study, it may be that we are seeing the limits of gender and gender binaries as a fully explanatory framework.

[25] James (1998), in her study of slang words for women, determines that some terms are being used in a more gender-neutral way by both men and women, and that women are leading the way in this process. Her conclusion problematizes established gender norms in similar ways to this analysis; she writes: "Such shifts towards more gender-neutral usage imply some convergence of gender norms and a blurring of the rigid lines separating the social categories 'woman' and 'man' in the university student population studied here" (James 1998: 413).

5.8   Conclusion

The emphasis on gender as a determinative factor has been problematized in recent feminist discourse analysis research. Variation in discourse patterns results from a complex interaction of many social factors such as race, socioeconomic status, ethnicity, age, and gender, not to mention all the local factors that create discourse communities (see, for example, Eckert and McConnell-Ginet 1998). It is a commonplace in scientific inquiry that the questions we ask can affect if not in some ways determine the answers that we generate. In this case, by basing our questions on an assumption of gender difference – and specifically on an assumption of a gender binary between masculine and feminine – we may well be setting parameters for the analysis that do not allow us to see the full implications of other factors involved. For example, as Bing and Bergvall (1998) point out, it is clear that binary, two-sex (and, therefore, often two-gender, as sex and gender so often get conflated) models tend to suppress difference within categories while emphasizing difference across them, and categories outside this binary model tend to get ignored if not erased. Arguing a similar point from a different angle, Romaine (1999: 32) notes that these binary pairings are clearly linguistically inadequate, given the existence of an array of other terms for human sexuality outside the binary (e.g., *homosexual*, *lesbian*, *transvestite*).

Cameron (1990: 86–87) raises the important question of whether binary oppositions exist in language to be discovered or whether we construct them as part of linguistic analysis; and if these oppositions reflect a way of thinking, is this innate or learned? But importantly, Cameron asks, whatever the answers to these questions, are the binaries that exist/are constructed for language equally applicable at every level of language? As linguists have often noted, binaries seem to be particularly relevant to certain phonological features (e.g., voicing), but the assumption of paired sounds to create phonological symmetry in our constructed representations of a language may sometimes be problematic. The use of binary features (e.g., ±MALE) in componential analysis has been problematized, as discussed above, but has semantic analysis left binaries behind with the "±" sign? In other words, much semantic analysis of words for men and women still rests on the assumption of gender as the most salient feature in the meaning of the words. Simply by defining lexical fields such as "male human being" and "female human being" (often with a subordinate distinction of age to separate adults from children) we create the gender categories in which to analyze the semantics of the terms in question. Bing and Bergvall (1998: 495) are particularly effective in speaking to this point:

> Because language is discrete and biased towards dichotomy and clear boundaries, the scalar values and unclear boundaries of reality are sometimes difficult to recognize and to accept; we must continually remind ourselves that reality and language can conflict. The many real-world continua hidden by language suggest a question: is our automatic division of

humans into female and male as justified as we think? Are the boundaries between them as clear as the words *female* and *male* suggest?

These two scholars raise the question in the context of discourse analysis, specifically the division of speakers into the categories male/masculine and female/feminine. But the question they ask is as applicable to the lexicon itself, as the wording of the question highlights.

The complexity of the theoretical questions raised in this kind of analysis of gender can be frustrating, especially as the questions can seem to problematize the obvious. Gender clearly is enormously culturally salient for Modern English speakers, and the norm is a heterosexual, binary masculine-feminine/male-female model, which is exactly what we see reflected in the language in the types of word pairings examined above, such as *man and woman, husband and wife,* as well as, of course, the pronouns *he* and *she*. While the English language makes many binary gender distinctions along these lines, languages do not have to; for example, spoken Chinese makes no distinction between masculine, feminine, and neuter in the third-person singular pronoun. And as linguists, we should not assume the cultural salience of particular gender models (i.e., our own norma-tive gender models) in the analysis of language in earlier periods. As argued in Chapter One, rethinking historical understandings of gender provides a critical understanding of the "natural gender system" of English grammar, and the same may well hold true for the lexicon. As linguists, we should question assumptions of gender binaries that inform our semantic analysis of the lexicon. The fact that normative cultural notions about gender play out in the lexicon does not mean that these are the only notions that play out in the lexicon, or that gender is always the most salient feature for words that can refer to men and women, boys and girls. The details of the analysis presented above make clear the slipperiness of notions such as symmetry and even prototypical meaning for words referring to male and female human beings within this framework. And questions such as whether a generic and gender-specific meaning can coexist privilege gender in a way that other factors are not always privileged. For example, for many words singular and plural meanings coexist (e.g., *you, sheep*), and given the lower cultural salience of number, the contradictory meanings encompassed by these words strikes us as less baffling and much less problematic. This question about gender binaries is particularly important here because it can make semantic slipperiness around the shifts of words between/among genders less "mystifying," as it may reflect a different reality of gender playing out in relation to other social constructions that cross male-female lexical fields.

In many ways, the results and analysis presented in this chapter raise as many questions as they begin to answer. At the same time, they provide a historical context in which to view the politically charged issues surrounding language and gender. The histories of these words are more complex than some modern dis-cussions allow – which is not to say that there are not fairly clear patterns, such as the derogation and sexualization of words referring to women. The fundamental point here may be that the cultural salience of gender makes it, in many ways, an overriding semantic factor for the words that English speakers use to talk about gendered beings. And it makes gender a critical focal point for feminist efforts at language reform. Our beliefs about gender do play out in our language, and by drawing attention to the ways in which gender plays out in language, feminist language reform has proven that it can become a part of the semantic factors that influence language change. To return to McConnell-Ginet's insightful observation, word meanings may change simply because they become focal points of social controversy and their historical interpretation is no longer unmarked or uncontested.

6   Implications for nonsexist language reform

The aim throughout this book has been not only to provide linguistic details that may help answer lingering questions about the development of gender in the English language, both in the grammar and in the lexicon, but also to show the ways in which this historical context can inform current debates about sexism in the language and language reform. A significant amount of time and attention has been paid to language in the feminist movement, in large part because, as both feminists and linguists argue, "language matters." (See Pauwels 1998 for an excellent cross-language survey of women's language reform efforts.) We do not know or understand the precise relationship of language to thought, but we do know that language can reflect social structures and attitudes, if not perpetuate them. And we know that in some ways, we can change language more easily than we can change attitudes. Whether or not changing language eventually changes attitudes remains an open question; clearly, however, the simple fact that language reform requires speakers to think about a linguistic construction and its possible social implications – be they sexist, racist, or otherwise discriminatory – brings a level of awareness of these issues to a speech community that might not otherwise be achieved. In other words, language reform movements contest the notion that language is a neutral medium for communicating ideas and force speakers to consider how their audience may perceive certain linguistic choices. And when speakers do use less, for example, sexist language, then the language is arguably not perpetuating sexist attitudes.

Such an outcome might seem a minor one to some, but the resistance to language reform evidenced in the history of English and other languages suggests that few if any reforms to language feel particularly "minor" to speakers. Language is integral to identity and to culture, no matter how we define these terms, and speakers tend to be very protective of their language, not wanting it to be unnecessarily "tinkered with." Yet, as Cameron argues persuasively in *Verbal Hygiene* (1995), the desire to regulate – if not "tinker with" – the language of others is natural to speech communities. Efforts to preserve older linguistic forms and attempts to introduce new politically correct forms all constitute acts of "verbal hygiene," as speakers work to control the language and tell others what is right and not right in language use. Even those of us in the field of descriptive linguistics are in a fundamental sense embarked on the same "hygienic" enterprise, although one hopes with more linguistic knowledge and informed goals. (For example, the premise of this book that the debate about sexist language will be better informed by historical context is, fundamentally, telling other speakers how better to think about their language and current usage debates.)

Despite general resistance to all kinds of language reform (from spelling to grammar to language policy) – and in the United States today to politically correct language reform in general to some extent – the feminist movement has been surprisingly successful in pushing through changes in the norms of accepted linguistic behavior, in writing particularly but also to some extent in speech. As described in Chapter Three, generic *he* is no longer assumed to be an acceptable alternative in singular generic constructions in most English style guides and writing manuals. As described in Chapter Five, women have reclaimed terms such as *woman* and *girl* for their own use, and have made it clear that, for example, *girl* is not an acceptable term for speakers outside the female community to use in reference to women in most circumstances.

It is easy to forget how far feminist language reform has come and how fast. Less than thirty years ago, in her revolutionary 1975 book *Language and Woman's Place* – the book that many scholars cite as the beginning of serious feminist linguistics – Robin Lakoff argued that it is not worth trying to change generic *he*.

> [O]ne should force oneself to be realistic: certain aspects of language are available to the native speakers' conscious analysis, and others are too common, too thoroughly mixed throughout the language, for the speaker to be aware each time he uses them. It is realistic to hope to change only those linguistic uses of which speakers themselves can be made aware, as they use them. One chooses, in speaking or writing, more or less consciously and purposefully among nouns, adjectives, and verbs; one does not choose among pronouns in the same way. . . . Perhaps linguistic training has dulled my perception, and this really is a troublesome question. If so, I don't know what to advise, since I feel in any case that an attempt to change pronominal usage will be futile. (R. Lakoff 1975: 44)

As Lakoff's later books attest in their abstention from the use of generic *he*, the pronouns have not been immune from language reform, and it has taken less than twenty-five years, an eye-blink in language change, for generic *he* to become generally unacceptable in written prose. This progress does not mean, however, that debates do not continue to rage over whether or not such changes should be made to the language. Here is a striking and recent example which required not only debate but also a vote.

On the ballot in the General Election of the State of Washington in November 1999 was City of Seattle Proposition No. 2, entitled "Gender Neutral Language." In the voters pamphlet published before the election, the City Attorney's Explanatory Statement reads:

1. The Charter as it Exists Now

Some sections of the City Charter, which was first adopted in 1946, still contain exclusively male gender references. For example, the Mayor and other City officers are referred to as "he," councilmembers are referred to as "councilmen," police officers are referred to as "policemen," and so forth. Such references have been replaced by gender-neutral references in some charter sections as those sections have been amended. However, not all charter sections have been changed to make their language gender-neutral.

2. Effect of the Proposition if Adopted

The City Charter would be amended so that all exclusively male gender references would be replaced with gender-neutral references. For example, "he" would generally be changed to "he or she," "councilman" would be changed to "councilmember," "policeman" would be changed to "police officer," and so forth. Some sentences could be rewritten to avoid awkward constructions, such as the repeated use of "he or she" or "his or her."

The statement for the proposition, prepared by the Seattle Mayor Paul Schell and President of the Seattle City Council Sue Donaldson, noted that these amendments would bring provisions "into line with the present needs and expectations of the citizens and officials of Seattle" and "more accurately reflect the makeup of the City's workforce." The statement against, prepared by Fred Bucke and Linda Johnson, two concerned citizens, must be quoted in full to capture the logic of their counterargument:

> We should not change the Seattle City Charter, an historic document, to reflect the politically correct nonsense of **our** time.
>
> It is common knowledge that in many documents, including legal documents, "he" is not a gender specific term anymore than historic, history or mankind are. Changing every "he" to "he/she" is absurd. It takes longer to say and sounds like a chocolate bar.
>
> Constitutions and Charters should only be amended on substantive matters and are not to be frivolously changed in order to salve the misguided hypersensitivities of nit-picking bureaucrats. The Seattle City Charter is our city's constitution, it deserves protection from needless meddling.

The rebuttal to this statement notes that preserving old, exclusive language is offensive to many citizens and that government documents should be as inclusive as possible. The authors also note: "Preserving archaic language serves no purpose." The rebuttal to the rebuttal reads:

> The fact that we have had many female City Council members underscores our argument that it has been universally understood that in the City Charter, as in many other documents, "he" is not a gender specific term. Turning everything into "he/she" and "her/him" wastes time and

needlessly interrupts the flow of language. Council members who just don't understand this common knowledge can be educated with the insertion of one sentence into the Charter "It is understood that, where applicable, he means she and vice versa." The fact that the Seattle City Council would waste time on this indicates that they are unable to identify items of importance.

This ballot anecdote effectively captures both the controversy and the pervasive misunderstandings that still surround the generic pronoun question and other feminist language reform. The opponents of the proposition present the common argument that language should not be meddled with, especially by hypersensitive politically correct language (or "nonsense") advocates. What this argument does not recognize, as is so often missing from debates about sexism in English, is the fact that the language was to some extent "meddled with" to put generic *he* in this document in the first place, as described in Chapter Three. And, of course, if language "meddling" is of no importance, why do the opponents waste their time trying to stop it? The counterargument to the proposition also raises the common notion that *he* can be gender-neutral. Here again is evidence of the ways in which linguistic scholarship has not yet successfully become a productive part of the discussion: the results of the many studies that indicate that *he* does not function as a generic for most speakers are clearly not available to many if not most speakers participating in the public debate. In addition, history has shown that *he* does not always include *she*: in 1879, for example, a move to allow female physicians to join the all-male Massachusetts Medical Society was stopped because the Society's by-laws described membership using the pronoun *he* (cited in Frank and Anshen 1983: 73). The suggestion of adding a sentence noting that "he means she and vice versa" is interesting not only because so few have proposed using *she* generically, but also because it seems highly unlikely that the authors themselves would endorse any amendment to change *he* to the "inclusive," generic *she*, with or without this caveat. (The reference to sounding like a chocolate bar may only unnecessarily involve Hershey's^{TM} in the controversy.) Suffice it to say, the people of Seattle seemed to see this kind of language reform as an item of importance, and the proposition passed by an overwhelming majority.

This debate in the voters pamphlet is of relevance to this book because it exemplifies the lack of linguistic information, particularly about the history of language but also about the meaning and power of words, that has so often characterized public debates about gender in the language. The statement against the proposition muddles truly gendered forms such as *he* and *mankind* with nongendered forms such as *history*, in an overblown attempt to mock nonsexist language reforms. The details presented over the past few chapters about the history of gender in English pronouns and selected nouns depict in part a history of sexism in both the English language and in grammars describing the English language. They also demonstrate the complexity of grammatical and semantic change – that generic *he* did not arise in a cultural vacuum or as the simple result of prescriptivism, and that the historical generic meaning of *man* does not transparently transfer to Modern English. One of the goals of this book is to make this kind of linguistic information more accessible to a wider audience who may choose to participate in discussions of how we wish to negotiate the relationship of gender in our speech community and gender in our language.

The fact that this concluding chapter discusses a ballot and voters pamphlet highlights the idea that the linguistic issues studied in this book have political implications, and feminist linguists will have to struggle with how to negotiate the values of scientific inquiry in linguistics and the values of political investment in feminism. As noted in the Introduction, pure "objectivity" is likely not possible in the study of language. The questions that we ask affect the answers that we find, and the assumptions and beliefs that we hold influence the questions that we ask. It is also, at the most fundamental level, difficult to escape from some of the categories that our language sets up as we employ language to describe and analyze the workings of language.

Language is a social instrument; to depoliticize it is to take the speakers out of the language. Languages do not exist or change without speakers, so in talking about language change, we are talking about speakers and their linguistic choices, be they conscious or unconscious. It is equally important to remember that language is spoken by people in language communities as they use language in "negotiating the social landscape," to borrow an evocative phrase from Mary Crawford (1995: 17). In this negotiation, speakers make strategic linguistic choices and constantly work to resolve the ambiguity inherent in language – and while some speakers may control language institutions, no speakers can fully "control" the language as it is used, maintained, and changed through social interaction. It is critical to analyze linguistic data carefully, to consider various interpretations in light of established linguistic models and theories for how language works and changes.

As the Seattle ballot attests, the debate over nonsexist language continues in the United States. Cameron (1995: 130–31) points out that in many ways, the rhetoric of the debate about politically correct language in the 1990s shows how little progress we have made in the past three decades: the arguments about the triviality of language and the mockery of proposed reforms echo the debates about feminist language reforms that arose as early as the mid-1970s. At the same time, it could be argued that the mockery is becoming more tempered, as nonsexist language usage becomes more standard in writing establishments (e.g., newspaper style guidelines, educational grammars). For example, William Safire, one of the best known language pundits in the US, took on nonsexist usage in his *New York Times Magazine* column of May 16, 1999: "Genderese: Looking for a masterful Webmistress?" In this column, Safire's question is not whether or not the language should be reformed to be less sexist, but whether or not we are going "too far too fast." And while he mockingly speculates about a female equivalent for *avuncular* (rooted in the Latin for "maternal uncle") in a more traditional attack on radical feminist prescriptions (in this case, Rosalie Maggio's *Nonsexist Word Finder*), his critique of *his or her* consists of the mild "space-consuming" and he even endorses as logical the use of *firefighter, police officer, mail carrier,* and *executive* as nonsexist alternatives of careers both women and men pursue. Safire's column is more about style than substance when it comes to nonsexist language reform – how to keep "the punch" in a good sentence. And his punchline is that a female webmaster herself endorses the "resolutely sexist" (his words) form *webmaster*. In other words, if the people who have the jobs do not mind the title, why should feminists tamper with it?

Of course, the same could have been said over the past few decades about female mail carriers who did not protest about the term *mailman*, or even feminists such as Robin Lakoff who did not protest about generic *he*. It does not constitute a strong argument that the terms are not sexist or that an effort to change them is ludicrous. In fact, Safire's critique raises a more interesting question in its assertion that *master* is "resolutely sexist." The historical morphological and semantic pairing of *master* and *mistress* is no longer fully applicable semantically in Modern English as the prototypical meanings of the two terms have diverged. *Master* and *Mr.* represent for most Modern English speakers two different lexical items, as *Master* is no longer used as a title and *mister* has become the standard pronunciation of the abbreviated form. It would also be difficult to argue that *-er* is a transparent masculine suffix in Modern English anymore, given words such as *writer* or *mail carrier* as non-sexist alternatives. Interestingly, even the suffix *-ster*, originally a feminine suffix and then considered a masculine suffix by the sixteenth century (Baron 1986: 120), seems to have become potentially generic as a productive suffix, as witnessed in the recently coined *spinster,* to complement *pundit* in descriptions of political commentary. (It will be interesting to see if this has any effect on the *bachelor–spinster* pairing.) The question here parallels the question raised by *guy* in Chapter Five: can a historically masculine term become gender-neutral or does etymology seal the word's fate? Is the prototypical meaning of *master* semantically masculine for Modern English speakers?[1] For the word *he*, studies indicate that the answer is yes – but I do not think that these results should be taken as a generalization that a gender-specific term cannot lose its gendered denotation or connotation if its prototypical meaning undergoes a significant shift (which is not the case with *he*).

As discussed in Chapter Five, while historical parallels can be informative, they are not always parallel let alone predictive. In other words, it seems possible for gender to lose salience for a term, if and when other meanings become more salient. It has not been problematized that a word can shift genders, so that, for example, masculine became no longer salient for *harlot* as it came to refer to women, or vice versa with *faggot*. The question remains as to whether gender can

---

[1] One factor to consider in the semantic shifts of the noun *master* is the possible effect of the verb *master*, first recorded in 1225 in the *OED*, with its more generic meaning of 'to get the better of, in a contest, etc.'

become simply not salient and the word, as a result, generic. Of course, if speakers determine that *master* or any other word "is" sexist in Modern English – that the history of *master* precludes it from being interpreted as anything but masculine – and problematize it as such, then it will be sexist, in the same way that *lady* is now seen as sexist, when it could, conceivably, have been reappropriated by women speakers rather than rejected. Once again, these statements are not meant to argue that *master* is not necessarily sexist, but rather to question the assumption that it is "resolutely sexist," so that we are forced to clarify our articulation of the relationship of gender and semantic change.

When we work in the earlier periods of English, we are clearly working within different parameters for language change: very low levels of literacy (particularly for women), very little standardization of the language until at least the Early Modern English period, and little to no available commentary about sexism in the language and/or speakers' attitudes about particular usages. This framework allows us, to some extent, to create neater stories of semantic change. In retrospect, the evidence allows us to create histories of when a word's prototypical meaning shifted and when, at a certain point, earlier meanings may have become obsolete; we have little evidence for speakers' debating new usages (which is not unusual given how much language change happens below the level of consciousness) or for speakers, at some point in a linguistic change, even being aware of an earlier usage. This last point is perhaps most crucial: with the rise of literacy, education, and standardization of the language, earlier meanings are now recorded longer, which gives them a historical power that they may not have had in times of "living memory" (as opposed to "written/recorded memory").

I am not sure that we as historical linguists yet fully understand the implications of standardization and particularly modern lexicography for semantic change. As Treichler (1989: 51) points out: "If discourse is the text from which a dictionary is constructed, a dictionary becomes the text that, in turn, constructs discourse." Dictionaries carry an enormous amount of authority for many speakers, and while this power will certainly not stop linguistic creativity and semantic change, it may preserve older meanings longer and, as importantly, have the power to affect words by their histories, even when their prototypical meanings have changed. The polysemy of words can often be seen as a living museum of some earlier, now peripheral meanings as well as current, more prototypical meanings; dictionaries then potentially add to that museum some historical artifacts of meaning. In this way, it is fascinating to think about the interplay of semantic change above and below the level of consciousness, as speakers embrace or reject the semantic changes of politically or socially important words – the ones that rise to the level of awareness and become the focus of debate.

Nonsexist language reformers can and have adopted various strategies for taking control of language above the level of consciousness (see Pauwels 1998). One of the more radical strategies is creating a woman-centered language, as French feminists have suggested and as Suzette Hayden Elgin has sought to do in her science fiction. Another is "linguistic disruption" to bring language itself to the foreground, by, for example, reclaiming derogatory terms, flouting grammatical gender concord in German, using *herstory* instead of *history*, or experimenting with nonsexist, nongendered, or differently gendered pronouns in literature (see Livia 2001).[2] Cameron (1990: 125) espouses this more disruptive approach, if feminists are seeking to change norms of language use:

> I do think it would be better if feminists operated with a more hard-headed, political notion of what we are trying to do. In my opinion we should be tampering with language not to tell the truth, but quite openly to shame the devil. It is disingenuous to claim that the conventions we propose are simply 'better' than the traditional ones (more accurate, more precise), because really it is a question of political and ideological preferences – the traditional usage embodies one view of the world, the feminist alternative a different one, and we need to make clear that *both* these views are politically non-neutral. We should therefore be honest enough to defend our tampering not in terms of its purported linguistic merits, but in terms of its political utility for raising consciousness, denouncing sexism and empowering women.

The strategies of language reform that have attempted to draw on arguments of accuracy are gender neutralization (i.e., discarding gender-specific terms in favor of generic terms, such as *poet* and *mail carrier*) and gender specification or feminization (i.e., making women visible through symmetrical specification of gender). (See Pauwels 1998: 112–16 for examples from a range of languages.) In English language reform campaigns, the stronger push has been for the creation or adoption of generic terms, in some ways moving away from the language's history of compounding with gender-specifiers (e.g., *wifmann* and *wæpmann*, *gay girl* and *knave girl*, *maiden child* and *knave child*). And what is so interesting about the history of these compounds is that the base generic form has taken many possible directions of semantic change, defying the notion of a historical pattern: *man* has specified to refer to males; *girl* has specified to refer to females; and *child* has remained gender neutral. The argument with *man* has been that the term specified to the subset of highest social salience, and the same could be said of the many terms under debate today: *doctor* and *lawyer* as unmarked masculine; *nurse* and *teacher* as unmarked feminine. As a result, compounding tends to be asymmetrical, reflecting prototypes rather than gender-balance: *female doctor* and *male nurse*. The exception to the push for a single generic term is the alternative *he or she* for generic singular pronouns, but as discussed in Chapter Three, the preference for singular generic *they* in the spoken language may override this prescription even in the written language.

"Naturally occurring" (i.e., not prescribed) language change tends to lag behind social change, although there are language reform movements attempting

---

[2] Pauwels (1998: 98) cites the use of generic singular *they* as an instance of linguistic disruption, and while this may be true in some written contexts, it does not seem to be disruptive for most speakers in the spoken language.

to reverse this order. One difference between some of the historical and the current examples of language change discussed in this book is the debate surrounding them, along with the major social changes that have happened in the past century with respect to the status of women. Thus, we see today an effort to help language "catch up" faster than it might otherwise (and *might* is a deliberate choice of wording here, given the argument that language can perpetuate belief systems). To echo the argument at the end of Chapter Five, the discussion about proposed language reforms toward nonsexist usage has the potential to benefit from some of the recent work in feminist theory which has destabilized the notion of gender, whether that be gender as performance (e.g., Butler 1990) or gender as a continuum (e.g., Bing and Bergvall 1998). Gender-specification relies on binary thinking about gender, as does the creation of a "women's language." The theoretical questioning of binaries is one of the most complex issues in language and gender research, for it is the moment when theories of language and the actual use of language can collide: although the questions we ask can affect the answers we find about gender differentiation, it is also true that speakers' belief in gender difference can perpetuate gender difference, be that in discourse patterns or in the grammar and lexicon of the language. It is here that we can see cultural belief systems played out in language at every level.

One of the great successes of feminist language reform has been politicizing language choices in the domain of gendered language, raising consciousness, and problematizing sexist forms. The question now may become, as feminist linguists and speakers generally think about "solutions," whether we are striving to make the language "gender equal" when we are referring to both men and women, or whether we are striving to make gender less salient if we are referring to both men and women. This does not mean that English speakers, or any other speakers, do not need or want to make gender distinctions when they speak. It is to say that speakers do not always need or want to make such gender distinctions.

The word *she* was selected as the word of the past millennium and in many ways, its choice captures the salience of feminism and the progress of women at this moment in history. The direction of language history in the ways that we talk about gender is impossible to predict. We could not have predicted the adoption of, for example, the words *she*, *boy*, or *girl* by English speakers, and in the same way, we cannot be sure what will happen to, for example, the terms *they* or *guy*. What we do know is that more of us, speakers of all genders, are talking about language change, as we negotiate the relationship of language and gender.

Appendix 1: Background on early English personal pronouns

This brief survey of some of the early linguistic developments in English personal pronouns is designed to provide useful background for the studies of the early English gender system and the gender shift described in Chapters Three and Four, as some forms of the third-person pronouns in Old and Middle English will look unfamiliar to Modern English speakers. In the process, this appendix explains linguistic curiosities such as the coexistence of *sh-* and *h-* forms for the feminine personal pronouns and the dialectal use of " 'em" in the plural.

Although by late Middle English, the language had lost most inflectional case endings on nouns, adjectives, and articles as well as grammatical gender, it preserved case and gender distinctions in the personal pronouns. In fact, Middle English not only preserved the distinctions from Old English, it also adopted new more distinctive pronominal forms: *they* and *she*. The distinct Old English third-person pronouns *he* (masculine), *heo* (feminine), and *hie* (plural) seem to have been merging in many Middle English dialects, at least in the written form, into a form often written *he*, about the time when the northern and midland dialects adopted the new pronominal forms *they* and *she*, which helped to preserve distinctions of number and gender in the personal pronouns. Like many of the structural changes that simplified the inflectional system and collapsed grammatical distinctions, the adoptions of the pronouns *they* and *she* appear to have been northern/east midland developments that spread southwards, preserving and/or reinforcing distinctions being lost outside the third-person pronoun system.

The basic Old English third-person pronoun paradigm (with common variants) can be summarized as follows (the charts are excerpted from Millward 1996: 100, 170):

| | Singular | | | |
	Masculine	Feminine	Neuter	Plural
Nominative	hē	hēo (hīe, hī, hīo)	hit	hīe (hī, hy, hīo)
Accusative	hine (hiene)	hīe (hī, hy)	hit	hīe (hī, hy, hīo)
Genitive	his	hiere (hire, hyre)	his	hiera (hira, hyra, heora)
Dative	him	hiere (hire, hyre)	him	him (heom)

By Middle English, the third-person pronoun paradigm looks more familiar, although the level of spelling variation found in Middle English texts can seem surprising to modern readers, and this chart juxtaposes many different dialectal forms of the period:

| | Singular | | | |
	Masculine	Feminine	Neuter	Plural
Subject	he	heo, sche, ho, he, ȝho, etc.	hit, it	he, hi, þei, ho, hie, þai, etc.
Object	him	hire, hure, her, heore, etc.	hit, it, him	hem, þem, ham, heom, þaim, þam, etc.
Possessive	his	hir(e), heore, her(e), etc.	his	here, þair, heore, hore, þar, etc.

Perhaps the most obvious difference between the two paradigms is the collapse of four grammatical cases in Old English into three in Middle English, as the dative and accusative cases collapse into one "object" case. Interestingly, the dative form of the masculine and feminine singular survives as the object form whereas the accusative form survives for the neuter, probably because this allows for differentiation between the masculine and neuter in object case. The neuter possessive form *its* does not appear until the sixteenth century (see Nevalainen and Raumolin-Brunberg 1994). The Middle English paradigm also shows the emergence of *sh-* forms for the feminine subject and *th-* forms for the plural throughout the paradigm. The historical origins of both forms are intriguing and revealing about a range of both internal and external forces and factors at work in the development of the language.

The origins of *they* are much clearer and less problematic than those of *she*. *They* represents a borrowing of the Old Norse form of the third-person plural pronoun. It was adopted into English in all cases of the pronoun; the nominative form generally entered the language first, followed by the oblique case forms, object and possessive. It is extremely rare for any language to borrow function words or any other words within the closed class of the lexicon, a fact which can make the adoption of *they* appear linguistically anomalous. If there were a need for a new pronoun in any given English dialect, a minor variant of either the third-person singular or plural pronoun that was more distinctive than the dominant form could have been selected and promoted to dominance within the existing Middle English pronoun paradigm. But given the assumption of close language contact between Old English and Old Norse in the Danelaw – contact which was likely a major factor in the fundamental structural changes in late Old English, as described in Chapter Two – the adoption of Old Norse function words does not appear as anomalous.

The question of how the pronoun *she* developed, whether it represents a borrowing or a native development, has been debated for the past century. The most comprehensive and plausible (but not necessarily unanimously accepted) explanation to date may be that proposed by Britton (1991), who favors a native development theory. Britton argues that first the Old English pronoun [he:o] shifted to [hjo:] / [ço:] (a palatalized fricative, often written by scribes as *ȝ(h)o*) through the resyllabification of the diphthong.[1] The second stage in the development of the *sh*-forms has provoked a great deal of controversy: how did [hj-] / [ç-] become [ʃ-]? No scholars have argued that the shift from [hj-] > [ç-] > [ʃ-] is phonetically impossible – it is well attested in many languages – but there has been little convincing evidence that the shift is natural in English. The development of [ʃ-] did occur in several English place-names (e.g., *Shetland*, *Shap*; for more details on Scandinavian-influenced place-names, see Ruud 1926: 201–204) but the geographic location of these names puts them squarely under Scandinavian influence, and it is well known that during this period, Norwegian underwent a consonant shift from [hj-] > [ç-] > [ʃ-]. Britton, however, reports his discovery in a survey of Scottish dialects of at least two other words in the English language which have undergone this consonant shift: 'huge' and 'hook' (pronounced in some Scottish dialects as [ʃudʒ] and [ʃʊk]). These two words provide possible proof that the shift is natural to English and that, therefore, the *sh*-forms (of pronouns and place-names) developed naturally in English,

---

[1] Old Norse underwent a context-free resyllabification of diphthongs in the eleventh century, but Britton argues that Scandinavian influence cannot account for the English change because the ȝ-forms appear in relatively early manuscripts in the southwest midlands, outside the Danelaw and therefore outside the sphere of Scandinavian linguistic influence. He proposes that the resyllabification took place due to the unstressed, marginal position of the pronouns, which does potentially explain how ȝ-forms appear in southern manuscripts but does not necessarily explain the prevalence of these forms (along with the *sh*-forms) in the north and east midlands. It is plausible that in these northern areas, there developed early on two variants of the feminine pronoun – one with initial *h*- (the reflex of the Old English form) and one with initial [hj-] / [ç-] (a native development in English influenced by or borrowed from Old Norse speakers) – which became options for all speakers within the dialects. The higher frequency of [hj-] and [ç-] forms in Old Norse could then have reinforced the legitimacy and use of such a feminine pronoun form in the English-speaking areas where Old Norse was also spoken.

independent of any Old Norse influence; they appear first and more often in the northern and eastern dialects because there were more words with initial [ç-] in this area due to Scandinavian influence.[2]

Given this evidence, there is reason to believe the consonant shift may be a natural development in English; at the same time, it is not necessary to shy away from explanations that stress the influence of contact with Old Norse as one factor in the development and preservation of these forms in the northern areas. In a close language contact situation, pronunciation and phonetic developments in one language could easily have repercussions in the other. And if late Old English could borrow a pronoun from Old Norse, there is no reason why Old Norse could not have influenced the development of a second pronoun in Old English.

Why did English speakers acquire new pronouns? The word *acquire* here should not be taken to imply conscious acquisition – this change, like most linguistic changes, probably happened primarily below the level of consciousness. Smith (1992:60) describes the rise of these new forms thus: "It would appear that the development of the English pronouns was essentially an unconscious piece of systemic regulation; we can see forms from a despised vernacular make their way into the 'standard' language. Plainly, these pronouns were not sociolinguistically 'fore-grounded' items."[3]   Interestingly this description seems to assume that the English language is fundamentally structured to have masculine, feminine, and plural pronoun distinctions, so that if these distinctions are lost through phonetic merger, new forms will be borrowed or developed to fill the empty slots within the given paradigm. But these grammatical categories of masculine and feminine in the personal pronouns are not linguistic universals, and the parallels or symmetry of the pre-existing system do not necessarily have to be maintained. There is no evidence that speakers need to make binary gender distinctions in language; but gender may be of such social salience that grammatical distinctions are maintained.

Many explanations of the success and the spread of the pronouns *they* and *she* out of the north have been functional in orientation. M. L. Samuels posits the avoidance of ambiguity as one of the fundamental principles of language change and one applicable to the Middle English pronoun situation: "[a]voidance of ambiguity means that of all the alternative forms available to a speaker, whether

---

[2] Samuels's work with Middle English dialect maps to analyze the spread of the new feminine pronoun forms both diatopically and diachronically supports the theory that the ʒ-forms represent an intermediate step between the *h*-forms and the *sh*-forms (1972: 114–16). They generally occur in the border areas between the new *sh*-forms in the north and the older *h*-forms in the south; the ʒ-forms never survive long in any area, and their border region pushes southwards throughout the period, anticipating the arrival of the *sh*-forms. Samuels carefully notes that by the time the new pronominal forms reach the southern areas, they may no longer have developed phonetically through the [hj-] or [ç-] stage; the southern dialects may simply have borrowed the distinctive *sh*-forms from their northern neighbors.

[3] Smith does not explain his grounds for labeling Old Norse as a "despised" vernacular.

in grammatical paradigm or lexical set, he [sic] selects only those that are clearest and least likely to give rise to ambiguity" (1972: 64). The pronoun *they*, therefore, was borrowed from Old Norse in response to a functional need for clearer communication since the Old English pronouns were phonetically merging, creating the great potential for ambiguity in reference. The potential for ambiguity was compounded by the reduction of verbal inflections to the point where distinctions were being lost between the singular and the plural in the past and present tenses. The same principle of ambiguity avoidance could hold for the success of *she* as a variant. In this case, the loss of distinctively gendered nominal inflections transferred all gender-marking functions to the pronouns, which could have heightened speakers' need to preserve the gender distinction in the pronominal forms.[4]

The adoption of the subject pronominal forms before the object and possessive forms can also be explained along functionalist lines. For the third-person plural, there is higher potential for ambiguity between the third singular and plural pronouns in subject position; in the oblique cases, the subject (and its number) is presumably already known. In addition, the nominative form in subject position generally receives greater stress in the sentence and is therefore more likely to be distinguished, as opposed to the often unstressed possessive and object forms. Even as late as the middle of the fifteenth century, *h*-forms appear in the south in oblique cases (Caxton printed some in his early documents), and scholars have noted that in some spoken dialects of English today, /həm/ is common as an object form of the third-person plural pronoun. The adoption of the distinct form *she* in the subject case and the retention of *h-* forms for the object and possessive could be explained similarly by the higher potential for ambiguity in subject position and the stress on the nominative form. In addition, since the plural pronoun forms seem to have shifted earlier, new *th*-forms in the oblique cases of the plural could have eliminated any potential ambiguity with the feminine.

Such functional theories could be taken to imply that English speakers *need* the distinction between the masculine and feminine in their pronouns in order to be able to communicate clearly, but it is important to note that there are numerous languages which flourish to this day without such distinctions (e.g., spoken Chinese makes no distinction between 'he' and 'she'). A related question is, was English ever really in danger of losing these pronoun distinctions? Was a merger, in fact, happening? While final vowels were undeniably being reduced in the spoken language and the forms for *he*, *heo*, and *hie* often appear to be merging in the surviving written manuscripts, these manuscripts cannot be taken as irrefutable proof that the spoken forms were merging within the dialect. They

---

[4] There are at least two explanations for why the *sh*-forms, which were originally marginal, became dominant and replaced the ȝ-forms. First, the *sh*-forms were more distinctive than the [hj-] or [ç-] forms in opposition to the third-person singular masculine pronoun *he*, and they were therefore selected from among the variant forms for the pronoun for communicative purposes. Second, /ç/ is a marginal phoneme within the language, so there may have been pressure to replace it with an acoustically similar and more common phoneme, and /ʃ/ would have been a possible substitution.

may have been becoming phonetically more similar, but not necessarily phonetically identical. It is equally probable that within each speaker's ideolect (if not within the dialect as a whole) the pronominal distinctions were preserved, even if subtly so. Scribal acrobatics to convey the differences between the pronouns in manuscripts do not have to reflect a merger of the forms in the spoken language: for example, the use of *hei* 'he' when it appears near *he* 'she' (Samuels 1972: 114). They could reflect a subtle difference in the forms' pronunciation which the scribe found difficult to transfer to vellum. In addition, as Labov has argued, speakers may perceive mergers that have not phonetically happened. The generations of speakers who adopted the new *th-* or *sh-*forms would not then have been necessarily recreating a gender or number distinction which had been lost in a previous generation of speakers; they would have been selecting (probably below the level of consciousness) a different, more distinctive variant of a still distinct form.

Appendix 2: Helsinki Corpus texts and methodology

Helsinki Corpus texts analyzed in Chapters Three and Four

Old English

The following Old English text excerpts from the Helsinki Corpus are included in the study described in Chapters Three and Four.[1]

OE I (pre-850 AD)	
Documents	*Documents 1*
Verse	*Cædmon's Hymn*
	Leiden Riddle

OE II (850–950 AD)	
Documents	*Documents 2*
Philosophy	*Alfred's Boethius*
History	*Chronicle MS A Early*
	Bede's Ecclesiastical History
	Ohthere and Wulfstan (MS L)
	Alfred's Orosius
Law	*Laws (Alfred's Introduction to Laws; Alfred; INE)*
Religious Treatises	*Alfred's Cura Pastoralis*
Prefaces	*Alfred's Preface to Cura Pastoralis*
Bible	*Vespasian Psalter*
Handbooks/Medicine	*Læceboc*
Verse	*Battle of Brunanburh*

[1] In the OE III and IV sections, it became apparent that the religious texts are grammatically conservative with respect to anaphoric gender agreement and they often contain very few anaphoric references to inanimate objects (e.g., in the excerpt from *Ælfric's Letter to Sigeweard*, of the 600 total anaphoric pronouns, only 1.3 percent refer to inanimate objects and another 0.5 percent to animals). In OE III, the *Blickling Homilies*, the *Old Testament*, and the *Paris Psalter* were included; the *West-Saxon Gospels*, *Lindisfarne Gospels*, or *Rushworth Gospels* were inspected for relevant data but not included.

OE III (950–1050 AD)

Documents	*Documents 3*
History	*Chronicle MS A Late*
	Ohthere and Wulfstan (MS G)
Geography	*Marvels*
Law	*Laws (Eleventh Century)*
Homilies	*Blickling Homilies*
Biography, lives	*Ælfric's Lives of Saints*
	Gregory the Great, Dialogues (MS H)
	Martyrology
Bible	*Old Testament*
	Paris Psalter
Prefaces	*Ælfric's Preface to Catholic Homilies I, II; Lives of Saints; Grammar; Genesis*
Science/Astronomy	*Byrhtferth's Manual*
	Ælfric's De Temporibus Anni
Handbooks/Medicine	*Lacnunga*
	Quadrupedibus
Verse	*Fates of Apostles, Elene, Juliana*
	Genesis
	Exodus
	Christ
	Kentish Hymn
	Andreas
	Dream of the Rood
	Exeter Book poems: the Wanderer, the Seafarer, Widsith, the Fortunes of Men, Maxims I, the Riming Poem, the Panther, the Whale, the Partridge, Deor, Wulf and Eadwacer, the Wife's Lament, Beowulf

OE IV (1050–1150 AD)

Documents	*Documents 4*
History	*Chronicle MS E*
Law	*Laws (Late; William)*
Religious Treatises	*Adrian and Ritheus*
	Ælfric's Letter to Sigeweard
	Solomon and Saturn
	Old English Vision of Leofric
Biography, lives	*Passion of St. Margaret*
	Gregory the Great, Dialogues (MS C)
Science/Astronomy	*Prognostications*

Early Middle English

The earliest Middle English part of the Helsinki Corpus (ME I) includes excerpts from the following texts (totaling over 113,000 words), all of which are included in the study described in Chapters Three and Four (the general dialectal origins of the texts as tagged in the Corpus are noted in parentheses).

ME I (1150–1250 AD)	
Handbooks/Medicine	*Peri Didaxeon* (southern)
Homilies	*The Ormulum* (east midland)
	Trinity Homilies (east midland)
	Vespasian Homilies (Kentish)
	Bodley Homilies (southern)
	Lambeth Homilies (west midland)
	Sawles Warde (west midland)
Religious Treatises	*History of the Holy Rood-Tree* (southern)
	Ancrene Wisse (west midland)
	Hali Meidhad (west midland)
	Vices and Virtues (east midland)
History	*The Peterborough Chronicle* (east midland)
	Layamon (west midland)
Biography	*Katherine* (west midland)
	Margarete (west midland)
	Juliane (west midland)

Methodology for the corpus-based studies in Chapters Three and Four

The studies in Chapters Three and Four are best described as empirical, corpus-based studies. However, it became apparent early in the studies that there are serious limits to how systematic and "objective" a study of this kind of syntactic phenomenon can be. It also became apparent how enormously time-consuming it has to be. For every one of the Helsinki Corpus texts included in these studies, I have recorded every instance of singular third-person anaphoric personal pronouns (17,912 total); for every one of these pronouns, the antecedent must be manually determined. In other words, there is no way to exploit the computerized nature of the Corpus for such a study as the relationship of the pronoun and antecedent noun can only be discovered by a close reading, and the spelling variation in Old and Middle English does not allow efficient searching of pronoun forms (e.g., Old English 'their' can be spelled *heora, hiera, hira*, etc.).

Moore (1921), Heltveit (1958), and Mitchell (1986) include only gender-distinctive forms of the third-person pronoun (i.e., masculine *he, hine*; feminine *heo, hie, hire*; and neuter *hit*) in their studies, but this study includes all singular forms.[2] To begin with, the forms *his* and *him* are "gender distinctive" with feminine antecedents because they indicate a non-feminine anaphoric reference. Second, the size of the gender-agreement "margin" for masculine antecedents is relevant to the picture of overall gender agreement: that is, the number of anaphoric pronoun references to masculine nouns that are potentially either masculine or neuter compared to how many are definitively masculine or definitively neuter. The ambiguity of the forms *his* and *him* with masculine antecedent nouns – the listener or reader would not have known with certainty whether such a pronoun was masculine or neuter, particularly during the transition period between systems – makes these two pronouns crucial to the gender shift, and it is, therefore, important to track the patterns of change in the use of these pronouns as well as in the use of gender-distinctive ones.

The pronoun *him* carries another problem for this kind of study, in addition to its nondistinctiveness between the masculine and neuter: its compound use as both a singular and plural dative form in many dialects (rather than the prototypical dative plural form *heom*). The singular feminine accusative form *hi(e)* creates a similar identification problem with the plural nominative and accusative form *hi(e)* in many dialects; in this case, however, the context or as importantly the verb-form almost always makes the referent clear. Context often helps distinguish the referent and number of the pronoun *him* also, as well as occasionally verb-forms, but the fluctuation between singular and plural with collective nouns in Old English often makes it almost impossible to know the number of the anaphoric pronoun.

For example, with the masculine noun *here* 'army,' the subsequent verbs and pronouns often shift between singular grammatical concord and plural notional concord. In the Winchester manuscript of the *Anglo-Saxon Chronicle*, the text fairly consistently switches number with this noun, as illustrated by the following two passages:

(1) Her for se **here** on Norþhymbre, & **he** nam wintersetl on Lindesse. (*Chronicle MS A Late* 72)

   'Here went the **army** to Northumbria, and **it (he)** took up winter-residence in Lindesse.'

(2) ða eode se **here** to **hiera** scipum . . . (*Chronicle MS A Late* 885)

   'Then went the **army** to **their** ships . . .'

---

[2] The demonstrative pronouns *se, seo, þæt* can be used independently in a subsequent clause or sentence to avoid repetition of the preceding noun (Mitchell 1986: §§316–27). If these pronouns occur between the antecedent noun and an anaphoric pronoun, they were recorded because they are gender distinctive in form. But no data was collected on their occurrences in constructions without anaphoric pronouns, as they did not survive into Modern English as gender-distinctive anaphoric pronouns.

The sentence in the next example from the *Chronicle*, therefore, is grammatically ambiguous:

(3)   for se here . . . & Brettas him wið gefuhton, & hæfdon sige, & hie bedrifon ut. (*Chronicle MS A Early* 82)

'Proceeded the army . . . And the Brits against it (him)/them fought, and had victory, and them drove out.'

Given evidence for variation within sentences and the effect of distance from the antecedent, the fact that the second anaphoric pronoun *hie* is clearly plural does not necessarily indicate the status of *him*. While these examples complicate data collection and analysis for these studies, they, more importantly, make it clear that anaphoric reference based on notional rather than grammatical concord occurs early in English, both for number as well as for gender.

One of the cornerstone features of this study is the compilation of a word count in addition to a token count. The word count is essential because a pure percentage of grammatical or natural gender agreement based on a token count (e.g., 85 percent of the anaphoric pronouns conflict with the natural gender of the antecedent) reveals little about the details of the variation or about the mechanisms involved in the shift. Some of the more intriguing questions that a word count can answer include which nouns are already showing fluctuation in gender agreement during the period, and, as importantly, which nouns are not. It is also clearly necessary to determine which antecedent nouns occur most frequently and could potentially skew the results if compared on a par with nouns that occur only once or twice.

In addition, all "other" instances of the neuter pronoun *hit*, both anaphoric and nonanaphoric, have been recorded. These pronominal references fall into two general categories (cf. Mitchell 1986: §§1485–90): (1) *formal subject* (or anticipatory subject); (2) *general reference*, or reference back to the general idea of the previous sentence or even larger grammatical unit (rather than back to one particular antecedent noun). The use of *hit* as a formal or existential subject in early English is very similar to Modern English, as the following example demonstrates:

(4)   Hit is gecueden ðætte ða stanas on ðæm mæran temple Salomonnes wæron sua wel gefegede . . . (*Alfred's Cura Pastoralis* 253)

'It is said that the stones in the great temple of Solomon were so well joined . . .'

The use of *hit* as a general reference back to an idea or a group of things, rather than to one specific noun, is quite common in early English, much like Modern English. In the medical text *Læceboc*, for example, the pronoun *hit* is often used to refer back to a mixture of things:

(5)   Læcedomas wiþ eagna miste, genim celeþenian seaw oþþe blostman, gemeng wið dorena hunig, gedo on æren fæt, wlece listum on wearmum gledum oþþæt **hit** gesoden sie. (*Læceboc* 26)

'Leechdoms for mistiness of the eyes: take celandine (swallow-wort) juice or blossoms, mix with humble bees' honey, put into a brazen vat, warm skillfully on warm coals, until **it** be boiled.'

The fine line between the use of the pronoun *hit* as a general reference anaphoric pronoun and as an anaphoric pronoun referring to a specific noun represents perhaps the biggest methodological difficulty in identifying antecedents for the study in Chapter Four. Throughout the Old and Early Middle English period, *hit* can be used as a general reference back to the idea of the sentence, so in cases where the logical antecedent of a *hit* reference is not a neuter noun, it seems perhaps prudent to classify that particular *hit* as a general reference: it is not, for example, referring to the pact itself but to the idea of breaking the pact. As a specific instance, in Alfred's Old English *Cura Pastoralis*, there appears the difficult passage:

(6)   he mæg ðy orsorglicor forbugan ða ðegnunga; ond næs swaðeah to anwillice ne forbuge he, swa we ær cwædon, ðonne he ongiete ðone ufancundan willan ðæt he **hit** don scyle (*Alfred's Cura Pastoralis* 51)

'[H]e can by this with less anxiety decline the **ministration**; and yet he too obstinately should not decline, as we earlier said, when he recognizes the divine will that he **it** must do.'

The pronoun *hit* could refer specifically to *ðenunga* 'ministry' (a masculine noun that often, as here, appears in the plural), or it could refer more generally to the accepting of the ministry. When it is possible to identify one noun phrase acting as the antecedent, it has been recorded for the study. When there is any serious question as to whether an idea, and not a specific noun, is being referred to with a neuter pronoun, or when no one antecedent can easily be determined, as in the above example, the neuter pronoun has been recorded as an instance of "general reference."

In a study of this size, there are numerous instances of sentences in which multiple noun phrases could all possibly serve as antecedents for a given anaphoric pronoun. In most cases, it is obvious from context which noun is meant, and in less clear cases, the gender of the pronoun often proves helpful in determining the antecedent. For example, in the following passage from the *Blickling Homilies* with two possible, synonymous antecedents (feminine *woruld* 'world' and masculine *middangeard* 'world'), the grammatical gender of the pronoun proves critical in determining the antecedent.

(7)   For þam þissere **weorlde** wlite noht, ne þisses **middaneardes** feȝernes, ac **he** is hwilwendlic, & feallendlic . . . (*Blickling Homilies* 130)

'Not at all because of this **world**'s beauty, nor this **world**'s fairness, but **it** (he) is transitory and perishable . . .'

The masculine pronoun *he* seems to refer back to *middangeard*, the closer of the two possible antecedent nouns.

The situation, as one can imagine, becomes more complex in alliterative poetry. If a sentence or longer passage contains a string of alliterating noun phrases standing in apposition, followed by the anaphoric pronoun *hit* referring back to the object in question, which of the preceding nouns should be selected as the antecedent? The closest one? The neuter one, wherever it may fall? The most prototypical one? The case is easier when the anaphoric pronoun is either masculine or feminine because generally the preceding masculine or feminine antecedent noun is fairly clear. But when the pronoun is neuter, it is very tempting to search for a neuter antecedent, and if only a masculine or feminine antecedent appears in the preceding string of text, it is even more tempting to assume human error and conclude that this particular *hit* must refer to something else or to the idea of the passage in general. The first 100 lines of *Beowulf* include a clear example of the problems in determining the antecedent in alliterative poetry:

(8) Him on mod bearn
 þæt **healreced** hatan wolde,
 medoærn micel, men gewyrcean
 þonne yldo bearn æfre gefrunon,
 ond þær on innan eall gedælan
 geongum ond ealdum, swylc him god sealde,
 buton folcscare ond feorum gumena.
 ða ic wide gefrægn weorc gebannan
 manigre mægþe geond þisne middangeard,
 folcstede frætwan. Him on fyrste gelomp,
 ædre mid yldum, þæt **hit** wearð ealgearo,
 healærna mæst . . . (*Beowulf* 67–78)

'It came into his mind, that he wanted to command the men to build a **hall-building**, a great **mead-hall**, [greater] than the children of men had ever heard of, and there within to distribute all to young and old, as God had given him except the public land and the lives of men. Then I widely heard [he wanted] to order the work to many a nation throughout the world, to adorn the **people's dwelling**. It happened in due time for him, speedily with [the work of] men, that **it** was quite ready, the **greatest of hall-buildings** . . .'

The most logical antecedent of the anaphoric neuter pronoun *hit* in terms of distance is *folcstede* 'dwelling-place,' a masculine noun. Two sentences previously, the two neuter nouns *heallreced* 'hall-building' and *meduærn* 'mead-hall' appear, standing in apposition, describing the same physical structure. And just after the *hit* in question, there appears the phrase *healærna mæst* 'greatest of hall-buildings,' *healærn* being a neuter noun perhaps in direct apposition to the pronoun. In a case as convoluted as this one, no antecedent noun has been selected for the study results; instead, this instance of *hit* has been recorded as a "general reference" – in other words, an instance when *hit* is used to refer to an idea, as could arguably be the case here if 'hall' is the underlying, almost prototypical idea in question.

The problems involved in identifying general reference uses of neuter pronouns, as opposed to antecedent-specific ones, and in handling multiple antecedents underscore some of the challenges of studying gender concord in anaphoric pronouns in any language at any point in time. Anaphora, in general, is a difficult grammatical phenomenon to examine due to the vagueness of its boundaries and the slippery distinction between exophoric reference (i.e., reference outside the discourse or text) and endophoric reference (i.e., reference within the discourse or text). A text-based study dramatically reduces the number of exophoric references: the reader rarely is confronted with a completely understood referent that stands outside the text. But even within a written context, the vagueness of any available definition of the antecedent and of the limits of anaphoric reference makes absolute precision difficult if not impossible.

Wales (1996: 22) remarks that actual speech and writing often involve competing antecedents for any one anaphoric pronoun; as a result, linguists cannot overemphasize "the importance of our own mental activity as users of English in both appreciating and resolving ambiguity, finding relevance in indeterminacy and, generally, in assigning the appropriate reference." In other words, as Wales phrases it, the onus is on the addressee to find the antecedent. In a historical case study of anaphora such as this one, the addressee is the linguistic historian who is many centuries removed from the texts and the language they contain, and the problems are often difficult to resolve. As I also note in Chapter Four, I believe this fact is critical to the results of the study for two reasons: (1) even as we look for and analyze general patterns, we must remember the "fuzziness" inherent in these kinds of statistics; and (2) this kind of ambiguity is exactly the kind of syntactic phenomenon that facilitates language change.

The advantage of a large sample size is that even with the required individual decisions on passages with vague or tangled anaphoric references and the relegation of a certain number of instances to "general reference," the overall trend of the results should still provide important insights into the mechanisms of this change. The statistics in Chapters Three and Four are presented as potentially revealing of larger trends, which may or may not be confirmed by future studies. And I hope that the specific examples culled from the texts themselves will be equally illuminating about the change in progress. Even with these potential pitfalls and ambiguities, large numbers of antecedents reveal the linguistic mechanisms at work in this syntactic change. The seeds of this gender shift are evident in Old English, and they blossom into patterns of natural gender concord in written early Middle English as the grammatical change diffuses through the grammar and lexicon of the language.

As importantly, these methodologically problematic passages highlight some of the critical linguistic factors involved in the shift. Speakers of early varieties of English were confronted with the same problems in antecedent identification that face the modern linguistic historian. The prevalent use of the neuter to refer back to general ideas or lists undoubtedly served only to encourage the eventual use of the neuter as a default anaphoric pronoun for all ideas and things being referred back to, no matter what their grammatical gender. The kind of ambiguity we see here in grammar echoes discussions of historical semantics and the inherent fuzziness of semantic categories. Meaning is constructed in the relationship between the speaker (or writer) and the hearer (or reader), and the ambiguity inherent in language and the possibilities for varying interpretations are critical components of language change, be it the gender shift or the semantic changes in words referring to men and women. In linguistic variation and ambiguity, at the level of the word or sentence or in discursive use, lie seeds of linguistic change.

References

Aitchison, Jean 1995. Tadpoles, Cuckoos, and Multiple Births: Language Contact and Models of Change. In J. Fisiak (ed.), *Linguistic Change under Contact Conditions*, 1–13. Berlin; New York: Mouton de Gruyter.

2001. *Language Change: Progress or Decay?* 3rd edn. Cambridge: Cambridge University Press.

August, Eugene R. 1992. Real Men Don't: Anti-Male Bias in English. In G. Goshgarian (ed.), *Exploring Language*, 6th edn, 238–48. New York: HarperCollins.

Bäck, Hilding 1934. *The Synonyms for 'Child', 'Boy', 'Girl' in Old English: An Etymological-Semasiological Investigation*. In E. Ekwall (ed.), *Lund Studies in English* II. Lund: A.-B. Ph. Lindstedts Univ.-Bokhandel.

Bäcklund, Ingegerd 1996. Males and Females in Jane Austen's World: A Study of Terms. In G. Persson and M. Rydén (eds.), *Male and Female Terms in English: Proceedings of the Symposium at Umeå University, May 18–19, 1994*, 9–28. Umeå: Umeå University; Uppsala: Distributed by Swedish Science Press.

Bailey, Charles J. and Karl Maroldt 1977. The French Lineage in English. In J. M. Meisel (ed.), *Langues en Contact – Pidgins – Creoles – Languages in Contact*, 21–53. Tübingen: TBL Verlag Gunter Narr.

Bailey, Richard 1991. *Images of English: A Cultural History of the Language*. Ann Arbor: University of Michigan Press.

1996. *Nineteenth-Century English*. Ann Arbor: University of Michigan Press.

Bain, Alexander 1879. *A Higher English Grammar*. New edn. London: Longmans.

Barber, Charles 1993. *The English Language: A Historical Introduction*. Cambridge: Cambridge University Press.

Barlow, Michael 1992. *A Situated Theory of Agreement*. New York: Garland.

Baron, Dennis 1986. *Grammar and Gender*. New Haven: Yale University Press.

Baron, Naomi S. 1971. A Reanalysis of English Grammatical Gender. *Lingua* 27: 113–40.

Batliner, Anton 1984. The Comprehension of Grammatical and Natural Gender: a Cross-Linguistic Experiment. *Linguistics* 22: 831–56.

Baugh, Albert C. and Thomas Cable 1978. *A History of the English Language*. 3rd edn. London: Routledge & Kegan Paul.

Beardsmore, H. Baetens 1971. A Gender Problem in a Language Contact Situation. *Lingua* 27: 141–59.

Beattie, James 1968 [1788]. *Theory of Language*. Reprint. Menston: Scolar Press.

Bebout, Linda 1984. Asymmetries in Male-Female Word Pairs. *American Speech* 59.1: 13–30.

1995. Asymmetries in Male/Female Word Pairs: A Decade of Change. *American Speech* 70.2: 163–85.

Bennett-Kastor, Tina L. 1996. Anaphora, Nonanaphora, and the Generic Use of Pronouns by Children. *American Speech* 71: 285–301.

Benson, Larry D. (ed.) 1987. *The Riverside Chaucer*. 3rd edn. Boston: Houghton Mifflin.

Bergvall, Victoria L., Janet M. Bing, and Alice F. Freed (eds.) 1996. *Rethinking Language and Gender Research: Theory and Practice*. London; New York: Longman.

Bing, Janet B. and Victoria L. Bergvall 1998. The Question of Questions: Beyond Binary Thinking. In J. Coates (ed.), *Language and Gender: A Reader*, 495–510. Oxford; Malden, MA: Blackwell.

Björkman, Erik 1969 [1900]. *Scandinavian Loanwords in Middle English*. New York: Greenwood Press.

Bloomfield, Morton W. and Leonard Newmark 1963. *A Linguistic Introduction to the History of English*. New York: Alfred A. Knopf.

Bodine, Ann 1975. Androcentrism in Prescriptive Grammar: Singular 'they,' Sex-indefinite 'he,' and 'he or she.' *Language in Society* 4: 129–46.

Bourcier, Georges 1981. *An Introduction to the History of the English Language*. (English adaptation by Cecily Clark.) Cheltenham: Stanley Thornes.

Bradley, Henry 1924 [1904]. *The Making of English*. London: Macmillan.

Bresnan, Joan, and Sam Mchombo 1986. Grammatical and Anaphoric Agreement. In A. M. Farley, P. T. Farley, and K. McCullough (eds.), *Papers from the Parasession on Pragmatics and Grammatical Theory at the Twenty-Second Regional Meeting* (Chicago Linguistics Society, 22), 278–97.

Britton, Derek 1991. On Middle English *She, Sho*: A Scots Solution to an English Problem. *North-Western European Language Evolution* 17: 3–51.

Brown, Goold 1982 [1828]. *The Institutes of English Grammar*. New York: Scholars' Facsimiles & Reprints.

Bryson, Bill 1990. *Our Mother Tongue: English and How It Got to Be That Way*. London: Penguin.

Buccini, Anthony F. Southern Middle English *Hise* and the Question of Pronominal Transfer in Language Contact. Unpublished paper.

Bullions, Peter 1983 [1846]. *The Principles of English Grammar*. New York: Scholars' Facsimiles & Reprints.

Burgschmidt, Ernst 1988. Gender in Modern English – Sub-systems and Variation. *Historical English: on the Occasion of Karl Brunner's 100th Birthday*, 219–30. Innsbruck: Institut für Anglistik, Universität Innsbruck.

Butler, Judith 1990. *Gender Trouble: Feminism and the Subversion of Identity*. New York: Routledge.

Cameron, Deborah 1990. *Feminism and Linguistic Theory*. 2nd edn. London: Macmillan.

1995. *Verbal Hygiene*. London: Routledge.

Cameron, Deborah and Jennifer Coates 1985. Some Problems in the Sociolinguistic Explanation of Sex Differences. *Language & Communication* 5: 143–51.

Campbell, Alistair 1959. *Old English Grammar*. Oxford: Clarendon.

Cassidy, Frederic G. (chief ed.) 1985–. *Dictionary of American Regional English*. Cambridge, MA: Belknap Press of Harvard University Press.

Cawdrey, Robert 1966 [1604]. *A Table Alphabeticall of Hard Usual English Words*. New York: Scholars' Facsimiles & Reprints. http://www.library.utoronto.ca/utel/ret/cawdrey/cawdrey0.html.

Champneys, A. C. 1893. *History of English*. London: Percival.

Christy, Craig 1983. *Uniformitarianism in Linguistics*. (Amsterdam Studies in the Theory and History of Linguistic Science, Series III, *Studies in the History of Linguistics*, 31.) Amsterdam; Philadelphia: John Benjamins.

Claiborne, Robert 1983. *Our Marvelous Native Tongue: The Life and Times of the English Language*. New York: Times Books.

Clancy, Steven J. 1999. The Ascent of guy. *American Speech* 74.3: 282–97.

Clark, C. 1957. Gender in the 'Peterborough Chronicle.' *English Studies* 38: 109–15.

1970. *The Peterborough Chronicle, 1070–1154*. 2nd edn. Oxford: Clarendon.

Clark Hall, J. R. 1960. *A Concise Anglo-Saxon Dictionary*. 4th edn. (With a Supplement by Herbert D. Meritt.) Toronto: University of Toronto Press.

Classen, E. 1919. On the Origin of Natural Gender in Middle English. *Modern Language Review* 14: 97–103.

1919. *Outlines of the History of the English Language*. London: Macmillan.

Coates, Jennifer 1996. *Women Talk: Conversation between Women Friends*. Oxford: Blackwell.

Cobbett, William 1986 [1832]. *A Grammar of the English Language*. New York: Scholars' Facsimiles & Reprints.

Cockayne, Thomas Oswald 1961 [1864]. *Leechdoms, Wortcunning and Starcraft of Early England*. London: Holland Press.

Comrie, Bernard 1999. Grammatical Gender Systems: A Linguist's Assessment. *Journal of Psycholinguistic Research* 28.5: 457–66.

Corbett, Greville G. 1991. *Gender*. Cambridge; New York: Cambridge University Press.

Cornish, Francis 1986. *Anaphoric Relations in English and French: A Discourse Perspective*. London; Sydney; Dover: Croom Helm.

Crawford, Mary 1995. *Talking Difference: On Gender and Language*. London: Sage.

Crystal, David 1995. *The Cambridge Encyclopedia of the English Language*. Cambridge: Cambridge University Press.

Curme, George O. 1931. *Syntax*. Boston: D. C. Heath.

Curzan, Anne 1998. When *It* Became All Things: A Study of the Rise of Natural Gender in English Anaphoric Pronouns. Unpublished dissertation.

1999. Gender Categories in Early English Grammars: Their Message to the Modern Grammarian. In B. Unterbeck and M. Rissanen (eds.), *Gender in Grammar and Cognition*, 561–76. The Hague: Mouton de Gruyter.

Dahl, Östen 1999. Animacy and the Notion of Semantic Gender. In B. Unterbeck and M. Rissanen (eds.), *Gender in Grammar and Cognition*, 99–115. The Hague: Mouton de Gruyter.

Dalton-Puffer, Christiane 1995. Middle English is a Creole and Its Opposite: On the Value of Plausible Speculation. In J. Fisiak (ed.), *Linguistic Change under Contact Conditions*, 35–50. Berlin; New York: Mouton de Gruyter.

Daly, Mary, conjurer, in cahoots with Jane Caputi 1987. *Websters' First New Intergalactic Wickedary of the English Language*. Boston: Beacon Press.

Danchev, Andrei 1997. The Middle English Creolization Hypothesis Revisited. In J. Fisiak (ed.), *Studies in Middle English Linguistics*, 79–108. Berlin; New York: Mouton de Gruyter.

Daniel, Neil 1992. *A Guide to Style and Mechanics*. Fort Worth: Harcourt Brace Jovanovich.

Dekeyser, X. 1980. The Diachrony of Gender Systems in English and Dutch. In J. Fisiak (ed.), *Historical Morphology*, 97–111. The Hague: Mouton de Gruyter.

Devis, Ellin 1801. *The Accidence or First Rudiments of English Grammar*. London.

Diensberg, Bernhard 1981. The Etymology of Modern English *Boy*: A New Hypothesis. *Medium Ævum* 50.1: 79–87.

1985. The Lexical Fields *Boy/Girl-Servant-Child* in Middle English. *Neuphilologische Mitteilungen* 86: 328–36.

Diller, Hans-Jürgen 1991. Pronoun and Reference in Old English Poetry. In D. Kastovsky (ed.), *Historical English Syntax*, 125–40. Berlin; New York: Mouton de Gruyter.

Dobson, E. J. 1940. The Etymology and Meaning of *Boy*. *Medium Ævum* 9.3: 121–54.

Domingue, Nicole Z. 1977. Middle English: Another Creole? *Journal of Creole Studies* 1: 89–100.

Dunayer, Joan 1995. Sexist Words, Speciesist Roots. In C. J. Adams and J. Donovan (eds.), *Animals and Women: Feminist Theoretical Explorations*, 11–31. Durham; London: Duke University Press.

Dykema, Karl W. 1960–61. Where Our Grammar Came From. *College English* 22: 455–65.

Eckert, Penelope and Sally McConnell-Ginet 1998. Communities of Practice: Where Language, Gender, and Power All Live. In J. Coates (ed.), *Language and Gender: A Reader*, 484–94. Oxford; Malden, MA: Blackwell.

Emerson, O. F. 1895. *The History of the English Language*. New York: Macmillan.

Erades, P. A. 1956. Contributions to Modern English Syntax: A Note on Gender. *Moderna Sprak* 50: 2–11.

Ervin, Susan 1962. The Connotations of Gender. *Word* 18: 249–61.

Farmer, J. S. and W. E. Henley (eds.) 1970 [1890–1904]. *Slang and Its Analogues*. Reprint. New York: Arno Press.

Fell, Christine, Cecily Clark, and Elizabeth Williams 1984. *Women in Anglo-Saxon England and the Impact of 1066*. London: British Museum Publications.

Fennell, Barbara 2001. *A History of English: A Sociolinguistic Approach*. Oxford; Malden, MA: Blackwell.

Fillmore, Charles J. 1978. On the Organization of Semantic Information in the Lexicon: Chicago Linguistic Society April 14–15, 1978. In D. Farkas, W. M. Jacobsen and K. W. Todrys (eds.), *Papers from the Parasession on the Lexicon*, 148–73. Chicago: Chicago Linguistics Society.

Fisher, John H. 1977. Chancery and the Emergence of Standard Written English in the Fifteenth Century. *Speculum* 52: 870–99.

Fisiak, Jacek 1977. Sociolinguistics and Middle English: Some Socially Motivated Changes in the History of English. *Kwartalnik Neofilologiczny* 24: 247–59.

Fodor, István 1959. The Origin of Grammatical Gender I & II. *Lingua* 8: 1–41, 186–214.

Fowler, Henry W. 1926. *A Dictionary of Modern English Usage*. Oxford: Clarendon Press.

Fowler, Henry W. and Francis G. Fowler 1906. *The King's English*. Oxford: Clarendon Press.

Frank, Francine and Frank Anshen 1983. *Language and the Sexes*. New York: State University of New York Press.

Gazdar, G., E. Klein and G. K. Pullum 1983. *Order, Concord and Constituency*. Dordrecht: Foris.

Geeraerts, Dirk 1997. *Diachronic Prototype Semantics: A Contribution to Historical Lexicology*. Oxford: Clarendon Press; New York: Oxford University Press.

Geipel, John 1971. *The Viking Legacy: The Scandinavian Influence on the English and Gaelic Languages*. Devon: David & Charles.

Gibbens, V. E. 1955. Shifts in Gender and Meaning of Nouns Designating the Sexes. *American Speech* 30: 296–98.

Goatly, Andrew 1997. *The Language of Metaphors*. London; New York: Routledge.

Goldstein, Norm (ed.) 1998. *The Associated Press Stylebook and Libel Manual*. Updated and Revised. Reading, MA: Perseus Books.

Görlach, Manfred 1986. Middle English – A Creole? In D. Kastovsky and A. Szwedek (eds.), *Linguistics Across Historical and Geographical Boundaries*, Vol. 1, 329–44. Berlin: Mouton de Gruyter.

Gouëffic, Louise 1996. *Breaking the Patriarchal Code*. Manchester, CT: Knowledge, Ideas & Trends.

Green, Jonathon 1996. *Chasing the Sun: Dictionary Makers and the Dictionaries They Made*. New York: Henry Holt.

Greenbaum, Sidney 1996. *The Oxford English Grammar*. London: Oxford University Press.

Greene, Samuel S. 1983 [1874]. *An Analysis of the English Language*. New York: Scholars' Facsimiles & Reprints.

Grimm, Jakob Karl Ludwig 1984. *On the Origin of Language*. Trans. by Raymond A. Wiley. Leiden: E. J. Brill.

Grossman, Ellie 1997. *The Grammatically Correct Handbook*. New York: Hyperion.

Hall, R. A., Jr. 1951. Sex Reference and Grammatical Gender in English. *American Speech* 26: 170–72.

Halliday, Frank E. 1975. *The Excellency of the English Tongue*. London: Gollancz.

Harris, Alice C. and Lyle Campbell 1995. *Historical Syntax in Cross-linguistic Perspective*. Cambridge: Cambridge University Press.

Harris, James 1765 [1751]. *Hermes, or a Philosophical Inquiry Concerning Universal Grammar*. 2nd edn. London.

Harvey, Thomas W. 1987 [1878]. *A Practical Grammar of the English Language*. New York: Scholars' Facsimiles & Reprints.

Heltveit, Trygve 1958. Attribute and Anaphora in the Gender System of English. *Norsk Tidskrift for Sprogvidenskap* 18: 357–69.

Henley, Nancy 1987. This New Species that Seeks a New Language: On Sexism in Language and Language Change. In J. Penfield (ed.), *Women and Language in Transition*, 3–27. New York: State University of New York Press.

Hines, Caitlin 1994. "Let me call you sweetheart": The WOMAN AS DESSERT metaphor. In M. Bucholtz, A. C. Liang, L. A. Sutton, and C. Hines (eds.), *Cultural Performances: Proceedings of the Third Berkeley Women and Language Conference*, 295–303. Berkeley: Women and Language Group.

    1999. Foxy Chicks and Playboy Bunnies: A Case Study in Metaphorical Lexicalization. In M. K. Hiraga, C. Sinha, S. Wilcox (eds.), *Cultural, Psychological, and Typological Issues in Cognitive Linguistics*, 9–23. Amsterdam: Benjamins.

Hines, John 1991. Scandinavian English: A Creole in Context. In P. S. Ureland and G. Broderick (eds.), *Language Contact in the British Isles: Proceedings of the Eighth International Symposium on Language Contact*, 403–27. Tübingen: Max Niemeyer Verlag.

Hooks, Julius N. and Ernst G. Mathews 1956. *Modern American Grammar and Usage*. New York: Roland Press.

Horn, Lawrence R. and Steven R. Kleinedler 2000. Parasitic Reference versus R-based Narrowing: Lexical Pragmatics Meets He-Man. Linguistic Society of America Convention, Chicago, 6 January. Unpublished paper.

Howe, Stephen 1996. *The Personal Pronouns in the Germanic Languages.* (Studia Linguistica Germanica, 43.) Berlin; New York: Walter de Gruyter.

Huddleston, Rodney D. 1984. *Introduction to the Grammar of English.* Cambridge; New York: Cambridge University Press.

Hughes, Geoffrey 1988. *Words in Time: A Social History of the English Vocabulary.* Oxford; New York: Blackwell.

1991. *Swearing: A Social History of Foul Language, Oaths, and Profanity in English.* Oxford: Basil Blackwell.

Ibrahim, M. H. 1973. *Grammatical Gender, Its Origin and Development.* Paris: La-Hay.

Jakobson, Roman 1966. On Linguistic Aspects of Translation. In R. A. Brower (ed.), *On Translation*, 232–39. New York: Oxford University Press.

James, Deborah 1998. Gender-Linked Derogatory Terms and Their Use by Women and Men. *American Speech* 73.4: 399–420.

Jespersen, Otto 1912. *Growth and Structure of the English Language.* 2nd edn. Leipzig: B. G. Teubner.

1924. *The Philosophy of Grammar.* London: G. Allen & Unwin; New York: H. Holt and Co.

1933. *Essentials of English Grammar.* New York: Henry Holt.

Johnson, Samuel 1882. *A Dictionary of the English Language.* Ed. Rev. H. J. Todd. Revised by Robert G. Latham. London.

Joly, André 1975. Toward a Theory of Gender in Modern English. In A. Joly and T. Fraser (eds.), *Studies in English Grammar*, 229–87. Paris: Editions Universitaires.

Jones, Charles 1967a. The Functional Motivation of Linguistic Change: a Study in the Development of the Grammatical Category of Gender in the late Old English Period. *English Studies* 4: 97–111.

1967b. The Grammatical Category of Gender in Early Middle English. *English Studies* 48: 289–305.

1988. *Grammatical Gender in English: 950–1250.* London; New York; Sydney: Croom Helm.

Jones, Richard F. 1953. *The Triumph of the English Language.* Stanford: Stanford University Press.

Jonson, Ben 1972 [1640]. *The English Grammar.* A Scolar Press Facsimile. Menston: Scolar Press.

Kanekiyo, T. 1965. Notes on Gender in English. *Philologica Pragensia* 8: 234–37.

Kastovsky, Dieter 1999. Inflectional Classes, Morphological Restructuring, and the Dissolution of Old English Grammatical Gender. In B. Unterbeck and M. Rissanen (eds.), *Gender in Grammar and Cognition*, 709–28. The Hague: Mouton de Gruyter.

Keller, Rudi 1994. *On Language Change: The Invisible Hand in Language.* Trans. by Brigitte Nerlich. London; New York: Routledge.

Kerl, Simon 1985 [1878]. *A Common-School Grammar of the English Language.* New York: Scholars Facsimiles & Reprints.

Kirkham, Samuel 1833. *English Grammar in Familiar Lectures.* New York: McElrath, Bangs, & Herbert.

Kitson, Peter 1990. On Old English Nouns of More Than One Gender. *English Studies* 71: 185–221.

Kittredge, George L. and Frank E. Farley 1913. *An Advanced English Grammar*. Boston: Ginn and Co.

Klaeber, Friedrich (ed.) 1950. *Beowulf and the Fight at Finnsburg*. 3rd edn. Lexington, MA: D. C. Heath.

Kleparski, Grzegorz A. 1996. Semantic Change in an Onomasiological Perspective. In G. Persson and M. Rydén (eds.), *Male and Female Terms in English: Proceedings of the Symposium at Umeå University, May 18–19, 1994*, 41–91. Umeå: Umeå University; Uppsala: Distributed by Swedish Science Press.

1997. *Theory and Practice of Historical Semantics: The Case of Middle English and Early Modern English Synonyms of* GIRL/YOUNG WOMAN. Lublin: University Press of the Catholic University of Lublin.

Kolln, Martha 1999. *Rhetorical Grammar: Grammatical Choices, Rhetorical Effects*. 3rd edn. Boston: Allyn and Bacon.

Kytö, Merja (compiler) 1991. *Manual to the Diachronic Part of the Helsinki Corpus of English Texts: Coding Conventions and Lists of Source Texts*. Helsinki: Department of English, University of Helsinki.

Labov, William 1978. On the Use of the Present to Explain the Past. In P. Baldi and R. Werth (eds.), *Readings in Historical Phonology*, 275–312. Pennsylvania: Pennsylvania State University Press.

1994. *Principles of Linguistic Change: Internal Factors*. Oxford; Malden, MA: Blackwell.

2001. *Principles of Linguistic Change: External Factors*. Oxford; Malden, MA: Blackwell.

Lakoff, George 1987. *Women, Fire, and Dangerous Things: What Categories Reveal about the Mind*. Chicago: University of Chicago Press.

Lakoff, George and Mark Johnson 1980. *Metaphors We Live By*. Chicago; London: University of Chicago Press.

1999. *Philosophy in the Flesh: The Embodied Mind and Its Challenge to Western Thought*. New York: Basic Books.

Lakoff, Robin 1975. *Language and Woman's Place*. New York: Octagon Books.

Langenfelt, Gösta 1951. *She* and *Her* Instead of *It* and *Its*. *Anglia* 70: 90–101.

Laqueur, Thomas 1990. *Making Sex: Body and Gender from the Greeks to Freud*. Cambridge: Cambridge University Press.

Lass, Roger 1987. *The Shape of English: Structure and History*. London: Dent.

1992. Phonology and Morphology. In N. Blake (ed.), *The Cambridge History of the English Language*, Vol. 2 (1066–1476), 23–155. Cambridge: Cambridge University Press.

Lehmann, Winfred P. 1958. On Earlier Stages of Indo-European Influence. *Language* 34: 179–202.

Le Page, Robert 1987. The Need for a Multidimensional Model. In G. Gilbert (ed.), *Pidgin and Creole Languages*, 113–29. Honolulu: University of Hawaii Press.

Lévi-Strauss, Claude 1967. Le Sexe des Astres. *To Honor Roman Jakobson: Essays on the Occasion of His Seventieth Birthday*, Vol. 2, 1163–70. The Hague: Mouton.

Liberman, Anatoly 1998. English *Girl* under the Asterisked Sky of the Indo-Europeans. In A. della Volpe and E. C. Polomé (eds.), *Proceedings of the Seventh Annual UCLA Indo-European Conference, Los Angeles, 1995*, 150–172. Journal of Indo-European Studies Monograph Number Twenty-Seven. Washington, DC: Institute for the Study of Man.

2000. The Etymology of English *Boy*, *Beacon*, and *Buoy*. *American Journal of Germanic Linguistics and Literatures* 12.2: 201–34.

Lighter, J. E. (ed.) 1994–. *Random House Historical Dictionary of American Slang*. New York: Random House.

Lightfoot, David W. 1979. *Principles of Diachronic Syntax*. Cambridge: Cambridge University Press.

Lippi-Green, Rosina 1997. *English with an Accent: Language, Ideology, and Discrimination in the United States*. London; New York: Routledge.

Lipton, Jack P. and Alan M. Hershaft 1984. "Girl," "Woman," "Guy," "Man": The Effects of Sexist Labeling. *Sex Roles* 10: 183–94.

Liske, Holly Bea 1994. The Status of the Sexes: A View Through Language. In K. Hall, M. Bucholtz, B. Moonwomon (eds.), *Locating Power: Proceedings of the Second Berkeley Women and Language Conference*, Vol. 2, 356–361. Berkeley: Berkeley Women and Language Group.

Livia, Anna 2001. *Pronoun Envy: Literary Uses of Linguistic Gender*. Oxford: Oxford University Press.

Lounsbury, T. R. 1891. *History of the English Language*. New York: Henry Holt.

Lüdtke, Helmut 1995. On the Origin of Middle and Modern English. In J. Fisiak (ed.), *Linguistic Change under Contact Conditions*, 51–53. Berlin; New York: Mouton de Gruyter.

Lunsford, Andrea and Robert Connors 1997. *The Everyday Writer*. New York: St. Martin's Press.

MacKay, Donald 1983. Prescriptive Grammar and the Pronoun Problem. In B. Thorne, C. Kramarae, and N. Henley (eds.), *Language, Gender and Society*, 38–53. Rowley: Newbury House.

Major, Clarence (ed.) 1994. *Juba to Jive: A Dictionary of African-American Slang*. New York: Penguin Books.

Malone, Joseph L. 1985. On the Feminine Pronominalization of Irish and English Boat Nouns. *General Linguistics* 25: 189–98.

Marckwardt, Albert H. and Fred G. Walcott 1938. *Facts about Current English Usage*. A Publication of the National Council of Teachers of English. New York: D. Appleton-Century Co.

Marcoux, Dell 1973. Deviation in English Gender. *American Speech* 48: 98–107.

Markey, Thomas L. 1982. Afrikaans: Creole or Non-Creole? *Zeitschrift für Dialektologie und Linguistik* 49: 169–207.

Markus, Manfred 1988. Reasons for the Loss of Gender in English. In D. Kastovsky and G. Bauer (eds.), *Luick Revisited: Papers Read at the Luick-Symposium at Schloß Liechtenstein, 15–18.9.1985*, 241–58. Tübingen: Gunter Narr.

1995. On the Growing Role of Semantic and Pragmatic Features in Middle English. In J. Fisiak (ed.), *Linguistic Change under Contact Conditions*, 161–78. Berlin; New York: Mouton de Gruyter.

Martyna, Wendy 1978. What Does 'He' Mean? Use of the Generic Masculine. *Journal of Communication* 28.1: 131–38.

1980a. Beyond the 'He/Man' Approach: The Case for Nonsexist Language. *Signs: Journal of Women in Culture and Society* 5: 482–93.

1980b. The Psychology of the Generic Masculine. In S. McConnell-Ginet, R. Borker, and N. Furman (eds.), *Women and Language in Literature and Society*, 69–78. New York: Praeger.

1983. Beyond the He/Man Approach: The Case for Nonsexist Language. In B. Thorne, C. Kramarae, and N. Henley (eds.), *Language, Gender and Society*, 25–37. Rowley: Newbury House.

Mathiot, Madeleine 1979. Sex Roles as Revealed Through Referential Gender in American English. In M. Mathiot (ed.), *Ethnolinguistics: Boas, Sapir and Whorf Revisited*, 1–47. The Hague: Mouton.

Mausch, Hanna 1986. A Note on LME Gender. *Studia Anglica Posnaniensia* 18: 89–100.

1989. Personal Pronouns and Markedness: An Interpretation of Grammatically Conditioned Changes. *Studia Anglica Posnaniensia* 22: 81–90.

McConnell-Ginet, Sally 1979. Prototypes, Pronouns and Persons. In M. Mathiot (ed.), *Ethnolinguistics: Boas, Sapir and Whorf Revisited*, 63–83. The Hague: Mouton de Gruyter.

1988. Language and Gender. In F. J. Newmeyer (ed.), *Linguistics: The Cambridge Survey*, 75–99. Cambridge: Cambridge University Press, 1988.

1989. The Sexual (Re)Production of Meaning: A Discourse-Based Theory. In F. W. Frank and P. A. Treichler (eds.), *Language, Gender, and Professional Writing; Theoretical Approaches and Guidelines for Nonsexist Usage*, 35–50. New York: Modern Language Association.

McIntosh, Angus 1956. The Analysis of Written Middle English. *Transactions of the Philological Society* 54: 26–55.

1989. Middle English Word-Geography: Its Potential Role in the Study of the Long-Term Impact of the Scandinavian Settlements upon English. In M. Laing (ed.), *Middle English Dialectology*, 98–105. Aberdeen: Aberdeen University Press.

McIntosh, Angus, M. L. Samuels, Michael Benskin, *et al.* 1987. *Linguistic Atlas of Late Mediaeval English*. Aberdeen: Aberdeen University Press.

McMahon, April 1994. *Understanding Language Change*. Cambridge: Cambridge University Press.

McWhorter, John 1998. *Word on the Street: Debunking the Myth of a "Pure" Standard English*. Cambridge, MA: Perseus.

Megginson, David 1994. He (pl) and Other New Old English Pronouns. *ANQ: A Quarterly Journal of Short Articles, Notes & Reviews* 7: 6–13.

Middle English Dictionary 1952–. Ann Arbor: University of Michigan Press. http://ets.umdl.umich.edu/m/med/.

Miller, Casey and Kate Swift 1977. *Words and Women*. New York: Anchor Books.

1980. *The Handbook on Nonsexist Writing*. New York: Lippincott and Crowell.

Miller, Thomas (ed.) 1959 [1890]. *The Old English Version of Bede's Ecclesiastical History of the English People.* (*EETS*, 95.) Oxford: Oxford University Press.

Mills, Jane 1989. *Womanwords*. London: Virago Press.

Millward, C. M. 1996. *Biography of the English Language*. 2nd edn. New York: Harcourt Brace Jovanovich.

Milroy, James 1992. *Linguistic Variation and Change*. Oxford: Blackwell.

2000. Historical Description and the Ideology of the Standard Language. In L. Wright (ed.), *The Development of Standard English, 1300–1800*, 11–28. Cambridge: Cambridge University Press.

Milroy, Lesley 1980. *Language and Social Networks*. Oxford: Blackwell.

Mitchell, Bruce 1986. *Old English Syntax*. Oxford: Clarendon Press.

Modern English Collection, Humanities Text Initiative, University of Michigan. http://www.hti.umich.edu/p/pd-modeng/.

Moe, Albert F. 1963. "Lady" and "Woman": The Terms' Use in the 1880s. *American Speech* 38: 295.

Moore, Samuel 1921. Grammatical and Natural Gender in Middle English. *Publications of the Modern Language Association of America* 36: 79–103.

Morris, Lori 1993. *Gender in Modern English: The System and Its Uses.* Unpublished dissertation.

Moulton, Janice 1977. The Myth of Neutral 'Man.' In M. Vetterling-Braggin, F. Elliston, and J. English (eds.), *Feminism and Philosophy*, 124–137. Totowa, NJ: Rowman and Littlefield.

    1981. The Myth of the Neutral 'Man.' In M. Vetterling-Braggin (ed.), *Sexist Language: A Modern Philosophical Analysis*, 100–115. New Jersey: Littlefield, Adams, & Co.

Mugglestone, Lynda (ed.) 2000. *Lexicography and the OED: Pioneers in the Untrodden Forest.* Oxford: Oxford University Press.

Mühlhäusler, Peter 1986. *Pidgin and Creole Linguistics.* Oxford: Basil Blackwell.

Mühlhäusler, Peter and Rom Harré 1990. *Pronouns and People: The Linguistic Construction of Social and Personal Identity.* Oxford: Blackwell.

Murray, K. M. Elizabeth 1977. *Caught in the Web of Words: James Murray and the Oxford English Dictionary.* New Haven; London: Yale University Press.

Murray, Lindley 1981 [1824]. *English Grammar.* New York: Scholars' Facsimiles & Reprints.

Mustanoja, Tauno F. 1960. *A Middle English Syntax* Part I. Helsinki: Société Néophilologique.

Namai, Kenichi 2000. Gender Features in English. *Linguistics* 38.4: 771–79.

Naro, Anthony J. and Miriam Lemle 1976. Syntactic Diffusion. In S. Steever, C. Walker, S. Mufwene (eds.), *Papers from the Parasession on Diachronic Syntax*, 221–40. Chicago: Chicago Linguistics Society.

Nevalainen, Terttu and Helena Raumolin-Brunberg 1994. Its Strength and the Beauty of It: The Standardization of the Third Person Neuter Possessive in Early Modern English. In D. Stein and I. Tieken-Boon van Ostade (eds.), *Towards a Standard English, 1600–1800*, 171–216. Berlin; New York: Mouton de Gruyter.

Newman, Michael 1997. *Epicene Pronouns: The Linguistics of a Prescriptive Problem.* New York, London: Garland.

Ng, Sik Hung, Kam Kuen Chan, Ann Weatherall, and Joanna Moody 1993. Polarized Semantic Change of Words Associated with Females and Males. *Journal of Language and Social Psychology* 12: 66–80.

Norberg, Catherine 1996. Chaucer's Women: Female Occupational Terms in *The Canterbury Tales*. In G. Persson and M. Rydén (eds.), *Male and Female Terms in English: Proceedings of the Symposium at Umeå University, May 18–19, 1994*, 115–34. Umeå: Umeå University; Uppsala: Distributed by Swedish Science Press.

Ogilvie, John 1882. *The Imperial Dictionary, English, Technological, and Scientific.* New edn. Ed. Charles Annandale. London: Blackie & Son.

Oxford English Dictionary 1989. 2nd edn. Oxford: Clarendon. *Oxford English Dictionary Online*: http://dictionary.oed.com.

Pauwels, Anne 1998. *Women Changing Language.* London; New York: Longman.

Penelope, Julia and Cynthia McGowan 1979. Woman and Wife: Social and Semantic Shifts in English. *Papers in Linguistics* 12: 491–502.

Persson, Gunnar 1990. *Meanings, Models and Metaphors: A Study in Lexical Semantics in English.* Stockholm: Almqvist & Wiksell International.

1996. Invectives and Gender in English. In G. Persson and M. Rydén (eds.), *Male and Female Terms in English: Proceedings of the Symposium at Umeå University, May 18–19, 1994*, 157–73. Umeå: Umeå University; Uppsala: Distributed by Swedish Science Press.

Persson, Gunnar and Mats Rydén 1995. The Project "Male and Female Terms in English": A Diachronic Study of a Semantic Field. In H. Kardela and G. Persson (eds.), *New Trends in Semantics and Lexicography*, 145–50. Umeå: Acta Universitatis Umensis.

Peyton, V. J. 1771. *The History of the English Language*. Reprint. Menston: Scolar Press.

Plag, Ingo 1994. Creolization and Language Change: A Comparison. In D. Adone and I. Plag (eds.), *Creolization and Language Change*, 3–19. Tübingen: Max Niemeyer Verlag.

Poussa, Patricia 1982. The Evolution of Early Standard English: The Creolization Hypothesis. *Studia Anglica Posnaniensia* 14: 69–85.

Robbins, Susan and Julia Stanley 1978. Going Through the Changes: The Pronoun *She* in Middle English. *Papers in Linguistics* 11.1–2: 71–88.

Roberts, Jane A. 1970. Traces of Unhistorical Gender Congruence in a Late Old English Manuscript. *English Studies* 51: 30–37.

Robins, R. H. 1971 [1951]. *Ancient and Mediaeval Grammatical Theory in Europe*. Reprint. New York: Kennikat.

Robinson, Fred 1968. European Clothing Names and the Etymology of *Girl*. In W. Arndt, P. Brosman, F. Loenen, W. Friederich (eds.), *Studies in Historical Linguistics in Honor of George Sherman Lane*, 233–40. Chapel Hill: University of North Carolina Press.

Rodgers, Bruce 1972. *The Queens' Vernacular: A Gay Lexicon*. San Francisco: Straight Arrow Books.

Romaine, Suzanne 1982. *Sociohistorical Linguistics*. Cambridge: Cambridge University Press.

1988. *Pidgin and Creole Languages*. New York: Longman.

1999. *Communicating Gender*. New Jersey; London: Lawrence Erlbaum.

Ross, A. S. C. 1936. Sex and Gender in the *Lindisfarne Gospels*. *Journal of English and Germanic Philology* 35: 321–30.

Rot, Sandor 1984. Inherent Variability and Linguistic Interference of Anglo-Old-Scandinavian and Anglo-Norman French Language Contacts in the Formation of Grammatical Innovations in Late Old English and Middle English. In N. F. Blake and C. Jones (eds.), *English Historical Linguistics: Studies in Development*, 67–86. Sheffield: Centre for English Cultural Tradition and Language, University of Sheffield.

Rudskoger, A. 1955. A Note on the Use of *she* for Inanimate Things in Australian. *Moderna Sprak* 49: 264–5.

Ruud, Martin 1926. *She* Once More. *Review of English Studies* 2: 201–204.

Rydén, Mats 1996. Aspects of Language Use. In G. Persson and M. Rydén (eds.), *Male and Female Terms in English: Proceedings of the Symposium at Umeå University, May 18–19, 1994*, 1–7. Umeå: Umeå University; Uppsala: Distributed by Swedish Science Press.

Safire, William 1999. Genderese: Looking for a Masterful Webmistress? *New York Times Magazine*, 16 May.

Sampson, Gloria P. 1979. Sociolinguistic Aspects of Pronoun Usage in Middle English. In W. C. McCormack and S. A. Wurm (eds.), *Language and Society: Anthropolgical Issues*, 61–69. The Hague: Mouton.

Samuels, M. L. 1963. Some Applications of Middle English Dialectology. *English Studies* 44: 81–94.

1969. The Role of Functional Selection in the History of English. In R. Lass (ed.), *Approaches to English Historical Linguistics*, 325–44. New York: Holt, Rinehart, and Winston.

1972. *Linguistic Evolution*. Cambridge: Cambridge University Press.

1988. *Dialect and Grammar*. In J. A. Alford (ed.), *A Companion to Piers Plowman*, 201–21. Berkeley, CA: Berkeley University Press.

1989. The Great Scandinavian Belt. In M. Laing (ed.), *Middle English Dialectology*, 106–15. Aberdeen: Aberdeen University Press.

Sandred, Karl Inge 1991. Nominal Inflection in the Old English of the Anglo-Saxon Land Charters: Change of Gender or Analogy? *Studia Neophilologica* 63: 3–12.

Sandström, Caroline 1999. The Changing System of Grammatical Gender in Swedish Dialects of Nyland, Finland. In B. Unterbeck and M. Rissanen (eds.), *Gender in Grammar and Cognition*, 793–806. The Hague: Mouton de Gruyter.

Sankis, Lizabeth M., Elizabeth M. Corbitt, and Thomas A. Widiger 1999. Gender Bias in the English Language? *Journal of Personality and Social Psychology* 77.6: 1289–95.

Schaffner, Paul. A Brief History of 'Man and Woman.' Unpublished Paper.

Schultz, Muriel R. 1975. The Semantic Derogation of Women. In B. Thorne and N. Henley (eds.), *Language and Sex: Difference and Dominance*, 64–75. Rowley, MA: Newbury.

Seppänen, Aimo 1985. The *who/what* Contrast in Germanic Languages. *Zeitschrift für Phonetik Sprachwissenschaft und Kommunikationsforschung* 38: 387–97.

Sigley, Robert and Janet Holmes 2002. Looking at *girls* in Corpora of English. *Journal of English Linguistics* 30.2: 138–57.

Simon, John 1980. The Corruption of English. In L. Michaels and C. Ricks (eds.), *The State of the Language*, 35–42. Berkeley, CA: University of California Press.

Sklar, Elizabeth S. 1983. Sexist Grammar Revisited. *College English* 45: 348–58.

Smith, Jeremy 1992. The Use of English: Language Contact, Dialect Variation, and Written Standardisation During the Middle English Period. In T. W. Machan and C. T. Scott (eds.), *English in Its Social Contexts*, 47–68. Oxford; New York: Oxford University Press.

Smitherman, Geneva 2000. *Black Talk: Words and Phrases from the Hood to the Amen Corner*. Revised edn. Boston: Houghton Mifflin.

Spender, Dale 1985. *Man Made Language*. London: Routledge & Kegan Paul.

Stanley, Julia (Penelope) 1977a. Gender-Marking in American English: Usage and Reference. In A. P. Nilsen, H. Bosmajian, H. L. Gershuny, and J. Stanley (eds.), *Sexism and Language*, 43–76. Illinois: National Council of Teachers of English.

1977b. Paradigmatic Woman: The Prostitute. In D. L. Shores and C. P. Hines (eds.), *Papers in Language Variation: SAMLA-ADS Collection*, 303–21. University: University of Alabama Press.

1978. Sexist Grammar. *College English* 39.7: 800–811.

State of Washington Voters Pamphlet: General Election November 2, 1999, Edition 12. Published by the Office of the Secretary of State, King County Records and Elections, and the City of Seattle.

Stein, Dieter 1986. Old English Northumbrian Verb Inflection Revisited. In D. Kastovsky and A. Szwedek (eds.), *Linguistics Across Historical and Geographical Boundaries*, Vol. 1, 637–50. Berlin: Mouton de Gruyter.

Stevick, Robert 1963. The Biological Model and Historical Linguistics. *Language* 39: 159–69.

Strang, Barbara 1970. *A History of English*. London: Methuen.

Sutton, Laurel A. 1995. Bitches and Skankly Hobags: The Place of Women in Contemporary Slang. In K. Hall and M. Bucholtz (eds.), *Gender Articulated: Language and the Socially Constructed Self*, 279–86. New York; London: Routledge.

Svartengren, T. Hilding 1927. The Feminine Gender for Inanimate Things in Anglo-American. *American Speech* 3: 83–113.

1928. The Use of Personal Gender for Inanimate Things. *Dialect Notes* 6: 7–56.

1954. The Use of Feminine Gender for Inanimate Things in American Colloquial Speech. *Moderna Spra. k* 48: 261–92.

Swanton, Michael (ed.) 1996. *The Anglo-Saxon Chronicle*. London: J. M. Dent.

Sweet, Henry 1871. *King Alfred's West-Saxon Version of Gregory's Pastoral Care*. (*EETS* 45, 50.) London: Oxford University Press.

1931 [1891]. *A New English Grammar: Logical and Historical*. 2 vols. Reprint. Oxford: Clarendon Press.

Talbot, Mary M. 1998. *Language and Gender: An Introduction*. Cambridge: Polity Press.

Thomas of Erfurt 1972. *Grammatica Speculativa*. With translation and commentary by G. L. Bursill-Hall. London: Longman.

Thomason, Sarah G. and Terrence Kaufman 1988. *Language Contact, Creolization, and Genetic Linguistics*. California: University of California Press.

Toon, Thomas 1985. *The Politics of Early Old English Sound Change*. New York: Academic Press.

1992. The Social and Political Contexts of Language Change in Anglo-Saxon England. In T. W. Machan and C. T. Scott (eds.), *English in Its Social Contexts*, 28–47. Oxford; New York: Oxford University Press.

Traugott, Elizabeth C. 1972. *A History of English Syntax: A Transformational Approach to the History of English Sentence Structure*. New York: Holt, Rinehart and Winston.

1973. Some Thoughts on Natural Syntactic Processes. In C. J. N. Bailey and R. W. Shuy (eds.), *New Ways of Analyzing Variation in English*, 313–22. Washington, DC: Georgetown University Press.

Treichler, Paula A. 1989. From Discourse to Dictionary: How Sexist Meanings Are Authorized. In F. W. Frank and P. A. Treichler (eds.), *Language, Gender, and Professional Writing; Theoretical Approaches and Guidelines for Nonsexist Usage*, 51–79. New York: Modern Language Association.

Trench, Richard Chevenix 1870 [1855]. *English, Past and Present*. 7th edn. London: Macmillian.

Trudgill, Peter 1983. *On Dialect: Social and Geographical Perspectives*. New York: New York University Press.

1992. Dialect Typology and Social Structure. In E. H. Jahr (ed.), *Language Contact: Theoretical and Empirical Studies*, 195–212. Berlin: Mouton de Gruyter.

Twain, Mark 1921. The Awful German Language. In *A Tramp Abroad*, Vol. 2, 267–84. New York; London: Harper & Bros.

Vachek, J. 1976. Notes on Gender in Modern English. *Selected Writings in English and General Linguistics*, 386–92. The Hague: Mouton.

van Marle, Jaap and Caroline Smits 1995. On the Impact of Language Contact on Inflectional Systems: The Reduction of Verb Inflection in American Dutch and American Frisian. In J. Fisiak (ed.), *Linguistic Change under Contact Conditions*, 179–206. Berlin; New York: Mouton de Gruyter.

Verstegan, Richard 1605. *A Restitution of decayed intelligence: in antiquities. Concerning the most nobel and renowned English nation.* Antwerp.

Visser, F. 1963. *An Historical Syntax of the English Language.* Leiden: E. J. Brill.

von Fleischhacker, R. 1888. On the Old English Nouns of More than One Gender. *Transactions of the Philological Society* 21: 235–54.

Vorlat, Emma 1975. *The Development of English Grammatical Theory, 1586–1737.* Leuven: Leuven University Press.

Wales, Katie 1996. *Personal Pronouns in Present-Day English.* Cambridge: Cambridge University Press.

Wallin-Ashcroft, Anna-Lena 1996. Male and Female Terms in 18th Century English Novels. In G. Persson and M. Rydén (eds.), *Male and Female Terms in English: Proceedings of the Symposium at Umeå University, May 18–19, 1994*, 175–95. Umeå: Umeå University; Uppsala: Distributed by Swedish Science Press.

Weber, Doris 1999. On the Function of Gender. In B. Unterbeck and M. Rissanen (eds.), *Gender in Grammar and Cognition*, 495–510. The Hague: Mouton de Gruyter.

Webster, Noah 1864. *An American Dictionary of the English Language.* Edited by Chauncey A. Gooderich and Noah Porter. Springfield, MA: G. & C. Merriam.

Welna, Jerzy 1980. On Gender Change in Linguistic Borrowing. In J. Fisiak (ed.), *Historical Morphology*, 399–420. The Hague: Mouton de Gruyter.

Werner, Otmar 1991. The Incorporation of Old Norse Pronouns into Middle English. In P. S. Ureland and G. Broderick (eds.), *Language Contact in the British Isles: Proceedings of the Eighth International Symposium on Language Contact*, 369–401. Tübingen: Max Niemeyer Verlag.

Wescott, Roger W. 1978 [1974]. Women, Wife-men, and Sexist bias. In *Verbatim: Volumes I and II*, 15–16. Essex, CT: Verbatim.

Whaley, C. Robert and George Antonelli 1983. The Birds and the Beasts: Woman as Animal. *Maledicta* 7: 219–29.

Whitney, William Dwight (ed.) 1889–1891. *The Century Dictionary.* New York: The Century Co.

Whorf, Benjamin 1956. Grammatical Categories. In J. B. Carroll (ed.), *Language, Thought, and Reality*, 87–101. Cambridge, MA: MIT Press.

Winchester, Simon 1998. *The Professor and the Madman.* New York: HarperCollins.

Wolfe, Susan 1980a. Constructing and Reconstructing Patriarchy: Sexism and Diachronic Semantics. *Papers in Linguistics* 13.1–2: 321–44.

1980b. Gender and Agency in Indo-European Languages. *Papers in Linguistics* 13.1–2: 773–93.

1989. The Reconstruction of Word Meanings: A Review of the Scholarship. In F. W. Frank and P. A. Treichler (eds.), *Language, Gender, and Professional Writing; Theoretical Approaches and Guidelines for Nonsexist Usage*, 80–94. New York: Modern Language Association.

Index